S0-BRZ-613

INDIVIDUAL SPORTS FOR MEN AND WOMEN

Individual Sports
FOR MEN AND WOMEN

---

by

RACHAEL B. YOCOM, BA., MA.
ASSOCIATE PROFESSOR PHYSICAL EDUCATION
UTAH STATE AGRICULTURAL COLLEGE

and

H. B. HUNSAKER, BS., MS.
PROFESSOR PHYSICAL EDUCATION
DEPARTMENT OF PHYSICAL EDUCATION
UTAH STATE AGRICULTURAL COLLEGE
LOGAN, UTAH

A. S. BARNES AND COMPANY
NEW YORK

Dedication

To our friends, who have helped in so many ways to make this book possible, our deepest thanks and our heartfelt appreciation.

THE AUTHORS

CONTENTS

FOREWORD

INDIVIDUAL SPORTS FOR MEN AND WOMEN is an attempt to condense the individual sports particularly applicable to co-recreation into one volume. Some "favorites" may have been omitted, due to the necessity for brevity.

The major contribution of this text lies in the skill analyses, and the visual, teaching, and verbal aids for instruction. It is not a text on method or "manner of presentation", nor does it presume to present any dogmatic technique or "way of doing". The material is presented for the use of the reader in any way that is generally accepted in educational theory.

INDIVIDUAL SPORTS FOR MEN AND WOMEN is *not* a radical deviation from general individual sports instruction, nor does it advocate exclusive co-educational instruction in individual sports. The main difference in point-of-view is embodied in the co-operative effort to present a skill analysis text of value to both men and women. The standards and policies of the National Section on Women's Athletics have been rigidly upheld. Educational, physiological, psychological, and sociological factors pertaining to men and women engaged in individual sport have been recognized, and provisions made for individual differences.

Further information covering specific purposes may be found in Chapter I, while the understanding and use of this text will be greatly facilitated by careful reading of Chapter II.

It is our wish that you find the book useful, and our hope that the spirit in which it is written may be fully understood.

The photographs were taken by Degn Studio, Logan, Utah, and we wish to express our special thanks to the Degn Studio staff for the many hours of time so graciously given.

RACHAEL B. YOCOM
H. B. HUNSAKER

Logan, Utah
1946

INDIVIDUAL SPORTS FOR MEN AND WOMEN

I

FUNDAMENTALS BASIC TO THE TEACHING TECHNIQUE IN INDI-VIDUAL SPORTS FOR MEN AND WOMEN

INTRODUCTION AND POINT-OF-VIEW

Introduction. Our present problems are, and in the future will be: curriculum content, instructional methods, major teacher training, measurement, "in-service" training for physical education, instructors, and scientific research.

Solutions to these problems dare not remain static; yet their initial basis must be established upon sound educational theory and scientific research. Some progress has been made, but it has been slow in comparison to the need. The time in which problems would normally require or attain solution tends to be accelerated by any kind of universal revolution. Such has been the influence of World War II. New teaching methods devised and used by educators in the armed forces, new discoveries in psychology and science, short courses, visual education, the emphasis on body conditioning, and the changing status of women in world affairs are just a few of the factors that will influence the solution to problems in physical education. Future changes such as densely populated areas, higher living standards, increased leisure, increased speed of living, new scientific discoveries, and the growing need for recreational guidance will constantly change the interpretation of educational theory, and thus influence physical education. In other words, public opinion and national and international progress or change are the stimuli that force program modifications within a profession, and like miniature pendulums, the programs of the various phases within a profession, swing back and forth as the stimuli decree. Teaching methods, theories, objectives, and philosophies follow as if magnetized to these pendulums. None of these should remain static so long that they become dogmatic:

yet constant changing to extremes seems just as dangerous to a profession.

General solutions to avoid constant radical change due to the influence of social forces. One possible solution to some of the problems in physical education would seem to lie in closer co-operation between the men's and women's physical education and the athletic programs. Such co-operation would require constant scientific research and analysis in physical education and every field that might have the slightest relationship to it. Past and present teaching and training methods will have to be analyzed in the light of the present and future needs of a constantly changing world. Controversies in theory, method, and principle must be discarded completely if physical education is to meet these needs successfully. Physical educators, educators, recreation leaders, health specialists, and coaches will have to see "eye-to-eye" on the total picture, rather than the narrow conception of their particular status in school and community programs. Each of these groups must understand the policies and standards of the others and respect and abide by them. Each group should welcome, offer, and accept advice on any phase of the physical education program, provided always that such advice is based upon proved scientific research, or acceptable and workable practice. Perhaps unity of purpose would be the logical key-word for such close co-operation.

POINT-OF-VIEW. One basic fundamental necessary to the successful use of any teaching technique, regardless of the method utilized, is a, point-of-view, or in other words, a philosophy. Such a philosophy must of necessity, if it is usable, avoid complexity and entanglement in verbosity, and develop, as do most philosophies, from experience, observation, and study.

Thus the philosophy upon which *Individual Sports for Men and Women* is based, is a simple one, and formulates a sound basis for instruction in skill analysis in individual sports activity. The principles which comprise this philosophy are as follows:

The necessity of co-operation. Close co-operation between men and women in physical education is a possible, and quite probable attainment, that has been realized, at least in part, by many in the profession. It is necessary if both groups are to realize the values derived through exchange of ideas concerning teaching aids, program organization, skill analysis, and methods of group instruction. The basic difference between the men's and women's physical education programs, of course, lies in physiological, and sociological differences in the sexes; therefore the program of activities varies in the amount and strenuousness of the activity and the type of competition approved for men's and women's programs. Individual sports vary in the strenuousness of individual play, rather than actual game modification. Thus the premise of co-operation becomes a logical and possible principle in the philosophy of individual sports for men and women.

The popularity of co-recreation. Men and women engage in individual sports activities as a means of co-recreation. The popularity of this type of recreation has steadily increased. The belief in the necessity of its consideration in planning present and future physical education programs arises not only from its increased popularity, but from opinions expressed by returned service men. The need will remain, and any philosophy must recognize the need in order to control and guide the development of the program to meet that need.

The growth of co-educational instruction in individual sports. The increase in co-educational instruction in individual sports activity has closely paralleled the growing popularity of co-recreation. This is especially true in colleges and universities where specific courses are offered for men and women in individual sports; however many secondary schools provide at least one day each week for co-recreation. While the instructional problem is always present in any class, it is a far greater problem in a class involving both men and women. Obviously one instructor is more logical than two for such a class; therefore the choice of using a man or a woman usually lies with the administrator. Whatever the choice, the instructor must be fully cognizant of the differences in the sexes, any game and style modifications necessary, the standards and principles of both the men's and women's programs, and the outcomes desired by both groups. Thus the principle of co-operation is strengthened and the necessity for competent instructors, trained to teach both men and women, is added to the philosophy of individual sports for men and women.

Initial instruction. Closely paralleling the problem of instruction in individual sports activity is the problem of initial instruction. Evidence is not sufficient at the present time to state the advisability of initial instruction of both boys and girls, particularly on the secondary level. Co-instruction in college has proved successful; since the physiological, sociological, and mental development of the participants has more nearly reached maturity. This does not preclude the necessity of the training mentioned previously in so far as secondary physical education instructors are concerned, since instructional aids must be given to boys and girls engaged in co-recreational periods as well as in the regular instructional classes involving only one sex.

The choice of method. The method, or manner of presentation, of an activity should be decided by each instructor. The method chosen is determined by the individual instructor's personality, educational training, experience, facilities, equipment, student personnel, and class segregation, and should have its basis in sound educational and psychological practice.

The importance of skill analysis. Skill analysis is important, and its necessity basic, to instruction in individual sports for men or women. Instruction without analysis usually results in demonstration by the instructor with commands to the student to attempt the skill demonstrated. Any physical education teacher should be able to analyze the skills in each sport and to teach the correct techniques. With the development of high speed cameras, the visualization of skills in sport is possible. This insures greater accuracy in skill analysis. The learning process is expedited if the skills to be learned are clearly visualized by the learner.

Summary. The principles which comprise this philosophy are reflected in the spirit in which *Individual Sports for Men and Women* is presented, and are applicable to both the men's and women's physical education programs. Obviously, the philosophy just propounded does not advocate the use of a specific method of instruction, nor the exclusive use of co-educational classes for individual sports instruction. It is, however, flexible enough to meet the needs of any teaching situation, and allows for close co-operation between the men's and the women's physical education departments; yet it also remains static enough to rigidly uphold the standards and principles of both programs and insure the desired outcomes of individual sports instruction.

PURPOSE

Specific remedies for any one of the problems of physical education must be formulated by the combined efforts and close co-operation of the whole profession. Individuals participate in these solutions only to the extent that their contributions are of value in the final solution. The seemingly endless scope of physical education, and the innumerable values within its many phases make these solutions complex, and relegate individual sports to a minor, though equitable part of the total program. Thus a book entitled *Individual Sports for Men and Women* cannot hope to avert an impending crisis; neither guarantee immunity from the influence of social forces; nor completely solve the problems of physical education; yet it may, by accomplishing the purposes for which it is written, contribute to the total body of knowledge necessary for the final solution of specific problems. A discussion of these purposes may present a clearer view of these problems.

Individual Sports for Men and Women is a text book intended for students, teachers, and participants of both sexes. In preparing this book, the following purposes have been paramount.

First. To bring the men's and women's programs into closer working relationship. This has been accomplished by rigid adherence to the standards and policies of both groups, while presenting material for use by both sexes, and by co-authorship, prove such close co-operation possible.

Second. To point out the basic differences and similarities in the technique of performance in, and teaching individual sports to, men and women. Thus the presentation of each skill recognizes any physiological, psychological, sociological, sex, and individual differences in men and women engaged in the same type of activity.

Third. To combine the best in teaching aids from the men's and women's physical education and the coaches instructional methods. Any volume purporting to present "the method" of teaching any sport is assuming the impossible. Technique, as used in this volume, is defined as a way of doing, and method, as a manner of presentation. Teaching aids are suggested "ways of doing," and the "manner of presentation" is believed to be the inherent right of each instructor. Physical educators, (men, women, and coaches), make daily use of teaching aids in presenting instruction to individuals engaged in activity. Each group employs the use of many teaching aids unknown or unused by the others. Only by close co-operation and free interchange of ideas can the ultimate in teaching success be realized, thus such a co-operative compilation of teaching aids has been a major purpose of this volume.

Fourth. To present a guide for co-educational classes in individual sports. Many schools have been offering co-educational classes in individual sports as a part of the physical education or the recreation program. Sometimes these are taught or supervised by men; sometimes by women. A text recognizing the differences between men and women in individual sports participation should bring about better understanding and closer co-operation regardless of which department was assigned the course, as well as benefit the students through better instructional aids.

Fifth. To present a skill analysis text for teacher training in physical education. Many physical education students are adept at demonstration; yet many fail miserably when asked to point out the specific point at which a performance was incorrect. The common reply to such a situation is to say: "No, that was wrong, do it this way.", and then the student proceeds to demonstrate. One of the usual faults of students attempting their practice or student teaching is failure to "break-down" or analyze an activity. For these reasons, skill analysis has been a major purpose.

Sixth. To present a guide for inexperienced teachers. The presentation of suggested "ways of doing" or teaching aids, has been an all important purpose, especially so when reviewing the needs of the inexperienced teacher. The aim has been to present a review of material already learned, teaching aids, verbal aids, and suggested class organization.

Seventh. To present a reference for experienced teachers. Experienced teachers often need a text that will give simple, logical, and concise aid in improving the particular teaching method used. This has been one of the purposes of this text.

Eighth. To present a text for "in-service" training of physical education instructors. The material in this volume has been used for "in-service" training of physical education instructors and has been so enthusiastically received, that it became an important reason for attempting the compilation of this material for publication, and automatically formulates the final purpose of this volume.

It is hoped the material in this text will contribute in some measure in the final solution to problems in instructional method, teacher training in physical education, and "in-service" training for the physical education instructor, as well as to stimulate closer co-operation between the men's and women's physical education, and the athletic programs for the best interests of the physical education profession.

EDUCATIONAL IMPLICATIONS

General Objectives. Any text whose philosophy is in agreement with the standards and principles of modern physical education, is naturally in accord with the general objectives of education and of physical education. Since these objectives are familiar to the profession of physical education, a re-statement is not necessary; however the educational implications of *Individual Sports for Men and Women* should be amplified in order to validate the philosophy upon which it is based. In so far as instructors and students in physical education are concerned, the educational values are so closely associated with the purpose of the text, that further amplification would result in unnecessary repetition; however the educational values to the majority of students engaged in required physical education activity would be realized through increased teaching success, rather than through intensive use of the text. Successful instruction in individual sports would realize the objectives of education and of physical education as they concern the development of good social habits and attitudes, love of wholesome play, neuro-muscular co-ordination, wholesome use of leisure time, and organic vigor.

The relationship of the general objectives and individual sport participation. Perhaps the logical procedure would be to discuss each phase of development in the order just presented; however the close relationship between them precludes the division of these phases into specific items for discussion. For example, individual sports participation might facilitate the development of good social habits and attitudes by student participation in sports activity requiring many of the same reactions to situations that will be met in community life. Co-educational activity of this kind will especially develop the understanding of both sexes necessary to enjoy playing together. The necessity for "give-and-take," the sport in playing together, the modification of styles of game for better enjoyment, and the courtesy inherent in individual sports are just a few of the values that will be learned and probably retained by the participants, and which will in turn aid in the development of good social habits and attitudes. Yet this same participation and instruction should, through the development of even a moderate degree of skill in a sport, develop a love of wholesome play, which will, if the student attains an average performance level, insure in part at least, the wholesome use of leisure time. Through continued practice and instruction, progress is made in neuro-muscular, particularly eye-hand, co-ordination; and the development of skills is increased. This participation should bring about some physiological development; however the degree of development would vary in direct ratio to the strenuousness with which the sport was played.

Summary. Actually it matters little whether individual sports are taught in co-educational classes or each sex instructed separately, in so far as the use of this text is concerned. Co-educational instruction is a problem that can be solved only by each individual instructor. The advantages and disadvantages of co-educational instruction must be weighed against the advantages and disadvantages of instructing a class of one sex. In any case, educational values are inherent in the activity, and the objectives of education and of physical education may be realized in part through correct instruction and participation in individual sports within a total physical education program.

PSYCHOLOGY AND THE ACQUISITION OF SKILLS

Methods in Learning. With the acceptance of physical education as a profession, and as an integral part of the educational program, came the responsibility of study in psychology of the acquisition of skills. Theories of learning, already advanced in psychology, provided a sound basis for the instructional methods selected by the physical education teacher.

However, many teachers failed to interpret psychological findings in terms of the teaching situation in its relationship to student learning. Others seemed more concerned with aligning themselves with, and proclaiming their allegiance to, only one theory of psychology. A good example of this is found in the unqualified acceptance, and general misunderstanding by teachers, of either the whole or the part method.

Common Elements in the Theories of Learning as Applied to the School Situation and to the Use of this Text. The problem in so far as the teacher is concerned is successful teaching with resultant student learning, rather than with a particular school of thought in motor learning. The main points in each of these have great value in the study of motor learning. It follows as well that these same points have great value in the school situation. The following attempt at enumerating the principles essential to motor learning is by no means complete; however it may serve to create a desire for further study in psychology and the acquisition of skills, and to strengthen the premise upon which much of this volume is based.

Principles Essential to Successful Motor Learning. It is quite generally agreed that motor learning is accomplished in the same manner as other forms of learning; and the theories of learning, while complete in themselves, are more applicable to the school situation and for use by the average teacher, if the common elements in each are used as a basis for instruction. No general formula can be applied to motor learning, for analysis of each situation and each individual is necessary. The general conditions affecting motor learning are: (1) environment suitable to learning; (2) motivation; (3) understanding of goals; (4) knowledge of progress; (5) repetition of opportunity; (6) maturity of the learner; (7) meaningful units strengthened by demonstration, visualization, verbal and manual guidance, and positive instruction; (8) allowing free rhythmic movement, in initial learning; and (9) variations or flexibility of performance.

(1) *Environment Suitable to Learning.* This includes the character of instruction (services of a good teacher); pleasant physical surroundings; good equipment; and adequate social stimulation. The first three problems are individual school problems and have no direct bearing upon the factual material in this volume; however the problem of adequate social stimulation is aided by individual sports through the popularity of co-recreation both in school and community life, and by the nature of an activity that is primarily recreational even in a class instructional period.

(2 & 3) *Motivation and Understanding of Goals.* Motivation in individual sports does not present a serious problem to instructors in this type of activity since the incentives are natural ones of use and interest. In every case the motivation should be intrinsically related to the teacher-desired and pupil-accepted goals, or other outcomes may result.

(4) *Knowledge of Progress.* Each student should be able to obtain information concerning the degree of success or failure made in attempting to attain the desired goal. Standardized tests for checking the progress in individual sports skills are not available in any number or degree of accuracy. Examinations of various types will aid the teacher in checking student progress; however the examining situation must be a natural one or internal tensions will be created within the learner, and an accurate progress check will be an impossibility. Long periods of no learning should be checked against the following: boredom by the student; external distractions; poor teaching; persistent, incorrect habits; radical changes in style; and ill health.

(5) *Repetition of Opportunity.* Opportunities to attempt the attainment of the desired goal are basic to learning, provided motivation is present. In individual sports this may be accomplished by independent student activity; short practice periods; spontaneous activity; and drill, provided the drill used attains a desired goal, does not become mechanical, the student understands its purpose, and it does not inhibit

natural, free action by the learner. Drill, as used in this text, exemplifies the characteristics just named; yet allows for regular time intervals in the performance, provided the time element is not made a limitation. In other words the rhythmic movement is important, although it should not be strictly enforced in the initial learning stages. Later the rhythm may be emphasized, and after a skill is learned, the actual count or time interval is not consciously performed.

(6) *Maturation Level.* A certain degree of maturity is necessary to learning, and the skills to be learned should be presented to the students in a manner they can grasp. The less maturation evident in the learner, the simpler the presentation must be. The greater the degree of maturation, the more complex the learning situation that can be grasped.

(7) *Meaningful Units.* Total units within a total sport have been designated as skills in this volume. The goal of each drill or activity unit must be understood by the learner. This is strengthened by demonstration (usually by the instructor); visualization (movie film or pictures in sequence); verbal guidance (must be used sparingly until the learner understands the terms for the movement to be formed. Verbal aids should always be clear and concise and adapted to each individual's learning problem); manual guidance (physical aid in performing a movement); and positive instruction (give positive aids. If errors are made, teach the correct pattern, do not try to stop the incorrect performance.). Each of these is covered in this volume.

(8) *Free Movement.* The importance of free movement has already been emphasized; however it should be stated that such free movement is allowed in the beginning of the learning period, and controlled, precision movements are expected as the learning progresses. This principle should be thoroughly understood in the use of the material in this volume since suggested teaching aids are not presented in detail.

(9) *Variations.* Individual differences in performance should be allowed in every type of motor activity. The skill pattern should be copied as closely as possible, but flexibility should be allowed to insure recognition of individual differences. This avoids regimentation into machine-like precision, which in itself detracts from the necessary spontaneity of the activity.

Summary. In these ways, the principles of a number of theories of learning as they apply to the acquisition of skills, may aid the teacher in successful instruction and thus benefit the learner through speedy and efficient learning. An attempt has been made to apply these same principles in the compilation of this volume, and demonstrates practical application of psychological theory. It has been emphasized previously, and now is repeated once again, that such applications are suggested "ways of doing" and the "method of presentation" is the inherent right of each individual instructor.

AUTHOR'S NOTE

Value is gauged by quality, and quality is determined by usefulness. Use is governed by understanding of purpose, which is regulated by knowledge of terms, particularly if the terms are a new coinage of expression, or terms that, over a period of years, have acquired various meanings. Thus an explanation of the nomenclature used in *Individual Sports for Men and Women* is presented to afford a better understanding of its purpose, and to facilitate its use.

II

APPLICATION OF TERMS

NOMENCLATURE

Teaching Premise. Each chapter pertaining to a specific individual sport is introduced by means of the teaching premise. It is presented for the use of the instructor only, and provides an opportunity to state conflicting thought in individual sports instruction without prejudice and with no attempt at analysis.

Teaching Progression. Teaching progression is used as a term, only in the table of contents for each chapter; yet the individual sports skills follow a definite pattern throughout the text. This should *not* be construed as a dogmatic selection of the order in which they should be presented to students. Many of the skills, for best results should be taught at the same time. For purposes of clarity and organization only, an attempt has been made to present them from the simplest to the most complex.

Individual Sport. The classifications of activity are many and varied, and the definition of individual sports seems to change with each classification. Thus the frequent use of the term, in this and many texts, is often misleading. Archery, badminton, fencing, golf, and tennis are the sports presented in this volume, and, although the use of the term individual sports is, in general, correct, it is used with full knowledge of other classifications. Standardized nomenclature has long been a need in the physical education profession, but until this is accomplished, it seems well to define the present use of a term.

Skill. Every sport is comprised of a number of skills. For example, skills in tennis include the forehand drive, the backhand drive, the services, the lob, the volley, and others. Thus the term as used in this text denotes the division of a sport into a number of separate movements or series of movements, which, when finally co-ordinated, guarantee some degree of performance.

Specific Skill Definition. Each skill in every sport is introduced by means of a definition or a brief statement of its use.

Skill Summary. Instruction in individual sport skills must begin with an explanation of just what the instructor wishes the student to attempt. This explanation should be clear, brief, and to the point. The skill summary is an attempt to formulate such an explanation of each skill analyzed.

Skill Analysis. In any text, written to aid sport instruction, the analysis of skills is of major importance. Although many methods are used in skill analysis, two types are more generally used. One type analyzes the action of parts of the body, while the other analyzes the steps within the skill. In other words the action of parts of the body describes the movement of wrist, head, trunk, feet, etc., as separate units. The steps within the skill describe the movements of all parts of the body as one unit throughout each step. The latter method will be used throughout this text, and presents a number of problems, when applied to a book for the use of both men and women. For example, skill analysis is actually a breakdown of a skill into steps or counts. Women, sometimes, refer to this as a rhythmic pattern; yet such a term would not appeal to the majority of men instructors and participants. Thus the final definition compromised with: *Skill analysis is a series of steps within the skill pattern.* This presented still another problem, that of the use of a term to designate the series of steps. Count 1, 2, 3, etc., seemed the most logical to use from the standpoint of class instruction, although the term step seemed more appropriate from the standpoint of theory; however theory was sacrificed at the altar of practical use in this instance, and counts were used. *It is essential to the success of the analyses to keep in mind the fact that counts do not mean formalized movement* to counts of 1-2-3-etc. *These counts must be smoothly co-ordinated to form the skill pattern, and are used merely to designate the order of action within the skill. Once the skill is learned, these counts may be entirely disregarded.*

Skill Illustration. In so far as it has been possible, action pictures have been taken to visualize an approved or accepted form of skill performance. Students were used for this purpose since it was felt they more nearly resembled the types of performance found in average participants. Individual illustrations were made by students selected especially for their ability to perform correctly the series of steps in the skill pattern. Group illustrations were taken at random from actual class instructional periods.

> NOTE: The illustrations which show action are flash photographs taken with a Speed-Graphic camera; therefore each single picture depicting a technique within the skill, actually was made from a complete performance of each skill. For this reason, and because students were used exclusively, some errors can be found. These are marked with an X, directly on the illustration, and in so far as possible, corrections are suggested.

Teaching Aids. In order to make full use of the teaching aids, it is necessary to understand that they are suggested "ways of doing" and the division into general and verbal is made for convenience in organization. The *general aids* or teaching techniques are, for the most part, suggested ways of group instruction to aid in teaching a large class in individual sport, and individual aids for correcting student errors. In so far as it has been feasible, these have been illustrated. Such teaching aids cover a number of lessons and may not follow the order desired by every instructor. *Verbal aids* are specific teaching techniques for use in correcting or aiding individual performance. These verbal aids describe the essence of what could be said to the student. Each instructor should shorten or lengthen these to fit class situations and student personnel. These aids are designated by the letters A-B-C-etc., and the corresponding letter on the illustration refers directly to that verbal aid.

Variations. Immediately following the teaching aids is a list of possible variations. These include possible individual differences, physiological differences, sex differences, etc., that might be found in style of play or in manner of performance.

Advantages. Many times one technique may have an advantage over another type of technique in the performance of a skill. For this reason, although it is closely related to variations, a separate unit has been included to list the advantages, and sometimes the disadvantages, of variations in performance. This is especially important in a book for the use of both men and women, because it affords a specific opportunity as well as a specific place, to designate the techniques that are particularly advantageous or hampering to either women's or men's performance.

Grip Illustrations. The grip illustrations are presented from four views. The top view illustrates the grip as seen by the player; the left side view is taken from the left side of the player; the right side view, from the right side of the player; and the bottom view is obtained by raising the grip toward the camera until that portion of the grip, usually completely out of sight, is in view. Thus the terms top, bottom, left and right of the handle, refer to these positions only.

Sport Terminology. Various terms in each sport, and points which need special emphasis have been added to the bottom of most of the pages. No attempt was made at any particular continuity; however the general usefulness of the information seemed important enough to include outside the general organization of the text.

TECHNIQUE

Technique of performance and technique of teaching. The term technique is, of course, a part of the nomenclature; however it is mentioned here as a separate unit to emphasize the two types of technique that are actually the basis for the compilation of this material. They are the technique of performance and the technique of teaching, or in terms mentioned previously, they are suggested ways of performing a skill, and suggested ways of aiding the learning process in a skill. These are so closely inter-related in the teaching situation that no division has been made between the two in the material presented.

SUMMARY

The nomenclature just presented is not entirely new to the profession of physical education, nor is its present use. The explanations of the use of terms should create a better understanding of the text, and it is hoped their organization within the text will add to the clarity and ease of its use.

III

ARCHERY

TEACHING PREMISE

THE popularity of archery today is due primarily to two factors, namely: scientifically balanced equipment and improved instruction in the art of shooting. The equipment of the modern archer is a far cry in balance, design, and types from that used by the yeoman. There are a number of forms of archery such as target shooting, hunting, clout shooting, archery golf, roving, the cross bow, etc. The equipment and technique of shooting differ to some extent with each form. The material in this chapter is presented for use in target shooting, and the term archery as used in this chapter refers to that form. Other forms of archery will be discussed very briefly; however, the analysis of skills is left for each individual instructor.

The skills and their analyses are presented from the simple to the complex and do not necessarily represent a rigid teaching progression. The general teaching aids are suggested ways of instruction for a large class and may form a basis for class drill.

Class drills may be used to advantage in speeding up the learning process in a large group; however, the individual aids are of greater value in the final outcome, since individual differences can be considered. Over-emphasis of drill, whether it be class or individual, may retard student learning, because the class becomes a period of mechanical drill performed to commands or counts. Thus the thrill of performance is lost, and the students lose interest. Commands and counts are useful, but should be discarded completely as soon as the student has mastered the basic fundamentals of the sport, and replaced with individual instruction in the form of verbal and physical aids.

A BRIEF HISTORY OF ARCHERY

The bow and arrow is one of the oldest implements known to man and, with the exception of fire, has done more than any other single agency to elevate man above the beast. The possession of better bows and arrows gave a country a decided advantage over another country.

England, because of the long bow, which was the machine gun of that day, was able to achieve great prominence in military prowess, which resulted in a higher economic and social status than her neighboring countries.

The bow was a universal piece of war equipment, as well as a means of livelihood, until 1600. In that year the gun replaced the bow and arrow. The Indians alone continued its use for lack of guns, and thus the bow and arrow has a closer association with them than with any other race.

Modern archery is primarily a form of recreation, and is generally applied to target shooting. In its present form, it resembles the archery of England and its Robin Hood; however better bows and arrows and technique of shooting have increased the skill of archers today to a degree that would be the envy of the most celebrated archers of old.

Many people believe the Indians to be the world's greatest archers. In reality they were very inaccurate with the bow and arrow. The bow and arrow to them was a means of livelihood, not a recreation, and like the yeoman of old, they hit their marks more because of estimation, at which they became very competent masters, than by aiming. Most modern archers shoot at a fixed target, and use an aiming technique.

Horace A. Ford, in 1848, was the first archer to formulate the principle of aiming, and this technique has improved archery scores materially.

Archery as a sport probably began in England about 1545 and its popularity continued to increase until in 1830 it became a national sport. In 1844, the first Grand National Meeting was held in New York. In 1859, Horace A. Ford made the highest score ever recorded to that time, in a Grand National Meet. His score for a double round was 245-1251. Since that time one other archer has made a comparable score of 255-1360.

The popularity of archery today is continually increasing, and the skill of modern archers has kept pace with this increase. Archery as a universal sport has proved its merit and is here to stay.

SELECTION, CARE, AND REPAIR OF EQUIPMENT

Bow

Selection. The target bows most widely used today are essentially the same as the bow used by the English yeoman; however such desirable characteristics as quickness of cast, balance, and smoothness of draw have been materially improved.

The bow should be about the same height as the archer using it.

Person 6 feet or more........ 6 foot bow.
Person 5½ to 6 feet....... 5½ foot bow.
Person 5 to 5½ feet...... 5 foot bow.

The weight of the bow should not be too heavy, especially for beginners.

Beginners: Men: 24-28 pounds.
Women: 20-26 pounds.
Experienced: Men: 28-35 pounds.
Women: 24-32 pounds.

Examine the bow for full draw test, even limb bend, excessive bend in handle or tips, and knots, tips, and cross grains. (Plate 1)

Care. Six general rules for proper care of the bow are as follows:
1. Do not pull past full draw.
2. String the bow properly.
3. Unstring the bow when it is not in use.
4. Warm up the bow before using it.
5. Never draw and release the bow without using an arrow.
6. Store the bow properly and in a dry place. (Plate 2)

Repair. Bow repair should be handled by an expert if possible. The most common repairs are tightening the handle piece, restoring an old bow by scraping, oiling, and varnishing the back, and restoring cast and power by shortening both limbs approximately two to three inches.

Arrows

Selection. Arrow selection should be based upon the size of the bow, and thus will fit each individual archer as closely as possible.

6 foot bow: 27-28 inch arrow.
5½ foot bow: 25-26-27 inch arrow.
5 foot bow: 23-24-25 inch arrow.

Examine arrows for straight shaft, good spine, good nocks, feathers and points. (Plate 3)

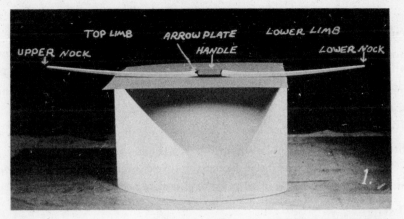

English Long Bow.

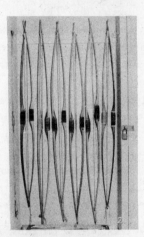

Archery Storage.

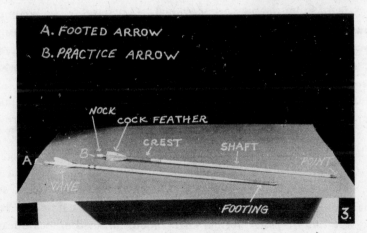

A. Footed Arrow. B. Practice Arrow.

Care and Repair. Arrows should be stored in an arrow case or cupboard, and wiped off after each use.

Repair for arrows consists of tightening or replacing nocks, points, and feathers. Replacement costs range from three to eight dollars per dozen arrows.

STRING

Selection, Care and Repair. A good string should have strength with little bulk, strong loops, and wrapping at the service piece. (Plate 4)

Avoid over-twisting and keep the service piece wrapped. The string should be waxed as often as necessary, and breaks repaired immediately.

TARGET

Selection. The standard target for archery should be 48 inches in diameter and can be made by machine or by hand. The machine made target is made by compressing short straw together and covering it on both sides with burlap and then binding it together. The hand made target is made by using long rye or bush straw wound together and stitched firmly. Target faces are made of oil cloth or paper. Oil cloth is generally considered more satisfactory. (Plate 5)

Care and Repair. Targets should be stored in a dry place when not in use. Care in handling will lengthen the life of a target.

Targets tend to loosen with use. This can be remedied by tightening the bindings, and prevented, to some extent, by placing cardboard or celotex between the target and the target stand.

QUIVERS, ARM GUARDS, AND FINGER TABS

Selection. A quiver is a receptacle for carrying or holding the arrows. Three main types are used: The leather pouch for carrying the arrows; the fiber cylinder mounted on a wooden base for indoor shooting; and the No. 1 galvanized wire loop for outdoor target shooting. (Plate 6)

Arm guards are made of leather or fiber and are laced or buckled around the bow forearm. These are not essential for archery instruction; but they prevent arm welts, especially with beginners, although even the best archers occasionally whip their arms with the bow string.

Constant shooting will cause the fingers to become sore and sensitive, and may result in inaccuracy in shooting. Finger tabs, if used, should be hard and stiff in order to allow for free release of the string. (Plate 7)

Care and Repair. Normal care should be used in handling and storage. Replacements should be made immediately.

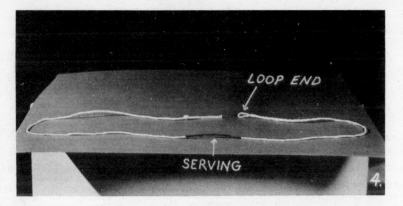

Bow String.

Archery Target.

A. Leather Pouch; B. Fiber
Cylinder; C. Wire Loop.

7

Arm and Finger Protection.

TEACHING PROGRESSION

STANCE

Stance is the position the archer assumes at the shooting line. It also includes the body position, (*not arm*) at the time of arrow anchor.

SKILL SUMMARY

Take an easy position with the feet 10 to 12 inches apart. This will vary with the height of the archer. Straddle the shooting line, with the shoulders at right angles to the target face. Point the left shoulder directly toward the target face and distribute the weight evenly beween both feet. Balance on the feet should be slightly toward the heels. Turn the face about ten degrees right of the target.

SKILL ANALYSIS AND ILLUSTRATION

Count 1. Straddle shooting line, feet 10-12 inches apart. Weight slightly toward heels.

Count 2. Shoulders at right angle with target. Left shoulder points toward target. Shoulders level.

Count 3. Head erect and level. Chin up. Eyes level. Face about 10 degrees right of target. Eyes turned toward the target. (Plate 8a, b, c)

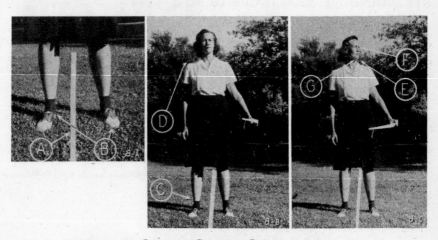

Count 1. Count 2. Count 3.

KEEP BODY ERECT. GOOD POSTURE IS THE KEY TO ACCURACY. ARROW ANCHOR: POSITION OF FULL DRAW.

GENERAL TEACHING AIDS

I. Explain and demonstrate the stance.

II. Use a student and call attention to the feet, head, trunk and weight positions.

III. Allow class to take positions at shooting line, and check position of feet, head, trunk, and weight distribution.

IV. *Student Drill:* Work in pairs, one student assuming the stance; the other, checking for errors.

VERBAL TEACHING AIDS

A. Straddle the shooting line.

B. Weight evenly distributed between both feet. (*Watch for shuffling of weight, usually to right foot.*)

C. Weight slightly toward heels. (*Weight toward balls of feet causes a body lean forward.*)

D. Shoulders level. (*Watch for hunching of left shoulder.*)

E. Face 10 degrees right of target. (*Face directly toward target causes string to be anchored on right side of face.*)

F. Eyes level. (*Avoids tilting of head.*)

G. Chin up. (*Gives proper chin and nose position for anchor. Dropping of chin to chest is common error.*)

AVOID SHIFTING WEIGHT TO RIGHT OR LEFT FOOT.

STRINGING OR BRACING THE BOW

Stringing or bracing the bow is the manner in which the bow is bent and the string secured in the bow nocks.

SKILL SUMMARY

Assume a position with the heels about 8 to 10 inches apart. Turn the right foot about 45 degrees to the right. Grasp the bow handle at the back in the right hand. Place the bottom end of the bow under the right instep. Extend the left hand up the top limb, resting the heel of the left hand on the upper limb below the string. Cup the thumb and index finger along the edges of the upper limb. Pull with the right arm throwing weight against the heel of the left hand and the right instep. At the same time, slip the left palm up the bow, and place the string in the nock with the fingers.

SKILL ANALYSIS AND ILLUSTRATION

Count 1. Grasp the bow handle. (*String away from body.*) Place lower bow nock under right instep.

Count 2. Place heel of left hand below string loop on top limb. Cup thumb and index finger below string along the sides of the bow.

Count 3. Pull with the right hand to relax string.

Count 4. Slip left palm up bow, and place string in nock with fingers.

Count 5. Check proper stringing, using fistmele. (Plate 9a, b, c, d, e)

Count 1. Count 2. Count 3.

Count 4. Count 5.

PROPER CARE IN USING THE BOW IS VERY ESSENTIAL TO THE LIFE OF THE BOW.

GENERAL TEACHING AIDS

I. Explain and demonstrate stringing the bow.
II. Form class in line in Count 1 position.
Assume Count 2 position.

Practice Count 3 until students can hold the weight of the bent bow on right instep and heel of left hand. Check by asking class to move the fingers of the left hand while the string of the bow is relaxed.

III. Demonstrate Count 4.
IV. Allow students to attempt placing the string in the nock.

V. Demonstrate unstringing the bow and allow students to attempt it.

VI. Demonstrate fistmele and have students check bows.

VII. *Student Drill:* String bows to counts used in SKILL ANALYSIS (page 23). Check with fistmele and assume correct stance. Unstring bow.

VERBAL TEACHING AIDS

A. Lower limb of bow does not touch. It is hooked *slightly* under right instep. (*Hooking under instep may break the lower limb of bow.*)

B. String away from body. Back of bow toward body.

C. Pull with right arm. Push with heel of left hand.

D. Thumb and forefinger place string in nock.

E. Be sure fingers do not get between string and bow. (*May pinch fingers.*)

F. Check to see that string is properly placed before weight is entirely shifted to the bow. (*Injury may result if string should slip from nock.*)

G. Check with fistmele for proper height of bow string. (*Overstrung bows are dangerous. Understringing lets string hit the arm in shooting.*)

NOTE: *Fistmele*

6 foot bows: 1 fistmele height, bow handle to string. (*Normal hand.*)

5 ½ foot bows: Bow string at middle of thumb nail.

5 foot bows: Bow string at bottom of thumb nail.

OVERSTRINGING IS HARD ON THE BOW, CHECK BY FISTMELE.

BOW GRIPS

Bow grip is the manner in which the archer takes hold of the bow preparatory to shooting.

SKILL SUMMARY

Assume the correct stance and hold the bow in the right hand. The bow is thigh high and parallel to the ground. Place the left hand on the bow grip so that the top portion of the bow handle is even with the outside part of the finger and thumb. Extend the fingers around the bow grip forming a grip with the thumb.

SKILL ANALYSIS AND ILLUSTRATION

Count 1. Bow in right hand and held parallel to ground.

Count 2. Place left hand on bow grip.

Count 3. Extend thumb and fingers around bow grip. (Plate 10a, b, c)

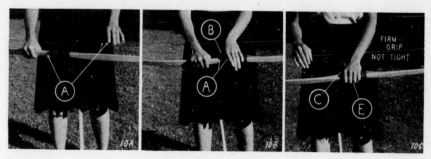

Count 1. Count 2. Count 3.

INCORRECT GRIP MAY CAUSE BOW STRING TO HIT THE WRIST.

GENERAL TEACHING AIDS

I. Explain and demonstrate the correct bow grip.

II. Check each individual to see that a proper grip is obtained and adjustments made for physical differences in hands, wrists, and arms. (See VARIATIONS.)

III. *Student Drill:* Assume correct stance. String bow. Check with fistmele. Assume bow grip in counts used in SKILL ANALYSIS (page 25). Elevate bow to a perpendicular position toward target. Check elbow point for alignment. Check for errors. Unstring bow.

VERBAL TEACHING AIDS

A. Outside of thumb and forefinger even with top of bow grip.

B. Second joint of thumb on body of handle between bow and string. (*Avoid getting thumb too far inside bow.*)

C. Grasp bow firmly, but not tightly between fingers and thumb. (*Allow for a certain amount of relaxation.*)

D. The pull should come on the base of the thumb. (*Gives better hand position.*)

E. Keep fingers together.

F. Flex hand slightly inward at wrist. (*Helps avoid hitting wrist with string.*)

G. Rotate elbow point. (*Turns point away from string.*)

VARIATIONS

1. In many women archers, the anatomy of the elbow makes it necessary to rotate the elbow point down and out to avoid hitting the elbow with the string at the time of release.

2. The grip may need adjustment for certain women archers, because of length of fingers and strength of grip. (Plate 11a, b, c)

Man's Bow Grip. Woman's Bow Grip. Correction to Protect Arm. (Women.)

RELAXATION IS IMPORTANT TO GOOD ARCHERY.

NOCKING

Nocking places the arrow on the bow with the string in the arrow nock. The arrow nock is the small slit at the end of the arrow.

SKILL SUMMARY

Assume the correct bow grip and hold the bow horizontally at the left side of the body, about hip high, parallel with the ground, and the string toward the body. Pick the arrow from the quiver with the right hand, using the thumb and index finger. Grasp the arrow between the ends of the feathers and the arrow nock. Place the arrow across the bow at the arrow piece, and twirl the arrow so that the cock feather is at right angles to the bow. Place the arrow nock on the string, using the left index finger as a guide. Secure the grip more firmly and flex the hand slightly inward.

SKILL ANALYSIS AND ILLUSTRATION

Count 1. Place bow at left side of body. Hip high and string toward body.

Count 2. Grasp arrow between thumb and forefinger in right hand.

Count 3. Place arrow across bow at arrow piece.

Count 4. Twirl arrow until cock feather is up, and place arrow nock on the string.

Count 5. Firm grip. Wrist flexed slightly inward. (Plate 12a, b, c, d)

Count 1. Count 2.

Count 3. Count 4.

Cock Feather Up and Arrow at Right Angles to String and Bow.

Arrow Piece: Found on outside of upper limb of bow near the bow handle.

Cock Feather: Feather at right angles to the arrow nock.

General Teaching Aids

I. Explain and demonstrate nocking the arrow.

II. *Class Drill:* String bow. Assume correct stance. Rotate bow toward body until the string is toward the hip.

III. *Class Drill:* Same as above adding nocking of arrow.

IV. *Nocking Drill:*

(1) Perform to explanation by instructor.

(2) Perform to counts as outlined in Skill Analysis.

(3) Perform to command: "Nock arrow."

VERBAL TEACHING AIDS

A. Bow at left side and hip high.

B. String toward body.

C. Use tips of forefinger and thumb to take arrow from quiver. (*Makes it easy to twirl arrow to find cock feather.*)

D. Place arrow across bow at arrow plate.

E. Twirl arrow after placing it on arrow plate so that cock feather is up.

F. Arrow at right angles to bow string.

PROPER CARE OF ARROWS WILL AID IN KEEPING THEM STRAIGHT.

VARIATIONS (Plate 13)

(1) Variation in nocking the arrow.

Count 1. Pick up arrow with thumb and forefinger. Check to see that the thumb is on the cock feather side of the end of the arrow.

Count 2. Place arrow on bow near arrow piece.

Count 1. Count 2.

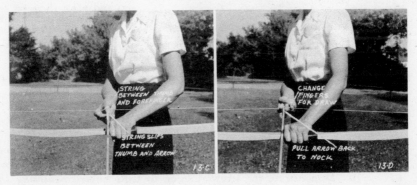

Count 3. Count 4.

Count 3. Slide arrow forward so that the string slips between thumb and arrow, leaving the string in space made by thumb and forefinger as it grips the arrow.

Count 4. Change fingers so that the arrow is held between the first and second fingers. The tips of these fingers are now up, and the arrow is pulled back until the string rests in the arrow nock.

ADVANTAGES

(1) There is no particular advantage in either type of nocking the arrow. Usually it is either a matter of individual preference or of using the type of nocking in which instruction was received.

ARROW GRIP

Arrow grip is the manner in which the fingers grip the arrow and hold it against the string after the arrow has been nocked.

SKILL SUMMARY

Nock the arrow. Turn the right hand palm up, and extend the index, second, and third fingers. Flex the thumb and little finger toward the palm of the hand in a modified Scout sign. Bring these three fingers up under the string so that the index finger is to the right of the arrow and the second and third fingers are on the left of the arrow. Flex the first joint of each finger and place on the string. Hold the arrow between the index finger and the second finger, with just enough pressure to keep the arrow nocked and at right angles to the bow.

SKILL ANALYSIS AND ILLUSTRATION

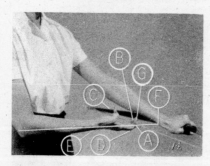

Count 1. Turn the palm up and take correct finger position. (Modified Scout sign.)

Count 2. Flex the first joint of the first, second, and third fingers and place them on the string. (Plate 14)

KEEP FINGERS AND WRIST RELAXED WHEN HOLDING ARROW.

GENERAL TEACHING AIDS

I. Explain and demonstrate the placement of fingers on the string.

II. Demonstrate the placement of fingers with the use of an arrow.

III. Demonstrate the arrow reaction to tense fingers. *Squeezing the arrow too tightly causes the arrow tip to jump away from the bow.*

IV. *Class Drills:*
   (1) Archers hold right hand up in modified Scout sign.
   (2) Place fingers on string.
                        Check for errors.
   (1) String bow.
   (2) Assume stance and nock arrow.
   (3) Place fingers on string and hold arrow.
                        Check for errors.

VERBAL TEACHING AIDS

A. First joint of fingers slightly flexed.
B. Use pads of fingers. (*Makes excessive flexing unnecessary.*)
C. Thumb and little finger slightly flexed to form a modified Scout sign.
D. Fingers form right angle with string.
E. Avoid flexing and extending the wrist joint. (*Excessive flexing causes arrow to move away from bow.*)
F. Arm in straight line from first knuckle of three fingers to elbow point. (*Causes majority of pull to come in the shoulders.*)
G. Keep grip pressure slight between first and second fingers. (*Pressure causes arrow point to move away from the bow.*)
H. Keep arrow nocked against string. (*Failure to keep arrow nocked causes string to foul arrow.*)

VARIATIONS

(1) A slightly deeper grip on the fingers is necessary for many women archers, because of lack of finger pad and finger strength.

DRAWING

   Drawing is the position assumed by elevating the left arm, turning the bow to a vertical position, and drawing the string back to the anchor position preparatory to shooting.

SKILL SUMMARY

   Nock the arrow, and assume the correct stance and arrow grip. Elevate the bow to a vertical position just above the target. The left or elevation arm is slightly bent. Bring the right arm across the chest. The right arm is bent at the elbow and forms a straight line from elbow to bow string. Spread the hands apart. Draw until the right hand reaches the anchor point. (See NOTE below.) Keep the right elbow shoulder high. At the same time that the right hand is brought to anchor point, extend the left hand to a point just short of full extension or a locked elbow. At full draw the arrow point is even with the back of the bow, and the string touches chin and nose tips.

   NOTE: *Anchor Point:* Bow string touches center of nose tip and chin point, and forefinger of right hand is under the jaw bone.

Skill Analysis and Illustration

Count 1. Bow at side and arrow nocked.

Count 2. Extend and lift left arm to raise bow to a vertical position at a point just above the target.

Count 3. Spread hands to anchor points. (Plate 15a, b, c)

Count 1. Count 2. Count 3.

The Majority of Pull Comes From the Shoulders and Right Arm.

General Teaching Aids

I. Explain and demonstrate drawing.

II. *Class Drill:* Elevate the bow by rotating the left arm outward, flexing the left wrist, and raising the bow to a vertical position.

Right Hand to Anchor Point.

Point for Shoulder Pull.

III. *Class Drill:* From the elevated position of the bow, have the class place right arms in position for the draw, but not holding the string. Draw the right hand to anchor position. (Plate 16)
Emphasis should be placed on the elbow position and the pull made by drawing the two shoulder blades together.

IV. To emphasize shoulder pull, touch a spot between the shoulder blades and ask archer to attempt to make the pull at that point. (Plate 17)

V. The archer should shoot practice arrows as soon as the fundamentals of safety, grip, draw, and release are learned.

VI. Correction of drawing technique should continue as the archer practices.

VERBAL TEACHING AIDS

A. Spread both hands apart simultaneously.

B. Avoid bending the left forearm at the wrist as the pull begins.

C. Keep fingers straight from first joint back. (*Cupping of fingers makes arrow jump away from bow.*)

D. Relax all joints of the right arm and hand, except the first joint of the three fingers on the string.

E. Keep right elbow shoulder high and parallel with the floor.

F. Pull largely through shoulder flexion.

G. Rotate left elbow point down if necessary to avoid being hit with the string. (See VARIATIONS.)

DO *NOT* RELEASE THE BOW STRING UNLESS THE ARROW IS NOCKED.

VARIATIONS

(1) Turning of the trunk slightly counter-clockwise may be necessary to avoid pulling directly against the left breast. Women should be advised to use this variation to avoid injury following the release.

(2) The anatomy of the elbow may make it necessary for some women to rotate the elbow down and out to avoid being hit by the string on the release. See page 27 for an illustration.

ANCHOR

Anchor is the position of full draw where the aiming is done preparatory to the arrow release.

SKILL SUMMARY

The anchor position is reached as the draw is completed. This position is fixed by the length of the arrow used; however the position for the correct length arrow is with the right forefinger under the right jaw bone. Hold the bow string firmly against the center part of the chin and the center of the nose tip. Keep the head erect, the eyes level, and the chin up. Extend a straight left arm towards the target with the bow in a vertical position. Check to see that the left elbow is *not* locked.

SKILL ANALYSIS AND ILLUSTRATION

Count 1.   Assume proper archery stance.

Count 2.   Pull arrow point to second knuckle of forefinger of left hand.

Count 3.   Drop chin to forefinger of right hand. Place center of nose tip on string. Place center of chin point on string. (Plate 18a, b, c)

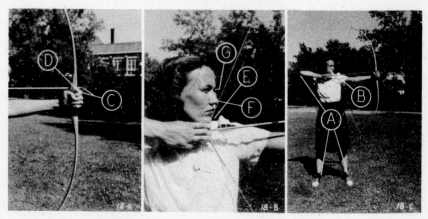

Count 2. Count 3. Full Draw and Anchor.

DEFINITE ANCHOR POINTS ARE PREREQUISITES TO GOOD ARCHERY.

GENERAL TEACHING AIDS

I.   Explain and demonstrate the anchor points.

II.   As the class drills for drawing, the anchor position should be stressed. This should be performed first without actually drawing the bow.

Full Draw. Anchor Point. Relaxation of Bow Without Arrow Release.

III. Preliminary to actual release, the archer should nock and draw an arrow to the anchor position, and then relax the draw without releasing the arrow. (Plate 19a, b, c)

IV. After the arrow has been drawn, it may be necessary to shoot several arrows before a comfortable anchor point has been achieved.

V. Correction of one point at a time may be necessary as the shooting continues.

VERBAL TEACHING AIDS

A. At the time of anchor, check body position and weight distribution.

B. Check head position. (*Tilting the head makes it impossible to obtain the correct anchor.*)

C. Draw to second knuckle of left index finger. (*DO NOT overdraw. This may break the bow or the arrow.*)

D. The arrow rests on top of the bow hand.

E. Chin tip on string.

F. Nose tip on string.

G. Eyes level.

PROPER STANCE SHOULD BE CHECKED AS ARCHER COMPLETES ANCHOR.

VARIATIONS

(1) *Cheek Bone Anchor:* (Plate 20)

Many archers prefer to draw the right hand back to the cheek bone for the anchor position. In this anchor position the index finger comes to rest immediately under the cheek bone.

(2) *Eye Anchor:* (Plate 21)

In this anchor position, the right hand is drawn back to a point on the side of the face. The thumb is hooked under the angle of the right jaw

Cheek Bone Anchor. Eye Anchor. Thumb Anchor.

bone and the fingers raised so that the arrow is thrown directly in line with the right eye.

(3) *Thumb Anchor:* (Plate 22)

The thumb anchor is very similar to the jaw bone anchor. Its chief variation is that the thumb is extended and rests on a point under the jaw bone.

ADVANTAGES

(1) *Cheek Bone Anchor:*
   a. Lessens angle of point of aim.
   b. Better for estimation shooting.
(2) *Eye Anchor:*
   a. Useful in sighting live or moving targets.
(3) *Thumb Anchor:*
   a. Individual preference of some archers.

DISADVANTAGES

(1) *Cheek Bone Anchor:*
   a. Beginning archers tend to vary length of pull.
   b. Allows head to tilt forward, and throws right eye to right of arrow.
   c. Archers unable to see target clearly at distances over 70-80 yards.
   d. Tendency to shoot to the left of the target is increased.
(2) *Eye Anchor:*
   a. Lack of fixed anchor position allows for head tilt.
   b. Awkward for most archers, because of the upward shifting of the shoulders to get the arms to the eye position.
(3) *Thumb Anchor:*
   a. Tendency to tilt head is increased.
   b. May cause improper draw.

POINT OF AIM

The Point of Aim is the establishment of a spot toward which the arrow tip must be pointed in order to hit the target.

SKILL SUMMARY

To establish a point of aim for target shooting, the archer should already have mastered such skills as stance, nocking, bow arm elevation, drawing, and release.

Draw to the anchor point. Make an estimation of the correct elevation needed to put the arrow on the target. Before releasing the arrow, check over the arrow tip to a point on the ground, which can be called an imaginary point of aim. Release the arrow. If the arrow hits high on the target, move the imaginary point of aim farther away from the target and shoot again with the new point of aim. If the arrow flight is too low, move the point toward the target and shoot again. Repeat this process until a point of aim is found.

Usually the third or fourth trial should establish a point of aim. When this is found, place a small object on the ground or wherever the point of aim was found. This object should be a contrasting color to the surface upon which it is used. (Plate 23a, b, c)

Below Target. On Target. Above Target.

AIMING

Aiming is sighting the arrow held at anchor position, preliminary to the release.

SKILL SUMMARY

Preliminary to taking the final shooting position at the shooting line, the archer establishes a point of aim. This point may be in front of the target, on the target, or above the target. Distance, length of arrow, size of bow, and the archer's anchor point are all factors in establishing this aiming point. As

Count 1. Count 2. Count 3.

the anchor points are reached, sight the arrow, by looking on the right side of the string, the left side of the bow, and over the point of the arrow to the point of aim.

SKILL ANALYSIS AND ILLUSTRATION

Count 1. Right eye directly over arrow. Sight right of bow string.
Count 2. Carry vision to arrow point at left side of the bow.
Count 3. Place arrow point on point of aim. (Plate 24a, b, c)

POINT OF AIM IMPROVES ACCURACY IN TARGET SHOOTING.

GENERAL TEACHING AIDS

I. Explain and demonstrate aiming.

II. *Estimation Shooting:* Estimation shooting begins on the first arrow release. The instructor or a student should aid the student in finding the proper arrow and bow elevation. (Plate 25a, b, c)

Draw Above Target. Estimation. Physical Aid.

III. Teach aiming as a skill *only after* the student has become acquainted with, and acquired some skill in, estimation shooting.

IV. DRAWING, ELEVATION, ESTIMATION, ANCHOR, AND RELEASE ARE TAUGHT PRIOR TO POINT OF AIM.

V. When a student acquires some degree of skill in estimation shooting, the use of point of aim should be encouraged. Ask the student to check a line over his arrow point to a spot where it seems to touch the floor, ground, or target. Place an object at that point and on the next shot, sight through to that point of aim to get the proper arrow elevation.

VERBAL TEACHING AIDS

A. Close left eye. (*May use both eyes if this is difficult.*)
B. Raise or lower the left arm to change elevation. (*Never raise or lower the right or anchor hand.*)

C. Use small, distinct object for point of aim. (*A large object causes inaccuracy.*)

D. Always use same spot on object for point of aim.

E. Begin draw from a point above the target. (*This allows a check for right and left of gold portion of target as the draw is made.*)

F. Release the arrow as the draw brings the arrow to the point of aim.

G. Avoid shooting on anticipation of point of aim. (*Wait until point of aim is clearly visible.*)

ESTIMATION SHOOTING: INDIVIDUAL JUDGMENT OF APPROXIMATE ARROW ELEVATION NEEDED TO HIT THE TARGET.

TWO ARCHERS WILL SELDOM HAVE THE SAME POINT OF AIM EVEN THOUGH SHOOTING FROM IDENTICAL POSITIONS.

RELEASE AND FOLLOW THROUGH

The release is the action in releasing the fingers from the string to allow the bow to cast, or shoot the arrow. The follow through is the position maintained until the arrow hits the target.

SKILL SUMMARY

As the anchor and aiming techniques are completed, straighten the fingers of the right hand, thus releasing the string from its anchor. Maintain the same general position until the arrow hits the target.

SKILL ANALYSIS AND ILLUSTRATION

Count 1. Straighten the fingers of the right hand.

Count 2. Allow the bow natural movement after release. Archer maintains same position as anchor position. (Plate 26a, b)

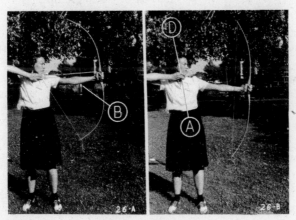

Count 1. Count 2.

PEEPING: DROPPING BOW BEFORE ARROW HITS TARGET. THIS IS NOT CONDUCIVE TO GOOD ARCHERY.

CAST: THE RELEASE OF THE BOW STRING WITH RESULTANT FLIGHT OF THE ARROW.

GENERAL TEACHING AIDS

I. Explain and demonstrate the Release and Follow Through.

II. *Student Drill:* Assume anchor position without the use of the bow string. Open fingers to release position and maintain contact with the chin in the correct anchor position. Check for errors.

III. *Watch For:* Shifting of the hand forward with the string, creating a fudging or creeping habit that hinders the bow cast.

IV. Constant checking is necessary to prevent errors in the release even after the fundamentals have been thoroughly learned.

VERBAL TEACHING AIDS

A. Extend fingers.
B. Avoid tenseness in the bow arm.
C. Keep the release smooth. (*Do not jerk.*)
D. Keep fingers of right hand in contact with chin.
E. Avoid moving left arm to the left or right.
F. Movement of bow arm very slight on follow through.

CREEPING: JERKING THE RIGHT HAND AWAY FROM THE CHIN POSITION. THIS IS A COMMON FAULT OF BEGINNING ARCHERS.

VARIATIONS (Plate 27)

(1) Drawing hand back until the bow string rolls off of the finger tips.

ADVANTAGES

(1) Easier to learn. Does not roll string.

DISADVANTAGES

(1) Release is not as smooth.

Roll Release.

PULLING THE ARROW

Pulling the arrow is the hand and finger action involved in removing the arrow from the target.

SKILL SUMMARY

Place the back of the left hand against the target with the arrow between the index and second finger. Grasp the arrow shaft near the target between the right thumb and finger tips. Turn the arrow as it is drawn from the target.

SKILL ANALYSIS AND ILLUSTRATION

Count 1. Place the back of the left hand on the target.

Count 2. Grasp the arrow shaft near the left hand with the thumb and fingers of the right hand.

Count 3. Turn the arrow and pull it from the target. (Plate 28a, b, c)

Count 1. Count 2. Count 3.

GENERAL TEACHING AIDS

I. Explain and demonstrate pulling the arrows.

II. Explain and demonstrate the variation of pulling the arrow. (See illustration above.)

III. Emphasize the importance of this skill in conserving both arrows and targets.

IV. Stress safety procedures in proceeding to the target after shooting. If class is shooting in a line and several targets are used, do not allow any student to proceed to pull the arrows until all are ready to do so.

VERBAL TEACHING AIDS

A. Back of hand on target.

B. Arrow between index and second fingers of left hand.

C. Grasp arrow in fingers tips of right hand.

D. Grasp arrow near target.

E. Turn arrow as pull is made.

VARIATION

(1) Using palm of hand rather than back of hand.

ADVANTAGE

(1) Individual preference.

SCORING THE ARROWS

A. Gold .... 9 points.
B. Red .... 7 points.
C. Blue .... 5 points.
D. Black .... 3 points.
E. White .... 1 point.
F. Petticoat 0

Target Points.

Arrows splitting line .... Highest ring is scored.
Arrows going through target ...... 5 points.
Arrows rebounding from target ... 5 points.
Arrows dropping from bow .... Counts as one shot unless equipment is broken, or the archer picks it up without moving from the shooting position.

SEE THE NATIONAL ARCHERY RULES FOR SPECIFIC INFORMATION ON HEIGHT OF TARGET, MEASURING SHOOTING DISTANCE, DETAILED RULES, ETC.

ARCHERY ROUNDS

YORK ROUND (Men)
72 arrows at 100 yards.
48 arrows at 80 yards.
24 arrows at 60 yards.

AMERICAN (Men)
30 arrows at 60 yards.
30 arrows at 50 yards.
30 arrows at 40 yards.

METROPOLITAN (Men)
30 arrows at 100 yards.
30 arrows at 80 yards.
30 arrows at 60 yards.
30 arrows at 50 yards.
30 arrows at 40 yards.

NATIONAL ROUND (Women.)
48 arrows at 60 yards.
24 arrows at 50 yards.

COLUMBIA (Women)
24 arrows at 50 yards.
24 arrows at 40 yards.
24 arrows at 30 yards.

METROPOLITAN (Women)
30 arrows at 60 yards.
30 arrows at 50 yards.
30 arrows at 40 yards.
30 arrows at 30 yards.

TEAM ROUND (Women)
96 arrows at 50 yards.

JUNIOR ARCHERS

JUNIOR METROPOLITAN ROUND   BOY SCOUT MERIT BADGE

30 arrows at 40 yards.	30 arrows at 50 yards.
30 arrows at 30 yards.	30 arrows at 40 yards.
30 arrows at 20 yards.	30 arrows at 30 yards.

ARCHERY CONTESTS

CLOUT SHOOTING

A very popular type of archery is the clout round developed by the National Archery Tournament. The target for the clout round is a large regulation style target marked on the ground with the same number of concentric circles as found on the standard size target. The gold in the clout target is nine and three quarter feet in diameter. The other circles are four feet eight inches wide with the outer circle forty-eight feet in diameter. The lines on the target are marked with lime, flour, or white tape. Men shoot 36 arrows from a distance of 180 yards, and the hits in the various circles score the same as on the standard size archery target.

ARCHERY GOLF

Archery golf is similar to golf in that the flight shot is substituted for the drive, and additional shots replace the fairway and iron shots. The target can be a small, straw ball, a marked surface on the ground, or a five inch cardboard mounted on a peg that can be turned toward the archer on each shot.

The course is similar to, or the same as, the regular golf course, with the total shots used to hit each target as the course score. This type of shooting is excellent for developing estimation shooting.

The Teaching Aids for each skill offer specific items suggested for use in the general activities listed below.

SUGGESTED CLASS ORGANIZATION

(60 minutes)

Initial Lessons (*1st three weeks*)

Introduction to Archery: History, Use, Organizations, etc.

Instruction in parts of bow, arrows, and equipment.

Instruction in proper equipment care.

Selection of equipment.

Class Organization.

Archery stance.
Stringing or Bracing the bow.
Nocking the arrow.
Anchor.
Drawing.
Release.
Pulling the arrows.
Estimation shooting at 20 yards.

4th through 8th week.
Continue individual instruction.
Continue shooting by estimation at 20 yards.
Stress value of estimation of arrow elevation.
Instruction in point of aim.
Point of aim shooting at 30 yards.
Vary class distance for drill in use of point of aim.

9th through 12th week.
Continue individual instruction.
Point of aim shooting at 40 yards.
Point of aim shooting at 50 yards.
Conduct class tournaments.
Conduct novelty shoots as desired.
Instruction in various types of games using the bow and arrow.
    (Many of these can be found in reference material.)

NOTE: Safety instruction should be paramount in every class.

Care should be taken to see that safety is practiced in each class period, and thoroughly understood by every student.

(1) No student should leave the shooting line until all bows are placed on their stands.

(2) No person should proceed to the target until all students shooting are ready to do so.

(3) No bow should be taken from the stands until all archers are behind the shooting line.

(4) Class members not shooting should remain two to three steps immediately behind the bow they expect to use.

(5) The student immediately behind the archer that is shooting should assist by watching for deviations from the accepted technique, and aid in correcting errors.

FURTHER REFERENCES

1. Ainsworth, Dorothy S.; Broer, Marion R.; Goss, Alice G.; Goss, Gertrude; Jennings, Evelyn; Pitkin, Bertha A.; Ryder, Florence: *Individual Sports for Women*, W. B. Saunders and Company, Philadelphia and London, 1943.
2. Lambert, Arthur W. Jr.: *Modern Archery*, A. S. Barnes and Company, Publishers, New York, 1929.
3. Official Sports Library for Women: *Individual Sports*, Archery, Fencing, Golf, and Riding. A. S. Barnes and Company, Publishers, 1945.
4. Reichart, Natalie and Kease, Gilman: *Archery*. A. S. Barnes and Company, Publishers, New York, 1940.
5. Rounsevelle, Phillip: *Archery Simplified*. A. S. Barnes and Company, Publishers, New York, 1931.
6. Sumption, Dorothy: *Archery for Beginners*. W. B. Saunders and Company, Philadelphia, 1932.
7. Tunis, John R.: *Sport for the Fun of It*. A. S. Barnes and Company, Publishers, New York, 1940.

IV

BADMINTON

TEACHING PREMISE

THE objective of this chapter is to present the fundamental skills in Badminton for beginner's instruction, and to improve the play of the more experienced player. The skills are presented from the simple to the complex and do not necessarily represent a rigid teaching progression. Some instructors, after teaching the grip, may wish to proceed to instruction of the forehand drive rather than the service.

The service presented has been found effective for deception and is especially adaptable to doubles play. Other variations are offered and are found by some instructors and players to be more effective.

The General Teaching Aids are only suggested drills. The use of them may prove effective in helping the learner acquire the skill more readily, and should not be over-used in class instruction.

In the discussion of the various skills or strokes, a specific stroke is selected for analysis with the understanding that other skills are possible. For example, in the forehand lob, there are nine specific strokes possible: front court; low, net high, and high; side court; low, net high, and high; and back court; low, net high, and high. Only one position was used for analysis. It may not be the most important, but the need for brevity made such condensation necessary. The other positions may be analyzed in the same manner as the skill selected.

Individual variations are necessary. In other words, fit the stroke to the individual rather than the individual to the stroke.

A BRIEF HISTORY OF BADMINTON

Badminton is centuries old, and originated from a game in India, called Poona.

The game as we know it today probably had its origin in England in 1873. A group of army officers who had served in India, christened it at the estate of the Duke of Beaufort. They called it Badminton, which was the name of the Duke's large, ancestral hall.

The game was only mildly popular in England until the first National Convention was held in 1898. This convention seemed to give the impetus necessary for greater participation.

The first Badminton Club was organized in the United States in 1878 by Bayard Clarke and E. Langdon Wilks. The First International Team Match was played in 1923 between a Canadian Club and the Original American Club of New York. Typical of the growth of Badminton is the comparison of club increase. In 1921 two clubs had been organized. Today, there are over 5,000.

It is quite generally agreed that the popularity of Badminton will continue to increase due to its adaptability for all age groups; the relatively low cost of equipment; and the small size of the court, which makes it possible for home use on the average sized lawn.

The amount of present participation alone warrants its inclusion in any physical education curriculum.

THE GAME

Badminton play requires stamina, speed, cleverness, and agility. Since the introduction of feinting, and deception shots, badminton experts have developed a tricky brand of play even more spectacular in its way than that of tennis.

Fundamentally, the game of Badminton is the same as a game in India called Poona. It is also similar to tennis in that it involves a racquet, net, and an object to be hit. It differs from tennis in that the playing court is about one half as large, the net is two feet higher, the service courts extend to the baseline, and the object hit is a shuttlecock rather than a ball. (Plate 1)

As a singles game (one player on each side) begins, the server stands any place desired in the right service court and serves diagonally across the net to the opponent's right service court. The serve must be made with the contact position of the racquet and shuttlecock below the server's waist, the head of the racquet below the wrist, and the feet in contact with the floor. Only one trial is allowed. The receiver must attempt to return the service. If this is accomplished, the shuttle is played back and forth until one player makes a fault, by hitting the shuttlecock out of bounds, into the net, or missing it entirely. If the serving side makes the fault, the side is down, the service goes to the opponent, and no points are made. If the receiving side makes the fault, a point

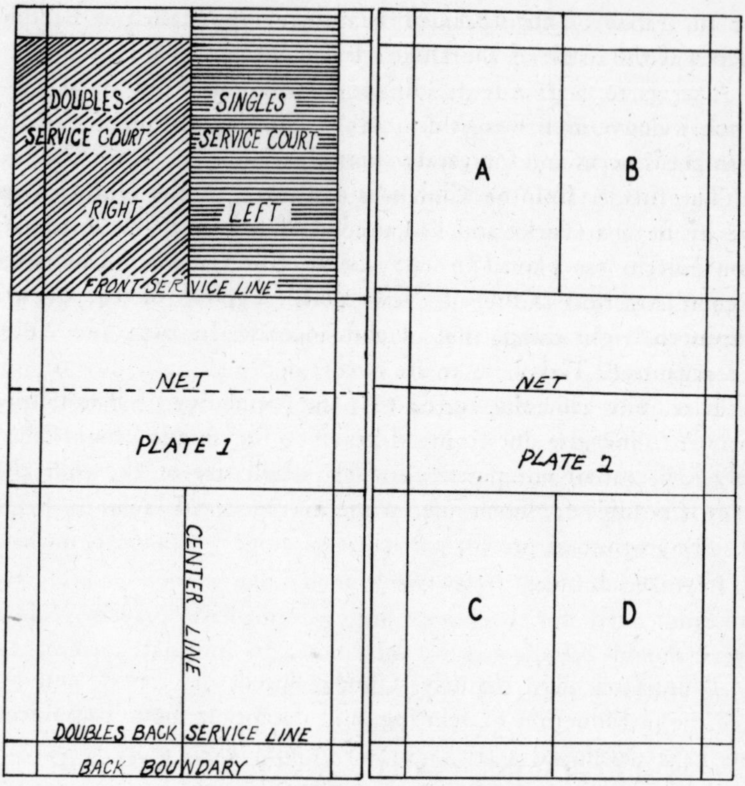

DOUBLES SERVICE COURT RIGHT

SINGLES SERVICE COURT LEFT

FRONT SERVICE LINE

NET

PLATE 1

CENTER LINE

DOUBLES BACK SERVICE LINE

BACK BOUNDARY

A   B

NET

PLATE 2

C   D

The Court. Game Explanation.

is made for the serving side, and the server and receiver move to the left to repeat the procedure outlined above in the left service court. The player serving continues to serve in alternate courts until a fault is made on the serving side. Each time a different side begins a service, the court from which the service is made, is determined by the score. If a serving player's score is even, (o, 2, 4, 6, etc.), service is begun in the right court; if it is odd, (1, 3, 5, 7, etc.), service is begun in the left court. Play continues until one player has accumulated enough points for game, which for women's singles is 11; for men, 15. Scoring in badminton singles is similar to volleyball scoring, in that the serving side is the only side that can make a point, while a fault made by the serving side, awards the service to the other side, and no point is made on the exchange of service. For rules regarding tie games and setting of the score, see the Official Guides on Badminton rules. (Plate 2)

In a doubles game (two people on each side), the play differs slightly from singles. As the game begins, team AB has the service.

See plate 2 above. This is decided by a toss or any other method desired. Player A serves to player D. If a point is made, A and B exchange courts, and A serves to C. If a fault is made, by the initial serving side (AB), the side is down, and the service goes to team DC. D, in the right court, begins the service and continues serving in alternate courts as long as points are made. If D or C make a fault, one down is called, and C serves from whatever court C occupied at the time the fault was made. C continues to serve until C or D make a fault, in which case, 2 downs are completed and the service returns to team AB. Whichever player occupies the right court, that player begins the service, and AB holds the service until they have made two faults, making 2 downs and loss of service. This continues until 15 points have been made. Thus two downs are allowed each serving side *except* on the initial service at the start of the game, and the serving side alternates courts, while the receiving side does not. See the official badminton scoring rules for tie games and setting of scores.

In mixed doubles, (men and women), the women's scoring system is recommended for beginners and intermediate players. Advanced players should be allowed to determine, by mutual agreement, the scoring system desired for length of game.

SELECTION, CARE, AND REPAIR OF EQUIPMENT

RACQUET

Selection. Select a racquet that is easy to handle and comfortable to grip. The racquet should be flexible, about five and one half ounces in weight, and strung with twenty gauge silk or gut string. Special care should be taken to check the weight of the racquet head. The racquet, held in the hand, should not feel heavy in the head. (Plate 3)

Care. Racquet strings should be kept tightly strung, and the racquet kept in a press and water-proof cover when not in use. Racquets should be stored in a warm, dry place.

All equipment should be marked and numbered. A number system that gives the equipment number and year purchased has proved successful. This system uses both a letter and a number. In A-12 for example, A designates the year purchased, and 12 indicates the number of the equipment.

Replacements should be made from time to time as breakage and loss from wear occur. Inventory should be taken at regular intervals.

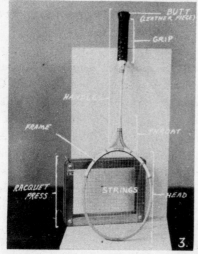

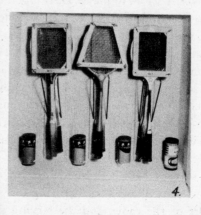

The Racquet.   Racquet Storage.

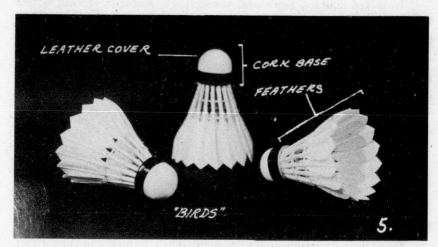

Shuttlecocks.

Such replacements as are needed can be secured from any standard sporting goods company.

There are many types of storage used successfully for the care of badminton equipment. The one presented here may not be the type preferred by the majority of instructors; however it has three values common to any correct storage. The storage space is warm and dry, the racquets hang evenly with no undue strain on the frames or strings, and the equipment is easily accessible for inventory and class use. (Plate 4)

Repair. Replace broken strings immediately. Warped racquets should be re-strung and placed in a press. Leather pieces on the butt of the racquet handles should be securely fastened.

SHUTTLECOCK

Selection. The official shuttlecock should weigh about 73 to 85 grams. The feathers should be of even length and well-matched. Shuttlecocks are made in three speeds: fast; medium; and slow. Generally, the medium speed indoor shuttle should be selected when play is indoors. The outdoor shuttlecock should be used for outside play only. (Plate 5)

Care and Repair. Shuttlecocks should be kept in a humidifier when not in use. Players should pick them up with the hands, rather than with the racquet. Feathers should be straightened after each point is made, and every effort should be made to avoid hitting the feathers with the racquet.

Repair of old shuttlecocks is almost impossible; however they last longer if the feathers are moistened slightly and straightened after each period of play.

COURT

Selection. The ideal badminton court should have a ceiling about forty feet high. The walls should be painted green or brown. The lighting should be from the sides, rather than from the ends of the court. all lines should be clearly marked for doubles and singles courts, and approximately one and one half inches in width. For safety purposes, as well as for good playing conditions, the floor should not be slippery.

Care and Repair. Badminton courts should be kept clean and free from marks. Courts should not be waxed. Lines should be repainted whenever necessary.

NET

Selection, Care, and Repair. The Official Badminton net should be used. This is usually made of brown net and bound with white tape.

Badminton nets should be mended immediately when breaks in the net appear. Rope ties last longer if they are waxed and metal clips used to fasten the net ropes to the net posts. Nets may be folded, rolled, or hung in storage.

Frayed rope and net tears are the most common repairs needed for badminton nets. Ropes should be replaced, and tears mended by tying broken ends together in the same net pattern. Brown string can be used for this.

GRIP

The Badminton Grip is the position of the hand as it grasps the racquet handle.

GRIP SUMMARY

The top portion of the handle falls between the thumb and forefinger, as the handle is grasped in the same manner as in the use of a small hatchet. The fingers extend around the right portion of the handle and the thumb around the left. The grip is primarily with the thumb and first and second fingers. The butt of the racquet is free in the hand. The little finger rests against the leather piece. The racquet head is raised above the level of the wrist. This cocking of the wrist, however, is illegal for serving and cannot be used in the service stroke.

GRIP ANALYSIS AND ILLUSTRATION (Plate 6a, b, c, d)

Top View: Top portion of handle falls between thumb and forefinger.
Right Side View: Fingers extend comfortably around the handle. Racquet above wrist level.
Left Side View: Thumb extends around handle. Butt of racquet is free in the hand. Racquet above wrist level.
Bottom View: Little finger rests against leather piece. Grip is primarily in thumb and first two fingers.

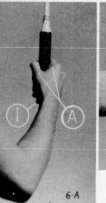  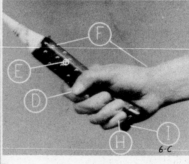 

Top View. Right Side View. Left Side View. Bottom View.

THE GRIP ON THE RACQUET SHOULD ALLOW FOR MAXIMUM WRIST FREEDOM.

GENERAL TEACHING AIDS

I. Explain and demonstrate the Badminton Grip.
II. How to obtain the Badminton Grip. (Plate 7a, b, c)

Step One. Step Two. Step Three.

(1) Hold the racquet in the left hand, handle toward the body, and the racquet face at right angles to the floor.

(2) Place the thumb and first two fingers on top of the racquet handle so that the top portion of the handle falls between the "V" made by the thumb and forefinger.

(3) Extend the fingers comfortably around the handle, gripping primarily with the thumb and first two fingers, and allowing the third finger to rest lightly against the handle, and the little finger to rest against the leather piece. Take the left hand away and cock the right wrist to raise the racquet head above the level of the wrist, leaving the butt of the racquet free in the hand.

III. Class may work in pairs, with No. 1's handing racquet to No. 2's, the latter, taking the correct grip. Both students check for errors. No. 2 hands racquet to No. 1, etc.

IV. Individual check by instructor for freedom of wrist action.

VERBAL TEACHING AIDS

A. Top portion of racquet falls between thumb and forefinger.

B. Fingers spread comfortably.

C. Wrist cocked. (*Greater wrist action in this position.*)

D. Thumb around left side of racquet handle.

E. Thumb extended along back of racquet handle in backhand grip. (*Gives more power to weak wrists in backhand strokes.*)

F. Racquet head above level of wrist. (*Illegal for service.*)

G. Grip with thumb and first two fingers. (*Aids wrist action.*)

H. Little finger rests lightly against leather piece. (*Grip position at end of racquet handle.*)

I. Butt of racquet free in hand. (*Wrist flexibility.*)

VARIATIONS

1. In the backhand strokes, it may be advisable for the player to place the thumb along the side of the racquet handle, rather than around it. (Plate 8)

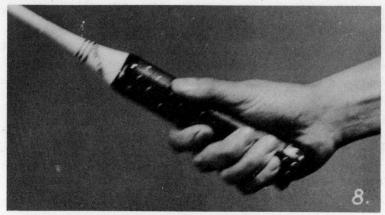

Left Side View of Backhand Grip.

2. Some players prefer to turn the racquet about five to ten degrees counter-clockwise from the regular grip.

ADVANTAGES

1. Backhand grip variation.
   Advantages: The variation of the thumb in the backhand grip, gives the player with a weak wrist, more power on the backhand stroke.
   Disadvantages: The movement of the thumb has a tendency to reduce the speed of the change from forehand to backhand.
2. Counter-clockwise variation.
   Advantages: This position gives the wrist a stronger forehand position; consequently a more powerful forehand stroke can be executed.
   Disadvantages: This position requires a shifting of the hand on the racquet on all backhand strokes. This further reduces the speed with which a change from a forehand stroke to a backhand stroke can be made.

READY POSITIONS
(STANCE)

Ready position is a term applied to the stance, or body position, assumed by a player when waiting for a service or a return of the shuttle.

FOR SERVICE

Assume a position with the feet slightly apart and the left foot just ahead of the right. Carry the body weight toward the balls of the feet and flex the knees slightly. Grasp the shuttle in the thumb and first finger of the left hand, so that the cork base points toward the court. Place the thumb on the outside of the feathers and the first finger just inside the feather tips. Bend forward from the waist so that the shuttle can be held at arms length from the body, below waist height, and directly in line with the racquet side. Use the forehand grip on the racquet, (backhand is legal), flex the right elbow until the forearm and upper arm form a right angle, and turn the right palm up, to place the racquet face directly below the base of the shuttle. (Plate 9)

For Receiving Service

Assume a position with the feet 8 to 12 inches apart, and one foot 6 to 8 inches ahead of the other. Bend the knees slightly and carry the weight on the balls of the feet. Rest the throat of the racquet in the fingers of the left hand. (Plate 10)

During Play

The body position changes very little from that assumed while waiting for the service. Carry the racquet well up and in front of the body, although not necessarily resting in the fingers of the left hand. (Plate 11)

> NOTE: Body build and sex will vary the ready positions particularly in relationship to width of stride, while the forward foot may vary according to individual preference.

ADVANTAGE POSITIONS

The advantage position is a term applied to the court position assumed by a player which will enable the player to cover the court in a minimum of time and with a minimum of effort.

For Service

The advantage position for serving is usually near the center line and approximately two steps back of the front or short service line.

For Receiving Service

The advantage position for receiving the service is generally about two steps back of the front or short service line, and midway between the center and the side line.

During Play

The advantage position during play is frequently called the "home" position, and is on the center line and approximately midway between the net and the baseline.

Ready Position Service. Receiving Service. During Play.

KEEP THE COURT COVERED AT ALL TIMES

DOUBLES "UP-AND-BACK" PLAY (After return of service.)

Net Player. The advantage position for the net player is on, or in front of, the intersection formed by the front or short service line and the center line.

Back Player. The advantage position for the back player is usually about two steps toward the net from the back service line, and slightly to the left of the center line. The back player shifts to the right of the center line if the net player moves left, and back again if the net player moves right.

NOTE: The advantage positions explained are optional; however beginners should be advised to use them.

ALWAYS BE READY TO MOVE. DO NOT CARRY WEIGHT ON HEELS.

SERVICE

The service is an underhand stroke used by each server at the beginning of each game, and after each point or down, to put the shuttle in play.

SKILL SUMMARY

Out-of-Hand Short Service. Assume the ready position for service within the service court. Extend the racquet wrist down and back. Swing the arm in a pendulum-like movement. Flex the racquet wrist and stroke forward and upward. Release the shuttle as the face of the racquet comes in contact with the base of the shuttle. Follow through in line with the intended shuttle flight. Contact with the shuttle must be made below the waist, with both feet in contact with the floor, and the racquet hand below the level of the wrist.

(See variations for toss, short, long, and driven services.)

SKILL ANALYSIS AND ILLUSTRATION (Plate 12a, b, c, d)

Count 1. Ready position for service.
Count 2. Extend racquet wrist and swing arm back.
Count 3. Swing arm forward, flex wrist, and contact shuttle.
Count 4. Follow through toward intended shuttle flight.

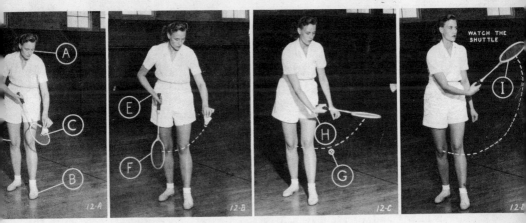

Count 1. Count 2. Count 3. Count 4.

WATCH THE SHUTTLE AT ALL TIMES.

MOVE IMMEDIATELY TO "ADVANTAGE POSITION DURING PLAY" AFTER SERVICE.

GENERAL TEACHING AIDS

I. Review the ready and advantage positions.

II. Explain and demonstrate the short (drop), out-of-hand service.

III. *Drill 1:* Plate 13)

All players on each side of the net, stand on the short service line facing the back of the court. Serve to count as described in the service skill analysis; however the count of 1 is also used to check wrist flexibility by extending and flexing the racquet wrist. Each student retrieves own shuttle, and the line forms on the back service line and faces the net. In this way, all students may practice the fundamentals of the service, regardless of the size of the class, and the drill can be counted by one student, while the instructor checks for individual errors.

IV. *Drill 2:* (Plate 14)

Players form a line on the short service line, all on one side of the net. Count as in Drill 1. Serve short drop service over the net and into the service court directly opposite from each student's position. Retrieve own service, and serve across the net from the opposite short service line. Check for and correct errors.

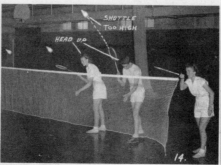

Group Drill No. 1. No. 2. Shuttle Toss for Toss Service.

V. *Drill 3:*

Divide the class by the number of courts available. Divide each of these groups by four. Numbers 1 and 3 form lines in opposite right service courts; numbers 2 and 4 in opposite left service courts. The first student in lines 1 and 2 assume the ready and advantage positions for service, and serve diagonally across the net to lines 3 and 4, with the short out-of-hand service. The serves are recovered by the first student in lines 3 and 4. The first student in lines 3 and 4 serve diagonally across the net. These students now go to the end of their respective lines, and the next students step up to repeat the drill. Counts are used as in Drill 2; however as skill increases, players disregard the counts and begin practice of placement of service. The positions of students in the right court should be changed frequently with those in the left court, in order to insure equal amount of practice from each position.

VI. Explain and demonstrate the long or lob out-of-hand service. See VARIATIONS page 59.

VII. Repeat drills used for short or drop service, using the lob service.

VIII. Place a rope or string about 12 to 16 inches above the net. Drop serves are to pass under the rope and lob serves over it.

IX. Explain and demonstrate the driven service. Repeat drills with this service. See page 59 for an analysis of the driven service.

X. Explain and demonstrate the toss service. See page 60 for an analysis of this service. (Plate 15)

XI. Placement practice for all types of service and for doubles and singles play. Practice varying types of service from either court.

NOTE: Forehand and backhand instruction should accompany instruction in the service.

VERBAL TEACHING AIDS

A. Watch the shuttle.
B. Weight toward balls of the feet. (*Quicker to move.*)
C. Shuttle base toward center of racquet.
D. Knees slightly flexed. (*Easier to move in any direction.*)
E. Extended wrist on backswing.
F. Racquet head below wrist level. (*Service rule.*)

G. Contact with shuttle made below waist level.

H. Flexed wrist on forward swing. (*More power on serve.*)

I. Follow through toward intended line of shuttle flight.

SERVE TO A *SPOT ON THE COURT*. DO NOT SERVE TO AN OPPONENT.

KNOW NET HEIGHT AND POSITION OF THE RECEIVER.

VARIATIONS

OUT-OF-HAND DROP (short) SERVICE previously described sends the shuttle from the server's advantage position just over the net to land just inside the short service line and in the correct service court.

OUT-OF-HAND LOB (Long) SERVICE sends the shuttle from the server's advantage position high into the air, over the net, to land just inside the back, or long, service line and in the correct service court.

OUT-OF-HAND DRIVEN SERVICE sends the shuttle from the server's advantage position in a low, fast, swift arc over the net to land in the back of the correct service court.

SKILL ANALYSIS COMPARISONS (See page 62 also.)

Count 1. *Drop; Lob; Driven:* Ready positions are identical.

Count 2. *Drop; Lob; Driven:* Backswings are identical.

Count 3. *Drop:* Swing arm forward, flex wrist, and contact shuttle.
Lob: Forward swing is harder and faster. Wrist flexion is more vigorously snapped through. Shuttle held slightly lower or dropped before contact.
Driven: Forward swing, wrist flexion more vigorous than in the lob.

Count 4. *Drop; Lob; Driven:* Follow through is always toward the intended shuttle flight; however the more vigorous the forward swing, the longer the follow through.

SKILL ILLUSTRATION SHOWING FLIGHT VARIATIONS (Plates 16, 17, 18)

TOSS SERVICE differs from the Out-of-Hand services only in the release of the shuttle, and a longer backswing. The shuttle is tossed in the air as the backswing is started and contacted in the air as it drops below waist level. The toss service may be used with the lob, drop and driven services. The toss service is an ADVANCED SKILL and is not recommended for beginners. (Plate 19a, b, c)

ALL RULES OF LEGAL SERVICE APPLY TO ALL SERVES. CONTACT POINT BELOW WAIST, RACQUET HEAD BELOW THE LEVEL OF THE WRIST, FEET IN CONTACT WITH THE COURT.

Drop Service. Lob Service. Driven Service Shuttle Flights.

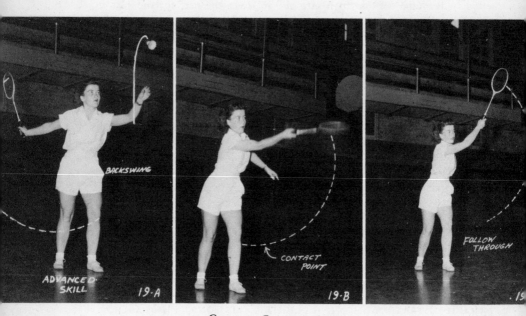

Count 1. Count 2. Count 3.

ADVANTAGES

OUT-OF-HAND SERVICE

Advantage: Easy to control. Excellent for teaching beginners to contact the shuttle and apply the rules of legal service.

Disadvantage: The swing of the racquet arm seems cramped due to the necessity of holding the left arm in a static position.

TOSS SERVICE

Advantage: The power of a full swing can be used for service. The backswing is free and natural, because the left arm can be used in opposition after the shuttle is tossed. Speed and length are easier to attain.

Disadvantage: The power and speed attained by a full backswing increases the difficulty in controlling the shuttle at the moment of impact when attempting different types of service.

DROP SERVICE

Advantage: The Drop Service is used in doubles play in order to force the opponents to hit a defensive stroke.

LOB SERVICE

Advantage: The Lob Service is used in a singles game to draw the opponent out of position. This service is easier to place in singles, because the service court is longer.

DRIVEN SERVICE

Advantage: The Driven Service is used as a surprise attack in both doubles and singles play.

THE LOB, DROP, AND DRIVEN SERVES ARE USED IN BOTH DOUBLES AND SINGLES PLAY. IT IS GOOD STRATEGY TO VARY THE TYPES OF SERVICE FREQUENTLY.

RETURN OF SERVICE

The return of the service is any stroke used to send the shuttle to the opponent's court after the service has been completed.

SKILL SUMMARY

Assume a ready stance in the advantage position for the return of the service and watch the shuttle at all times.

SKILL ANALYSIS

The service is generally returned with a lob, drop, or drive. A smash or kill is seldom possible, since a well-placed service makes such a stroke impossible. Detailed analysis of these skills can be found in the following pages.

SKILL ILLUSTRATION

See the illustrations of drop, lob, and drives, for the type of return is governed by the type of service, and the court position of the opponent.

A PROPERLY RETURNED SERVE SHOULD BE AN OFFENSIVE SHOT.

WATCH FOR RACQUET ARM AND EYE SIGNALS FROM THE OPPONENT.

GENERAL TEACHING AIDS

I. Explain and demonstrate the footwork used in covering the court.

II. *Footwork Drill 1:*

Count 1. Face the net in ready position for play.

Count 2. Pivot on the left foot, and step back with the right for a forehand stroke, side to the net.

Count 3. Face the net as in Count 1.

Count 4. Pivot on the right foot, and step back with the left for a backhand stroke, right side to the net.

Repeat the drill moving toward the net.

III. *Footwork Drill 2:*

Count 1. Assume service ready and advantage positions.

Count 2. Move to advantage position for play.

Count 3. Move to right and toward net.

Count 4. Move to advantage position for play.

Repeat Drill for each direction from "advantage position for play."

IV. *Footwork Drill 3:*

Combine Drills 1 and 2. (i.e.: Move toward net and to the right, pivot to place left side to net for a forehand shot, etc.)

NOTE: Many returns are made with such speed that correct footwork is impossible. Get into position if possible but return the shuttle.

VERBAL TEACHING AIDS

A. Short, quick steps.

B. Side to net if possible.

C. Run on balls of the feet.

D. Keep weight forward.

E. Be ready to move in any direction.

DO NOT OVER-DRILL—THIS KILLS INTEREST.

UNDERHAND FOREHAND CLEAR

(LOB)

The Underhand Forehand Clear is an underhand return of the shuttle that carries it in a high arc, so that it will fall deep in the opposite court.

SKILL SUMMARY

Assume a position with the left side to the net, and the left foot ahead of the right. Swing the racquet down and back in a full backswing, weight on the right foot. Extend the wrist as the backswing is made, but keep the right arm straight. Swing the racquet forward as the weight transfers to the left foot, and flex the wrist as the shuttle contact is made. Aim for a spot high above the center of the opposite court, and follow through toward the line of intended shuttle flight.

SKILL ANALYSIS AND ILLUSTRATION (Plate 20a, b, c, d)

Count 1. Ready position for play, left side to net.

Count 2. Full backswing, wrist extended, arm straight, weight on right foot.

Count 3. Swing racquet forward, right arm straight. Flex wrist quickly as shuttle is hit.

Count 4. Follow through toward shuttle flight.

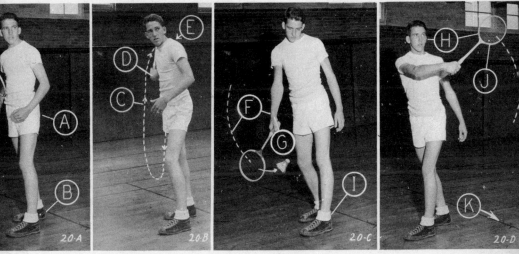

Count 1. Count 2. Count 3. Count 4.

Move to "Home" Position After Return is Completed.

General Teaching Aids

    I. Review the lob service.

    II. Explain and demonstrate the Underhand Forehand Clear.

    III. Drill class in counts outlined in skill analysis.

        (1) To explanation by instructor.

        (2) To slow counts.

        (3) To fast counts.

        (4) Without counts.

    IV. *Drill:* No. 1's serve to No. 2's forehand. No. 2's return the service with the Underhand Forehand Clear. Repeat drill with No. 2's serving to No. 1's.

    V. Instruction in Underhand Backhand Clear.

    VI. Rally with Underhand Clear Shots.

Verbal Teaching Aids

A. Left side to net.

B. Weight on right foot.

C. Swing racquet down and back. (*Full backswing.*)

D. Wrist extended fully.

E. Arm straight.

F. Swing down and up on forward swing. Wrist leads.

G. Snap wrist through as shuttle is hit. (*Aids power.*)

H. Aim high in opposite court.

I. Transfer weight to left foot.

J. Follow through toward intended shuttle flight.

K. Move to "home" position after stroke is completed.

KEEP LOBS HIGH AND DEEP IN OPPOSITE COURT.

VARIATIONS

Variations in stroking the Underhand Forehand Clear will result from the speed with which the return has to be made, the spot to which the shuttle was returned by the opponent, and the distance the shuttle must be hit, rather than from the use of different techniques. The explanations presented in the following pages show only a few of these and refer to court positions of the shuttle only.

FRONT COURT (*Low*)

Count 1. Step forward toward shuttle with left foot. Drop racquet to low position, wrist ahead of racquet face.

Count 2. Swing racquet back in as full a backswing as possible.

Count 3. Swing racquet upward toward shuttle.

Count 4. Snap wrist upward to contact shuttle. Follow through and return to "home" position.

BACK COURT (*Deep*)

Count 1. Move to back of court, left side to net. Weight on right foot.

Count 2. Take a full backswing. Wrist fully extended.

Count 3. Transfer weight to left foot, swing forward, wrist leading, and snap wrist as quickly as possible as contact with the shuttle is made. Hit against a straight left leg.

Count 4. Follow through toward the point at which the shuttle was aimed. (*The follow through is naturally longer, since the swing was more vigorous.*)

UNDERHAND BACKHAND CLEAR
(LOB)

The Underhand Backhand Clear is an underhand backhand return of the shuttle that carries it in a high arc, so that it will land deep in the opponent's court.

SKILL SUMMARY

Assume a position with the right side to the net, the right foot ahead of the left. Swing the racquet down and back across the front of the body, in a full backswing. Flex the wrist and bend the elbow in order to obtain as complete a backswing as possible. Swing the racquet down and up to meet the shuttle. Allow the wrist to lead until the contact point is reached, and then snap the wrist through as vigorously as possible. Transfer the weight to the right foot as the forward swing is started. Aim for a spot high above the center of the opposite court, and follow through toward the line of intended shuttle flight.

Skill Analysis and Illustration (Plate 21a, b, c, d)

Count 1. Right side to net and full backswing, wrist flexed, bent elbow.

Count 2. Swing racquet forward, wrist leading.

Count 3. Arm straightens, snap extension of wrist to meet shuttle.

Count 4. Follow through toward shuttle flight.

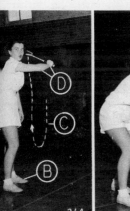   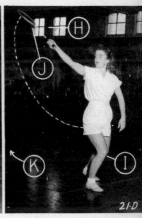

Count 1. Count 2. Count 3. Count 4.

General Teaching Aids

I. Explain and demonstrate the Underhand Backhand Clear.

II. This should be taught at the same time as the Underhand Forehand Clear; therefore the same type of drills and General instruction can be used.

III. As skill increases in the use of the Underhand Clear strokes, advise students to attempt to place their clear shots in the back corners of the opposite court.

Verbal Teaching Aids

A. Right side to net.

B. Weight on left foot.

C. Swing racquet down and back.

D. Arm bent, wrist flexed at top of backswing.

E. Swing down and up on forward swing.

F. Right arm and leg straight as shuttle is hit.

G. Snap wrist through as shuttle is hit. (*Extension.*)

H. Aim high in opposite court.

I. Transfer weight to right foot.

J. Follow through toward intended shuttle flight.

K. Move to "home" position after stroke is completed.

VARY THE UNDERHAND CLEAR SHOTS FROM RIGHT TO LEFT SIDE OF OPPONENT'S COURT.

VARIATIONS

As in the variations of the Underhand Forehand Clear, the analyses presented in the following pages show only a few variations that might result from the court position of the shuttle as the Underhand Backhand Clear is performed.

FRONT COURT (*Low*)

Count 1. Step forward toward shuttle with right foot. Drop racquet to low position, wrist ahead of racquet face.

Count 2. Swing racquet back in as full a backswing as possible.

Count 3. Swing racquet upward toward shuttle.

Count 4. Snap wrist upward to contact shuttle. Follow through and return to "home" position.

BACK COURT (*Deep*)

Count 1. Move to back of court, right side to net, weight on left foot.

Count 2. Take a full backswing, wrist and elbow flexed.

Count 3. Transfer weight to left foot and swing forward vigorously, wrist leading and arm straight. Snap wrist quickly as contact with the shuttle is made and hit against a straight right leg.

Count 4. Aim high and follow through. (*The follow through will be longer, since the swing is vigorous.*)

FOREHAND DRIVEN CLEAR

The Forehand Driven Clear is a sidearm stroke that contacts the shuttle at a point approximately waist high and sends the shuttle in a high arc to land deep in the opposite court.

SKILL SUMMARY

Assume a position with the left side to the net, and the left foot ahead of the right. Swing the racquet back parallel with the court in a full backswing, the wrist cocked and fully extended, weight on the right foot. Keep the racquet head slightly above the wrist and flex the elbow to obtain a free backswing. Transfer the weight to the left foot, and swing the racquet forward, wrist leading. Contact the shuttle out away from the body and insure power by snapping the wrist to full flexion. Aim high in the center of the opposite court, and gain the necessary shuttle height by an upward follow through and a slightly open racquet face at contact with the shuttle.

SKILL ANALYSIS AND ILLUSTRATION (Plate 22a, b, c)

Count 1. Full backswing parallel to court, weight on right foot, racquet head above wrist.

Count 2. Forward swing out and away from body. Arm straightens, weight on left foot.

Count 3. Snap wrist to full flexion, racquet face slightly open. (Not illustrated.)

Count 4. Follow through to a point higher than shuttle contact and toward intended shuttle flight.

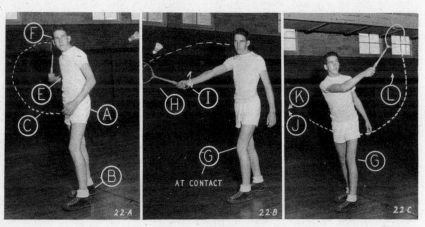

Count 1. Count 2. Count 4.

GENERAL TEACHING AIDS

I. Explain and demonstrate the Forehand Driven Clear.

II. Demonstrate the similiarities and differences between the Forehand Driven Clear and the Underhand Forehand Clear.

III. Drill class in the same general manner as used for the Underhand clear strokes.

IV. Instruction in Backhand Driven Clear.

V. Rally with Clear shots. Check to be sure students do not run around the shuttle to avoid backhand strokes. Check for individual errors as play continues, and caution students to vary the type of Clear shots used.

VI. As skill increases, practice for placement to right or left in back of opposite court.

VERBAL TEACHING AIDS

A. Left side to net.

B. Weight on right foot.

C. Backswing parallel to court.

D. Wrist cocked.

E. Elbow flexed.

F. Racquet head above wrist.

G. Transfer weight to left foot.

H. Swing racquet out and away from body.

I. Wrist leads.

J. Snap wrist to full flexion at shuttle contact.

K. Racquet face slightly open at contact.

L. Follow through toward line of intended shuttle flight.

BACKHAND DRIVEN CLEAR

The Backhand Driven Clear is a backhand stroke that contacts the shuttle at a point approximately waist high, and sends the shuttle in a high arc to land deep in the opposite court.

SKILL SUMMARY

Assume a position with the right side to the net, and the right foot ahead of the left. Swing the racquet across the body, and parallel with the court in a full backswing. Cock the wrist and keep the weight on the left foot. Flex the elbow to obtain a free backswing. Transfer the weight to the right foot, and swing the racquet forward, wrist leading and keeping the racquet head slightly above the wrist level. Contact the shuttle out and away from the body with a straight right arm. Snap the wrist to full extension as the shuttle is hit with the face of the racquet slightly open. Aim high in the center of the opposite court, and gain the necessary shuttle height by an upward follow through.

SKILL ANALYSIS AND ILLUSTRATION (Plate 23a, b, c, d)

Count 1.   Full backswing parallel to court, weight on left foot, racquet head above wrist, and elbow flexed.

Count 2.   Forward swing out and away from body. Arm straightens, weight on right foot.

Count 3.   Snap wrist to full extension, racquet face slightly open as shuttle is hit.

Count 4.   Follow through toward point of aim and intended shuttle flight.

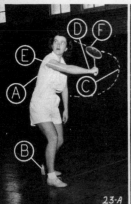

Count 1. Count 2. Count 3. Count 4.

RETURN TO "HOME" POSITION AFTER THE STROKE IS COMPLETED.

GENERAL TEACHING AIDS

I. Explain and demonstrate the Backhand Driven Clear.

II. Demonstrate the similiarities and differences between the Backhand Driven Clear and the Underhand Backhand Clear.

III. Drill class in the same general manner as used for the Underhand clear strokes.

IV. Rally with Clear shots.

V. Practice for placement.

VERBAL TEACHING AIDS

A. Right side to net.

B. Weight on left foot.

C. Backswing parallel to court.

D. Wrist cocked.

E. Elbow flexed.

F. Racquet head above wrist.

G. Transfer weight to right foot.

H. Swing racquet out and away from body.

I. Snap wrist to full extension at shuttle contact.

J. Racquet face slightly open at contact.

K. Follow through toward line of intended shuttle flight.

FOREHAND OVERHEAD CLEAR

The Forehand Overhead Clear is an overhead stroke in which the shuttle is contacted at racquet height above and to the right of the head, and sends the shuttle in a high arc to land deep in the back of the opposite court.

SKILL SUMMARY

Assume a position with the left foot forward, and the right foot back, the body rotated slightly to the right sidelines, weight on the right foot. Swing the racquet head down toward the court, bend the right elbow and raise the hand to approximately the height of the top of the head. This hyper-extends the wrist and the racquet hangs head down behind the shoulders. Shift the weight to the left foot and bring the racquet head up in an arc over the head. Straighten the arm and snap the wrist up toward the point of aim as the shuttle is contacted to the right and just in front of the body. Keep the racquet face open at shuttle contact. Aim toward a point high above and past center of the opposite court. Follow through in the direction of intended shuttle flight.

SKILL ANALYSIS AND ILLUSTRATION (Plate 24a, b, c, d)

Count 1. Drop racquet back, transfer weight to right foot, and rotate body toward sidelines.

Count 2. Bend right elbow and raise hand to head height.

Count 3. Shift weight to left foot, swing racquet forward and up-
          ward. Straighten arm, snap wrist up toward point of aim
          and contact shuttle at racquet height to the right and in
          front of the body.

Count 4. Follow through toward intended shuttle flight.

Count 1. Count 2. Count 3. Count 4.

Meet Shuttle at Highest Possible Point of Racquet Reach.

General Teaching Aids

I. Explain and demonstrate the Forehand Overhead Clear.

II. *Class Drill:* Raise racquet above and to the right of the head
to check approximate position of shuttle contact. From ready position drop
racquet back, adduct wrist and raise hand to head height allowing racquet head
to hang below wrist and behind the shoulders.

III. *Class Drill:* Place racquet behind back as in Count 2 of skill
analysis. Attempt movements of forward swing and follow through.

IV. General instruction to counts as used in previous instruction in
the clear strokes.

V. Check individuals for errors in stance, grip, starting position,
height of shuttle contact, follow through, etc.

NOTE: The Backhand Overhead Clear is a difficult stroke and is
seldom used because the correct height and distance are hard to
attain. For this reason, students should be advised to substitute the
Backhand clears already learned or the Circular Overhead Clear.

VI. Instruction in the Circular Overhead Clear.

VII. Game situation, using services and Clear shots.

Verbal Teaching Aids

A. Left foot forward, right foot back.

B. Weight on right foot.

C. Swing racquet down toward court.
D. Hand high behind head.
E. Racquet head hangs down behind shoulders.
F. Transfer weight to left foot.
G. Forward swing straightens arm.
H. Contact point at height of racquet reach in front of and to right of body.
I. Face of racquet open at contact.
J. Wrist flexion toward point of aim.
K. Aim high and follow through.

SUBSTITUTE A BACKHAND CLEAR OF A TYPE ALREADY LEARNED FOR THE OVERHEAD BACKHAND CLEAR. DO NOT RUN AROUND THE SHUTTLE IN ORDER TO TAKE A FOREHAND CLEAR.

CIRCULAR OVERHEAD CLEAR

The Circular Overhead Clear is an advanced skill in which the shuttle is contacted at racquet height above and to the left of the head, but with the use of a circular racquet swing over the head and the forehand grip, stance, and general body position.

SKILL SUMMARY

Assume a position with the left foot forward, and the right foot back, the body rotated slightly to the right sidelines, weight on the right foot. Swing the racquet out to the right and parallel with the floor, racquet head leading, arm straight, until the racquet head points toward the back of the court. Bend the elbow and hyper-extend the wrist, and bring the racquet around the head until the wrist and hand are behind and above the head, and the open racquet face is beyond the back of the left shoulder. Transfer the weight to the left foot, and swing the racquet forward and upward, face open, to contact shuttle at racquet's reach to the left and above the body. Aim the shuttle high and past center of the opposite court. Flex the wrist toward the point of aim and follow through in line with intended shuttle flight.

SKILL ANALYSIS AND ILLUSTRATION (Plate 25a, b, c, d)

Count 1. Swing the racquet out and to the right, racquet head leading, weight on right foot, arm straight.

Count 2. Bend elbow, hyper-extend the wrist, and bring racquet, face open, to a position beyond the back of the left shoulder.

Count 3. Transfer weight to left foot, straighten arm, and swing forward and upward to contact shuttle.

Count 4. Follow through toward intended shuttle flight.

THE CIRCULAR OVERHEAD CLEAR IS AN ADVANCED SKILL AND IS NOT RECOMMENDED FOR BEGINNERS BECAUSE THEIR BACKHAND SKILLS HAVE NOT YET BECOME FIXED.

Count 1. Count 2. Count 3. Count 4.

GENERAL TEACHING AIDS

I. Explain and demonstrate the Circular Overhead Clear.

II. Point out similarities and differences between the Overhead Forehand Clear and the Circular Overhead Clear.

III. Class drill to imitation of demonstration by the instructor; to commands; to slow count; to fast count; and without the use of counts.

IV. Follow the same general procedure for teaching the Circular Overhead Clear as was used in the instruction of other types of clear strokes.

V. *CAUTION:* If the Circular Overhead Clear is taught too soon, the students will use it in preference to a backhand clear; therefore it should not be taught until the various types of backhand strokes have been mastered.

VERBAL TEACHING AIDS

A. Left foot forward, right foot back.
B. Weight on right foot.
C. Swing racquet out and back. (*Parallel to court.*)
D. Arm straight.
E. Bend elbow, hyper-extend wrist.
F. Racquet beyond back of left shoulder.
G. Racquet swung around head.
H. Transfer weight to left foot.
I. Arm straight on forward swing.
J. Flex wrist toward point of aim.
K. Follow through toward intended shuttle flight.

WATCH THE SHUTTLE AT ALL TIMES.

FOREHAND DRIVE

The Forehand Drive is a stroke used to pass the opponent and make a speedy placement shot. It is usually used for net high returns; however the height at which the drive may be made varies from approximately the knees to the shoulders.

SKILL SUMMARY

Stand with the left side to the net, weight on the right foot, and swing the racquet back parallel to the court, and in line with the intended point of shuttle contact. Cock the wrist to keep the racquet head above wrist level, and flex the elbow to complete a full backswing. Transfer the weight to the left foot, and swing the racquet forward parallel to the court, with the wrist leading and the arm straight. Snap the wrist to full flexion and contact the shuttle out and away from the body and opposite the left foot. Follow through just above the contact point of the shuttle, in line with net height, and toward the intended shuttle flight.

SKILL ANALYSIS AND ILLUSTRATION (Plate 26a, b, c, d, e)

Count 1. Left side to net, begin backswing, and transfer weight to right foot.
Count 2. Full backswing, wrist cocked, elbow flexed.
Count 3. Forward swing, wrist leading, weight on left foot.
Count 4. Snap wrist to full flexion and contact shuttle.
Count 5. Follow through toward intended shuttle flight.

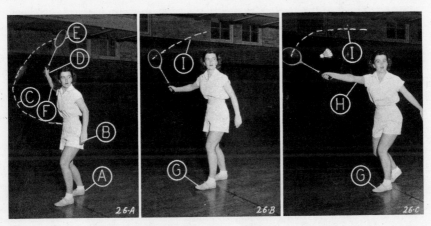

Count 1. Count 2. Count 3.

KEEP THE DRIVES LOW.

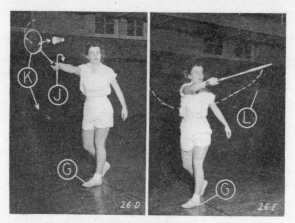

Count 4. Count 5.

General Teaching Aids

I. Explain and demonstrate the Forehand Drive.

II. Face the same direction as the class and take them through a short period of drill in the forehand drive, without the use of a shuttle. Allow them to continue and check for errors.

III. Drill to commands, to counts, and without counts.

IV. Partners assume positions on opposite sides of the net and rally using the forehand drive.

V. Short period of play using the services, clears, and drives.

VI. Teach the Backhand Drive at the same time as the Forehand Drive is taught.

VII. Explain and demonstrate the similiarities and differences in the Drives and the Driven Clears.

Verbal Teaching Aids

A. Weight back on right foot on backswing.

B. Left side to net.

C. Backswing parallel to court.

D. Wrist cocked.

E. Racquet head above wrist level.

F. Elbow flexed.

G. Weight on left foot on forward swing.

H. Arm straight on forward swing.

I. Forward swing parallel to court.

J. Snap wrist to full flexion at shuttle contact.

K. Contact point away from body and opposite left foot.

L. Follow through in line with intended shuttle flight.

Teaching Aids Cover Days, and Sometimes Weeks of Instructional Material. Do Not Attempt to Make the Student

Proceed to Further Instruction Until the Previous Lessons Have Been Satisfactorily Mastered. Avoid Speeding Up Instruction in Order to Cover a Certain Amount of Material Each Class Period. Classes Differ in Ability to Learn Quickly.

THE BACKHAND DRIVE

The Backhand Drive is a stroke used to send the shuttle low across the net to pass an opponent, and to place the shuttle deep in the opposite court.

SKILL SUMMARY

Stand with the right side to the net, weight on the left foot, and swing the racquet back parallel to the court, and in line with the intended point of shuttle contact. Cock the wrist to keep the racquet head above wrist level, and flex the elbow to complete a full backswing. Transfer the weight to the right foot, and swing the racquet forward parallel to the court, with the wrist leading and the arm straight. Snap the wrist to full extension and contact the shuttle out and away from the body and opposite the right foot. Follow through just above the contact point of the shuttle and toward intended shuttle flight.

SKILL ANALYSIS AND ILLUSTRATION (Plate 27a, b, c, d, e)

Count 1. Right side to net. Begin backswing and transfer weight to left foot.

Count 2. Full backswing, wrist cocked, elbow flexed.

Count 3. Forward swing, wrist leading, weight on right foot.

Count 4. Snap wrist to full extension and contact shuttle.

Count 5. Follow through toward intended shuttle flight.

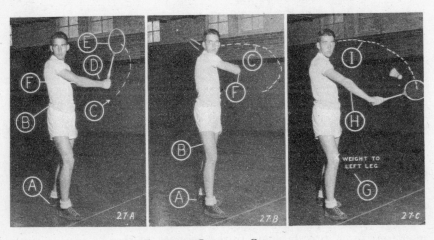

Count 1. Count 2. Count 3.

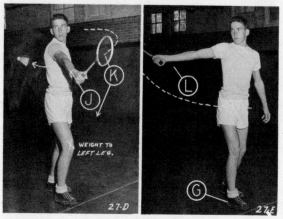

Count 4. Count 5.

PRACTICE THE BACKHAND DRIVE AS MUCH OR MORE THAN THE FOREHAND DRIVE.

GENERAL TEACHING AIDS

I. Explain and Demonstrate the Backhand Drive.

II. Face the same direction as the class and take them through a short period of drill in the backhand drive, without the use of a shuttle.

III. Drill to commands, to counts, and without counts.

IV. Partners assume positions on opposite sides of the net and rally using the forehand drive.

V. Short period of play using services, clears, and drives.

VERBAL TEACHING AIDS

A. Weight on left foot on backswing.

B. Right side toward net.

C. Backswing parallel to court.

D. Wrist cocked.

E. Racquet head above wrist level.

F. Elbow flexed.

G. Weight on right foot on forward swing.

H. Arm straight on forward swing.

I. Forward swing parallel to court.

J. Snap wrist to full extension at shuttle contact.

K. Contact point away from body and opposite right foot.

L. Follow through in line with intended shuttle flight.

FOREHAND SMASH
(KILL)

The Forehand Smash is a forehand stroke which contacts the shuttle at the height of the racquet reach, and sends the shuttle with great speed and force directly down to the opposite court.

SKILL SUMMARY

Assume a position with the left foot forward, and the right foot back, the body rotated slightly to the right sidelines, weight on the right foot. Swing the racquet head down toward the court, bend the right elbow and raise the hand to approximately the height of the top of the head. This hyper-extends the wrist and the racquet hangs head down behind the shoulders. Shift the weight to the left foot, arch the back, and bring the racquet head up in an arc over the head, wrist leading and arm straight. Contact the shuttle at the highest point that can be reached by snapping the wrist, to bring the racquet ahead of the wrist, and down to follow through toward the intended shuttle flight. The follow through is made with the arm, shoulders, and body in order to give additional power and speed to the wrist snap. (NOTE: The arm may be brought across the body to the left side, or down on the right side in the follow through.)

SKILL ANALYSIS AND ILLUSTRATION (Plate 28a, b, c, d)

Count 1. Drop racquet back, transfer weight to right foot, and rotate body toward sidelines.

Count 2. Bend right elbow and raise hand to head height.

Count 3. Shift weight to left foot, swing racquet forward and upward, wrist leading. Arch back, straighten arm, and snap wrist so that racquet head is directed down toward shuttle flight.

Count 4. Follow through with arm, shoulders, and body toward intended shuttle flight. This aids the power and speed imparted by the racquet and wrist action.

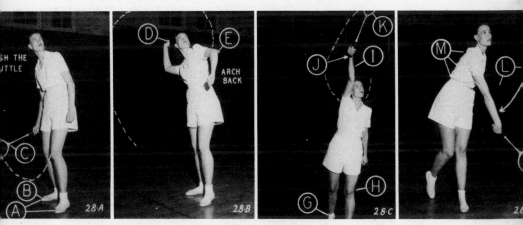

Count 1. Count 2. Count 3. Count 4.

GENERAL TEACHING AIDS

I. Explain and demonstrate the Forehand Smash.

II. Demonstrate the differences and similarities in the Forehand Smash and the Forehand Overhead Clear.

III. Use the same general teaching procedure as in the drives and clears.

IV. Students may work alone by hitting the shuttle straight into the air, and then attempting to smash it into the opposite court.

VERBAL TEACHING AIDS

A. Left foot forward, right foot back.

B. Weight on right foot.

C. Swing racquet down toward court.

D. Hand high behind head.

E. Racquet head hangs down behind shoulders.

F. Arch back.

G. Keep feet in contact with the court.

H. Transfer weight to left foot.

 I. Forward swing straightens arm, wrist leads.

J. Snap wrist to bring racquet head into shuttle.

K. Contact point at height of racquet reach in front of body. (*Lower: shuttle will hit net or go out of court. Farther back: shuttle will travel high.*)

L. Wrist flexion toward point of aim. (*Spot on opposite court.*)

M. Bring arm, shoulders, and body into follow through.

THE NEARER THE SHUTTLE TO THE NET, THE GREATER THE WRIST SNAP AND THE SHORTER THE FOLLOW THROUGH.

BACKHAND SMASH

(KILL)

The Backhand Smash is a backhand stroke which contacts the shuttle at the height of the racquet reach, and sends the shuttle with great speed and force directly down to the opposite court.

SKILL SUMMARY

Assume a position with the right foot forward, and the left foot back, the body rotated slightly left toward the left sidelines, and the weight on the left foot. Swing the racquet head down toward the court, bend the right elbow and raise the hand to head height. This allows the racquet head to hang down behind the shoulders. Transfer the weight to the right foot and bring the racquet head up in as high an arc as possible to contact the shuttle at the highest possible point in front of the body. Let the wrist lead the forward swing until the contact point is nearly reached. Snap wrist forcibly to bring racquet head into shuttle and down toward opponent's court. Follow through toward the line of intended shuttle flight. The follow through is usually completed to the right side; however it may be finished on the left side if desired.

Skill Analysis and Illustration (Plate 29a, b, c, d)

Count 1. Drop racquet back, transfer weight to left foot, and rotate body left.

Count 2. Bend right elbow and raise hand to head height.

Count 3. Shift weight to right foot, and swing racquet forward and up, wrist leading. Snap wrist to contact shuttle.

Count 4. Follow through toward line of desired shuttle flight.

Count 1. Count 2. Count 3. Count 4.

Keep the Contact Point of Racquet and Shuttle High and in Front of the Body.

General Teaching Aids

I. Explain and demonstrate the Backhand Smash.

II. Demonstrate the similarities between the Forehand and the Backhand Smash.

III. Use the same general teaching procedure as in the drives and clears.

IV. Rally using all strokes learned.

V. Short tournament period using shortened game score.

Verbal Teaching Aids

A. Right foot forward, left foot back.

B. Weight on left foot.

C. Swing racquet down toward court.

D. Hand high near head.

E. Racquet head hangs down behind shoulders.

F. Transfer weight to right foot.

G. Forward swing straightens arm, wrist leads.

   H. Snap wrist to bring racquet head into shuttle.

   I. Contact point at height of racquet reach in front of body.

   J. Wrist extension toward point of aim. (*Down toward spot on opposite court.*)

   K. Follow through toward line of intended shuttle flight.

LESS FORCE IS ATTAINED IN A BACKHAND THAN IN A FOREHAND SMASH.

FOREHAND DROP

A Forehand Drop is a return of the shuttle with a forehand stroke so that it just clears or rolls over the net to land near the net in the opposite court.

> NOTE: The Forehand Drop may be made from any level, and the grip, stance, backswings, and forward swings are identical with the forehand strokes at each level; however the wrist checks the momentum of the racquet at the moment of impact and follow through, causing the shuttle to drop close to the net in the opposite court. For this reason, very brief skill analyses only are presented. General Teaching and Verbal Aids remain the same as for all forehand strokes at the various levels, with the exception of the wrist check and follow through.

> OVERHEAD DROP (*Forehand*)
> Count 1. Beginning of backswing.
> Count 2. Full backswing.
> Count 3. Forward swing.
> Count 4. Wrist check, contact, and follow through.

> UNDERHAND DROP (*Forehand*)
> Count 1. Beginning of backswing.
> Count 2. Full backswing.
> Count 3. Forward swing.
> Count 4. Wrist check, contact, and follow through.

> DRIVEN DROP (*Forehand*)
> Count 1. Beginning of backswing.
> Count 2. Full backswing.
> Count 3. Forward swing.
> Count 4. Wrist check, contact, and follow through.

VERTICAL AND CROSS COURT FOREHAND NET DROP SHOTS WILL BE EXPLAINED IN DETAIL LATER IN THIS CHAPTER.

BACKHAND DROP

A Backhand Drop is a return of the shuttle with a backhand stroke so that it just clears or rolls over the net to land near the net in the opposite court.

> NOTE: The Backhand Drop may be made from any level, and the grip, stance, backswing, and forward swings are identical with the backhand strokes at each level; however the wrist checks the momentum of the racquet at the moment of impact and follow through, causing the shuttle to drop close to the net in the opposite court. For this reason, very brief skill analyses only are presented. General Teaching and Verbal Aids remain the same as for all backhand strokes at the various levels, with the exception of the wrist check and the follow through.
>
> OVERHEAD DROP (*Backhand*)
> Count 1. Beginning of backswing.
> Count 2. Full backswing.
> Count 3. Forward swing.
> Count 4. Wrist check, contact, and follow through.
>
> UNDERHAND DROP (*Backhand*)
> Count 1. Beginning of backswing.
> Count 2. Full backswing.
> Count 3. Forward swing.
> Count 4. Wrist check, contact, and follow through.
>
> DRIVEN DROP (*Backhand*)
> Count 1. Beginning of backswing.
> Count 2. Full backswing.
> Count 3. Forward swing.
> Count 4. Wrist check, contact, and follow through.

VERTICAL AND CROSS COURT BACKHAND NET DROP SHOTS WILL BE EXPLAINED IN DETAIL LATER IN THIS CHAPTER.

WATCH THE SHUTTLE, THE FASTER IT TRAVELS, THE LESS FORCE NECESSARY FOR A DROP SHOT.

DISGUISE THE DROP SHOT BY A FULL BACK AND FORWARD SWING BEFORE THE WRIST CHECKS THE MOMENTUM.

FOREHAND VERTICAL NET DROP

The Forehand Vertical Net Drop is a forehand wrist action, racquet stroke involving very little racquet movement and which sends the shuttle straight up, barely over or touching the net, to drop straight down the opposite side of the net.

Skill Summary

Assume a stance with the left foot forward and the right foot back. Extend the racquet out away from the body and toward the point of shuttle contact, the face of the racquet fully open, or turned up toward the ceiling. Extend the wrist slightly for a small backswing, and flick the wrist quickly to send shuttle just over the net. The weight is forward and the follow through is negligible.

Skill Analysis and Illustration (Plate 30a, b)

Count 1.   Assume a stance, left foot forward, right foot back. Extend racquet away from body with face open.

Count 2.   Extend the wrist slightly for a small backswing.

Count 3.   Flick the wrist to send shuttle over net.

Count 4.   Very little, if any, follow through.

Counts 1 and 2, 3 and 4.

Contact Shuttle at the Highest Possible Point to Avoid Having to Lift or Flick the Shuttle Any Greater Distance Than Necessary.

Keep the Weight Forward on All Net Drop Shots.

General Teaching Aids

I.   Explain and demonstrate the Forehand Vertical Net Drop.

II.   Students check wrist action by holding racquets at arm's length, face open, and moving racquets up and down with wrist action.

III.   Students work in pairs on opposite sides of the net, attempting to perform the vertical net drop.

IV.   Continue individual practice and check for errors.

A. Left foot forward, right foot back.
B. Extend racquet out away from body.
C. Right arm straight, hand in supination.
D. Racquet face open.
E. Contact shuttle at highest possible point.
F. Aim for the tape.
G. Slight backswing.
H. Flick wrist quickly, but gently.
I. Keep weight forward.
J. Slight follow through.

AIM FOR THE TAPE. WATCH THE SHUTTLE HIT THE RACQUET STRINGS.

BACKHAND VERTICAL NET DROP

The Backhand Vertical Net Drop is a backhand wrist action, racquet stroke involving very little racquet movement and which sends the shuttle straight up, barely over or touching the net, to drop straight down the opposite side of the net.

SKILL SUMMARY

Assume a stance with the right foot forward and the left foot back. Extend the racquet out away from the body and toward the point of shuttle contact, hitting surface of racquet parallel with the ceiling and the hand in pronation. Flex the wrist slightly for a small backswing, and flick the wrist quickly to send shuttle just over the net. The weight is forward, and the follow through is slight.

SKILL ANALYSIS AND ILLUSTRATION (Plate 31a, b)

Count 1. Assume a stance, right foot forward, left foot back. Extend racquet away from body, hitting surface up and hand in pronation.
Count 2. Flex the wrist slightly for a small backswing.
Count 3. Flick the wrist to extension and contact shuttle.
Count 4. Keep weight forward. Little follow through.

DO NOT TOUCH THE NET.

GENERAL TEACHING AIDS

I. Explain and demonstrate the Backhand Vertical Net Drop.
II. Students check wrist action by holding racquets in position of Count 1 of SKILL ANALYSIS and repeating Counts 2 and 3 a number of times.
III. Students work in pairs on opposite sides of the net, attempting to perform the vertical net drop.

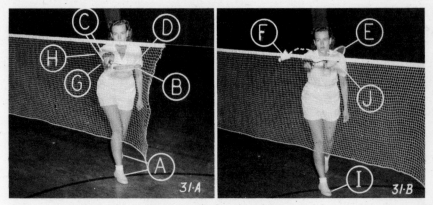

Counts 1 and 2, 3 and 4.

IV. Continue individual practice and check for errors.

V. Use GENERAL TEACHING AID III above, performing both forehand and backhand vertical net drops.

VERBAL TEACHING AIDS

A. Right foot forward, left foot back.
B. Extend racquet out away from body.
C. Right arm straight, hand in pronation.
D. Racquet surface parallel with ceiling.
E. Contact shuttle at highest possible point.
F. Aim for the tape.
G. Slight backswing by wrist flexion.
H. Flick wrist quickly and gently. (*Extension*)
I. Keep weight forward.
J. Slight follow through.

WORK FOR WRIST CONTROL AND CLOSE NET CLEARANCE.

CROSS-COURT FOREHAND NET DROP

The Cross-Court Forehand Net Drop is a forehand, wrist action, racquet stroke involving very little racquet movement, and which sends the shuttle diagonally across from right to left, barely over or touching the net, to land close to the net and in the opposite diagonal court from which the stroke was made.

SKILL SUMMARY

Assume a stance with the left foot forward and the right foot back. Extend the racquet out away from the body and toward the point of shuttle contact, the face of the racquet slightly open, and the hand in semi-supination.

Extend the wrist slightly for a small backswing, and flick the wrist quickly from right to left to send the shuttle just over the net and cross-court. The weight is forward, and the follow through is negligible.

SKILL ANALYSIS AND ILLUSTRATION (Plate 32a, b)

Count 1. Left foot forward, right foot back. Extend racquet away from body, hand in semi-supination.
Count 2. Extend the wrist slightly for a small backswing.
Count 3. Flick the wrist quickly from right to left.
Count 4. Very little follow through.

Counts 1 and 2, 3 and 4.

USE SAME GENERAL TEACHING AND VERBAL AIDS AS FOR VERTI-CAL NET DROPS.

CROSS-COURT BACKHAND

The Cross-Court Backhand Net Drop is a backhand, wrist action, racquet stroke involving very little racquet movement, and which sends the shuttle diagonally across from left to right, barely over or touching the net, to land close to the net in the opposite diagonal court from which the stroke was made.

SKILL SUMMARY

Assume a stance with the right foot forward and the left foot back. Extend the racquet out away from the body and toward the point of shuttle contact, the hitting surface of the racquet turned to the player's right, and the hand in semi-pronation. Flex the wrist slightly for a small backswing, and flick the wrist quickly from left to right to send the shuttle just over the net and cross-court. The weight is forward, and the follow through is slight.

SKILL ANALYSIS AND ILLUSTRATION (Plate 33a, b)

Count 1. Right foot forward, left foot back. Extend the racquet away from the body, the hand in semi-pronation.

Count 2. Flex the wrist slightly for a small backswing.

Count 3. Flick the wrist quickly from left to right.

Count 4. Weight forward, little follow through.

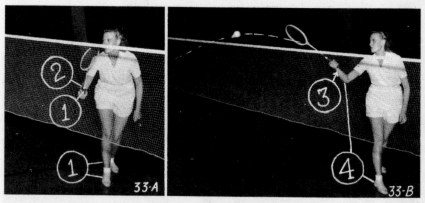

Counts 1 and 2, 3 and 4.

USE SAME GENERAL TEACHING AND VERBAL AIDS AS FOR VERTICAL NET DROPS.

STRATEGY FOR BEGINNERS

(SINGLES)

The initial service and receiving position vary with most Badminton players and depend on the type of play, the opponent's strong and weak strokes, and the player's own ability. The following suggested court positions may be considered fundamental positions, and in certain instances, may vary because of any one or a combination of the above named factors.

SERVICE-(Singles) (Plate 34)

A, the server, may vary the service from Positions 1, 2, and 4. This is largely dependent upon the position which B assumes as a receiving position, although it may also be governed by the type of play used by player B.

Singles Service Positions.

Position 1.

Position 1 is a strong position for the player with an effective drop serve and an average lob service. From this position, the server should move to X, or home, position as soon as the service is completed.

Position 2.

This position gives a good angle for the server, but in singles, it is weak for defense against drop shots. It is weak, because the server must move very quickly after the service to protect the backhand against a drop return, which in turn leaves the forehand vulnerable for a cross-court drop shot.

Position 3.

Position 3 is an effective position for doubles play and is valuable in singles if the server has an effective lob, and is slow in covering the court.

Position 4.

Position 4 is especially good for the beginner, who has not developed an effective service, and has not learned the type of return to anticipate from an opponent's position.

RECEIVING- (Singles)

The receiver should assume a court position that will protect the court against all types of serves. A position too close to the front service

line leaves a player vulnerable to a lob serve. A deep position places
the player at a disadvantage for recovering drop serves. The initial position should be about five to six feet back from the front service line, and
approximately midway between the center and the side lines. (Plate 35)

Singles Receiving Positions.

1. If A serves from No. 1 position, the best position for player B
   is at No. 1. In this position player B can cover the front court
   in one step. Usually this will necessitate a long stride and a long
   reach with the racquet, especially for drop shots to the front
   corners of the court. The back court can be covered with one
   long, or two short steps, and a back pivot.

2. If A serves from No. 2 position, player B should protect the
   court from approximately near No. 2 position. Serves from the
   No. 2 position will probably fall toward the back of the court
   or near the front left corner.

3. If A serves from either No. 3 or No. 4 positions, player B should
   assume the No. 3 court position. This position is very nearly in
   the center of the court.

The receiver should study the strong and weak points of the opponent's serve, and of the court position assumed immediately after the
service. This will determine to some extent the court position assumed
for receiving the service, and the type of return to make. Placement of
the service return, and variation of lob and drop returns will prove
valuable assets in game strategy.

STRATEGY FOR BEGINNERS
(Doubles)
Up and Back Play (Plate 36)

Up and Back Play Positions.

The initial positions of the server and the receiver in doubles, are generally the same as in singles, although the positions for the serve, and after the service, will be dependent upon the style of play adopted. This style should be agreed upon before play begins. One particular style is up-and-back with rotation occurring when the net player is drawn into a disadvantageous position.

1. If server A stands at or near position No. 1, then partner A' should assume a position near No. 1.' A' must be near enough to protect the court if a return is made to the front of the left court.

2. If server A stands at position No. 2 then partner A' should assume a position near No. 2'.

3. Play after the service should find A at, or near, No. 2 position, and A' near position No. 2'. These two positions may be considered fundamental court positions for doubles play, and the essential positions for up-and-back play.

There are certain exceptions to up-and-back play, and in these cases the players rotate. These usually occur when the net man is drawn into a disadvantageous position.

(1) A is drawn to the rear of the court by a high lob serve. A′ immediately goes to the net and becomes the net player, with A remaining in the back court.

(2) A is drawn to the right front corner of the court, and a return is played to the left front corner with a drop shot. A′ takes this play, and A moves to the back position.

(3) Partners should agree on the following points of strategy before the game begins.

    (a) Net player is the server and the receiver.

    (b) Initiative of play left to net player.

    (c) The back player calls for rotation when the net player is in a disadvantageous position.

Beginners should be advised to place the shuttle so that the opponent will have to move to make a return; to vary the returns made from the front court, to the back court, and from left to right; and to use all the strokes in which instruction has been received.

A more detailed discussion of court strategy, and other types of doubles play, may be obtained from the books listed in the reference material. Space did not permit further amplification in this chapter.

WATCH THE SHUTTLE. TRY FOR PLACEMENT OF RETURNS. USE THE WRIST.

The Teaching Aids for Each Skill Offer Specific Items Suggested for Use in the General Activities Listed Below.

SUGGESTED CLASS ORGANIZATION
(60 *minutes*)

GENERAL DAILY LESSON PLAN

Dress	10 minutes
Roll Call and Preliminaries	3 minutes
Warm-up Period	10 minutes
Explanation and Demonstration of New Skills	5 minutes
Instruction and Drill in New Skills	10 minutes
Class Practice or Play	12 minutes
Shower and Dress	10 minutes

NOTE: As the class progresses, the length of the drill period shortens, and the play period increases. The explanation and demonstration period may be shifted to accompany the play period, using group and individual aids.

    The time allowed for showering and dressing for class depends upon each teaching situation.

WEEKLY LESSON PLAN

SUGGESTED ACTIVITY

1st three weeks.

Explain care and use of equipment.

Explain Badminton etiquette.

Demonstration of Game.

Class organization.

Instruction in stance, grip, stroking, wrist action, and footwork.

Instruction in various types of services.

Instruction in Underhand Clear (Lob).

4th through 8th week.

Instruction in rules of the game. (Singles and doubles.)

Instruction in forehand and backhand drives.

Instruction in forehand and backhand smash.

Instruction in forehand and backhand drop shots.

9th through 12th week.

Instruction in court strategy and stroke deception.

Class Progressive tournament.

Class tournament.

Practical tests.

Written tests.

NOTE: It should be understood that many of these activities are interchangeable, or may be used each week, particularly those listed in the 9th through the 12th week period. Special types of activities and game situations for each class period are in addition to those listed for the weekly schedule.

FURTHER REFERENCES

1. Ainsworth, Dorothy S.; Broer, Marion R.; Goss, Alice G.; Goss, Gertrude; Jennings, Evelyn; Pitkin, Bertha A.; Ryder, Florence: *Individual Sports for Women.* W. B. Saunders and Company, Philadelphia and London, 1943.
2. Devlin, J. F.: *Badminton for All.* Doubleday, Doran and Co., New York, 1937.
3. Jackson, Carl H. and Swan, Lester A.: *Better Badminton.* A. S. Barnes and Company, Publishers, New York, 1939
4. Jackson, Carl H. and Swan, Lester A.: *Badminton Tips.* Detroit: Sport Tips and Teaching Aids, 16801 Parkside, 1938.
5. Official Sports Library for Women: *Badminton Guide.* A. S. Barnes and Company, Publishers, New York, 1945.

V

FENCING

TEACHING PREMISE

THE following analyses of skills in fencing include foil fencing only, because of its more general use, and greater popularity, in school instruction. The techniques of these skills may not conform to a single school of fencing, although the French foil is used exclusively, and emphasis is placed upon French methods. Any deviations result from an attempt to simplify and to clarify initial group instruction. In so far as it is possible, the skills are presented from the simple to the complex, and do not necessarily represent a rigid teaching progression; nor are they complete. Intermediate and advanced fencing instruction would most certainly require the full use of the additional references listed, and such skills included in this material are not accompanied by teaching aids.

> NOTE: Fencing masks and jackets should be worn at all times. It was necessary to omit the use of them in some illustrations in order to be able to recognize the students and so segregate the pictures for numbering the plates.

A BRIEF HISTORY OF FENCING

A brief history of foil fencing cannot hope to present a complete picture of the many centuries in its development to its present science. At best it can deal only in generalities and must sacrifice human interest in favor of factual material.

Originating from the days of warfare by sword, and emerging as a direct outcome of duels, foil fencing underwent many modifications. The first official ban to prevent dueling was issued in Spain in 1480, and during this century the first books on fencing were written. Spain, perhaps, deserves the credit for the first great schools. Gradually, as the science of fencing increased, the weapons became lighter, and Spain, Italy, and France developed styles of fencing and foil modification. The Italian foil retained a foreshortened modification of the crossbar of a sword. The Spanish foil modified this crossbar to facilitate stronger finger grip, while the French foil eliminated the bar entirely. The Italian school of fencing influenced the style of fencing in Italy, Australia, Germany, Hungary, and South America. The Spanish school influenced the style of fencing in Spain and Portugal. The French school of fencing influenced the style of fencing in France, Central America, England, and the United States. The French school of foil fencing is probably the most popular style universally, and most certainly merits particular consideration from fencing enthusiasts.

The 19th century brought fencing across the Atlantic and in 1894, the Intercollegiate Fencing Association was founded by three Eastern universities. This association now includes a number of universities from that area. Fencing, in its early beginnings in the United States was dominated by Annapolis and West Point. Intercollegiate championships were held in the East. As the popularity of fencing grew, the Amateur Fencers League of America was formed and provided competition for the Pacific Coast. The National Collegiate Athletic Association, the Y.M.C.A., the Turnvereins, the Public School Athletic League, and the National Interscholastic Foil Competition were a few of the groups which afforded competition for college, community, and secondary school fencers. The National Section on Women's Athletics of the American Association for Health, Physical Education, and Recreation approved fencing as a part of a total physical education and intramural program for women, and published official guides for women. The popularity of fencing has increased tremendously in the last five decades, and its science and values have been firmly established.

THE BOUT

Participation in competitive fencing between two opponents is afforded by the bout. The object of the bout is for each fencer to make a touch without being touched. A touch is made by bringing the point of the foil in contact with the target.

The target differs slightly for men and women, although in general terms it is the torso. Front target lines extend from the top of the collar to the groin lines for the men. The back of the target differs only in the lower line, which ends at a horizontal line connecting the tops of the hip bones. This same horizontal line determines the lower limit of the target lines for women both in front and in back. The difference in these target lines for men and women is in the lower limit of the front of the target. In both cases, the legs, head, and arms up to the shoulders are excluded from the target area. The target may be divided into four sections by bisection horizontally and perpendicularly. These sections may be easily remembered through the use of the terms inside high, inside low, outside high, and outside low.

The regulation fencing strip or platform is usually a long, narrow, rubber strip 40' long and 5' 11" and 6' 6" wide, plainly marked in the middle. The contestants assume positions of attention at either end of the strip, with the mask in the left arm and the foil in the right hand. They advance toward the center of the strip until they are about ten feet apart. The salute is given, and the on guard position assumed. By means of attacks, parries, advances, retreats, lunges, and recoveries, they attempt to score five touches to win the bout. As each touch is made, the fencer *who was touched* acknowledges the touch by coming to the position of attention and raising the foil to a perpendicular position in front of the face, while pointing with the left hand to the place where the touch was made. Touches made by the fencer should never be acknowledged until the opponent acknowledges, or a judge recognizes, a touch. The bout terminates when a fencer has made five touches. The fencers usually remove masks and shake hands at the end of a bout. This is a matter of courtesy, as is the mutual agreement of not talking, when participating in fencing.

Four Judges and one Director control the bout. The judges stay five feet away from, and one foot behind, the fencers. They move with the fencers and remain five feet away and one foot behind the fencers at all times. The director stands thirteen feet away and an equal distance from the fencers. (Plate 1)

Fencing Bout.

Official Rules and Fencing Strip Regulations:

Amateur Fencers League of America, 25 Beaver Street, New York City, c/o Dr. Ervin S. Acel, Scty. *Individual Sports Guide,* Official Sports Library for Women, Published for the National Section on Women's Athletics by A. S. Barnes and Company, Publishers, New York. Address 67 West 44th Street, N. Y. (18).

SELECTION, CARE, AND REPAIR OF EQUIPMENT

Equipment selection is especially important in fencing since the initial expense in incorporating fencing into an instructional program is greater than most sports. The initial costs are increased because students do not, as a general rule, acquire fencing equipment for personal use until they have learned to fence, and experienced the enjoyment of the sport. Intelligent selection presupposes a thorough knowledge of the equipment necessary for fencing instruction. The following facts about the equipment are necessary to such selection.

FOIL SELECTION (Plate 2)

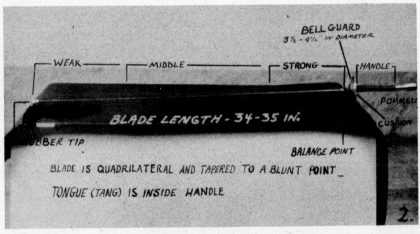

French Foil. (*Average Weight* 12½ *Ounces.*) Flexible Blade: Advanced Fencers; Sturdy Blade: Beginning Fencers.

Care. The care of equipment often becomes a controversial issue when one type is set forth as the best. Space is the greatest single factor governing the storage of equipment, while ease of equipment issue, regulates the type of storage within that space. The following diagram is offered merely as a type of storage and issue that has proved successful from the standpoint of cage issue, where space is not at a premium. (Plate 3)

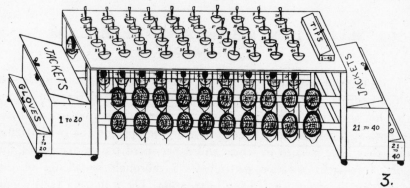

Fencing Equipment Storage Rack.

Repair. Any number of variations are possible in this type of storage rack, permitting modification for amount of equipment, size of storage space, and availability for class use.

Regardless of the type of storage used, all equipment should be numbered and checked out and in by the students. Blades should be checked and straightened, masks mended, buttons sewn on jackets, tears mended, and replacements made immediately when needed. All defects in equipment used should be reported by the students as soon as they are discovered.

Immediate repair will save materially on the cost of replacement. The most common damage to fencing equipment, and suggested methods of repair, are as follows:

Foils: Broken Blades—Repair by welding.

Worn Leather Pads—Repair by leather shop or shoe shop.

Crooked Blades—Repair by hand pressure, or by placing the convexity up and drawing from guard to tip under left foot, or straightened by machine shop.

Worn threads on Pommel or Tang—Repair by re-threading at a machine shop.

Worn cord on Handle—Repair by re-winding by students, or sporting goods company.

MASK

Selection. (Plate 4)

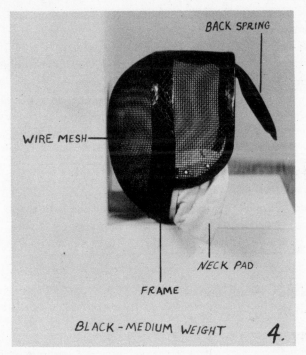

Black Fencing Mask. *May be Purchased in White.*

Repair. Worn Leather—Repaired by leather shop, or shoe shop.

Broken Laces for Neck Cloths—New laces from shoe repair shop.

Damaged Wire Net—Mended by machine shop.

Soiled Neck Pads—Immediate cleaning, laundry mending tears.

If repair is impossible, replacements should be made immediately in order to maintain the original amount of equipment. Replacements may be made through most sporting goods companies or through the following fencing equipment companies. These are listed alphabetically and their place in the list does not denote preference of equipment.

Castello Fencing Equipment Company, Inc., 55 East Eleventh Street, New York City.

Greco Fencing Co., 19 West 34th Street, New York City.

The American Fencing Equipment Co., 124 Augur Street, Hamden, Connecticut.

Vince Fencing Equipment, Inc., 202 East 44th Street, New York
City.

JACKETS

Selection. (Plate 5)
Modifications: Purchase large size sweat shirts.
              Arms and front are quilted with cotton and muslin.
Repair. Tears—Mended by laundry.
        Lost buttons—Mended by laundry, or sewn on by cage
        attendant or gymnasium matron.
        Soiled—Cleaned by laundry as soon as they become soiled.

GLOVES

Selection. (Plate 6)
Substitution: Old pigskin gloves.
Repair. Tears—Mended by leather shop, or glove shop.
        Soiled—Cleaned by leather shop.

LUNGING MATS AND TARGETS. (Plate 7a, b)

COSTUME

Regulation gymnasium suit.
Tennis shoes.

THE GRIP

The grip is the manner of holding the foil. This should be completely mastered before attempting further fencing skills.

GRIP SUMMARY

Place the thumb on the convex part of the handle and the first two
joints of the index finger directly opposite on the concave part of the handle,
about ¼ to ½ inch from the guard. Close the rest of the fingers naturally
around the handle. Rest the pommel against the center of the wrist and supinate
the hand so that the fingernails are up and the thumbnail is toward the right.

GRIP ANALYSIS AND ILLUSTRATION (Plate 8a, b, c, d)

Top View: Hand in supination, fingernails pointing up, and the
        thumbnail toward the right. Pommel rests against the center
        of the wrist.
Left Side View: Fingers spread easily, grip in tips of fingers, handle
        away from palm of hand. Wrist straight.
Right Side View: Thumb on convex part of handle, first two joints
        of index finger directly opposite on the concave part of the
        handle. Both about ¼ to ½ inch from the guard.
Bottom View: Thumb extended directly up the convex portion of
        the handle.

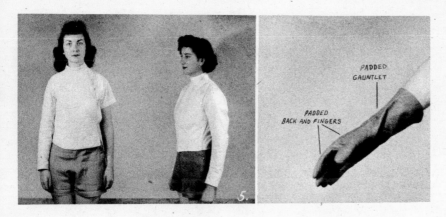

Fencing Jackets. Front View: Half Jacket; Side View: Full Jacket. Fencing Glove. (*Light Weight Leather.*)

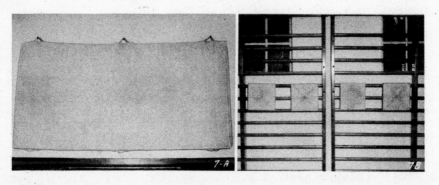

Lunging Mat. (*Regular Tumbling Mat.*) Lunging Targets. (*Padded Canvas on Wooden Frames.*)

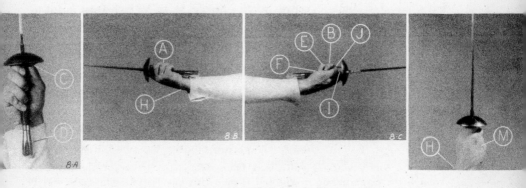

Top View. Right Side View. Left Side View. Bottom View.

GENERAL TEACHING AIDS

I. How to Obtain the Correct Fencing Grip. (Plate 9a, b, c, d)

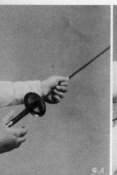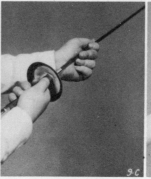

Foil in Left Hand, Handle Toward Body, Convex Side Up. Place Thumb Directly Up Convex Side, ¼ to ½ Inch from Guard, and First Two Joints of Index Finger Directly Opposite Thumb on Concave Side of the Handle, ¼-½ Inch from the Guard. Wrap Other Fingers Comfortably Around Handle, Tips Against Narrow Side of Handle. Supinate Hand. Fingernails Up, Thumbnail Toward Right, Pommel Against Center of Wrist.

II. Check individuals for possible errors.

III. Point out differences in size in facets of grip.

IV. Demonstrate checking points for each individual.

VERBAL TEACHING AIDS

A. Palm up.

B. Fingernails point up.

C. Thumbnail toward right.

D. Pommel against center of wrist.

E. Fingers spread easily.

F. Grip in tips of fingers.

G. Handle away from palm of hand.

H. Wrist straight.

I. Thumb up convex part of handle, ¼ to ½ inch from guard.

J. First two joints of index finger opposite thumb on concave part of handle, ¼ to ½ inch from guard.

K. Thumb and index finger on broadest parts of handle.

L. Curve of thumb and hand fits curve of handle.

M. Grip firm, not too tight.

N. Index finger acts as fulcrum. (*Do not grip with index finger.*)

O. Control the foil with the thumb and index finger.

P. Second, third, and fourth fingers merely steady the blade.

VARIATIONS

Any variations will result from differences in size of the hand, although the construction of the foil is such that the grip modifications will be negligible.

ADVANTAGES

The correct grip is necessary to the successful performance of all further fencing skills; therefore initial learning in the correct way has its advantages in speedier learning, and increased success in the future performance of fencing skills.

ATTENTION

The position of attention is as basic to fencing as the grip. It is the initial position for beginning and ending all bouts and classes, since it is the preliminary position in the salute.

SKILL SUMMARY

Stand erect facing the opponent, foil gripped correctly in the right hand, mask in the left. Place the right foot parallel, and the left foot horizontal, to the fencing strip, heels touching and forming a 90 degree angle. Leave the feet in this position and rotate the body until the right shoulder is toward the opponent. Turn the head to the right and look directly at the opponent. Tuck the mask, hip high, under the left arm. Extend the right arm toward the opponent until the tip of the foil is within 6 inches of the floor, and the foil and arm form a straight line. Rotate the hand until the thumb is up and the fingernails point to the left.

SKILL ANALYSIS AND ILLUSTRATION (Plate 10a, b, c)

Count 1. Assume stance facing opponent, foil in right hand, mask in left.

Count 2. Place feet at right angles, heels touching, and rotate body to left, turn head to right.

Count 3. Tuck mask under left arm, extend right arm and rotate hand to normal position.

Count 1. Count 2. Count 3.

GENERAL TEACHING AIDS

I. Explain and demonstrate the position of attention.

II. *Mask Drill:* To tuck mask hip high under left arm. (Plate 11a, b, c)

Mask Held Face Down at Sides of Head Spring by Thumb and Fingers. Turn Mask in Toward Body. Tuck Mask Under Left Arm, Top of Mask Forward, Chin Pad Toward Rear, and Face of Mask Under Upper Arm.

III. Explain, demonstrate, and perform to verbal explanation.

IV. Perform to counts designated in SKILL ANALYSIS.

V. Disregard counts when position of attention is learned.

VERBAL TEACHING AIDS

A. Assume stance facing opponent.

B. Foil gripped correctly in right hand.

C. Hold mask face down, grip sides of spring with thumb and fingers.

D. Feet at right angles, heels touching.

E. Right foot parallel, left foot horizontal to fencing strip.

F. Right shoulder toward opponent.

G. Turn head and look directly at opponent.

H. Mask tucked under left arm. (See TEACHING AIDS.)

I. Top of mask forward.

J. Neck pad toward the rear.

K. Extend arm and foil in a straight line toward opponent.

L. Foil tip 6 inches from the floor.

M. Rotate hand to left, thumb up and finger-nails to the left.

N. Knees straight, but not rigid.

VARIATIONS

1. a. Mask held under left arm, neck pad toward the floor, face of mask toward opponent, and top of mask under upper arm. Hand is under the bottom of the mask. (Plate 12)

b. Mask is held by the spring, left arm is straight, and mask hangs from left arm. It is not tucked under the arm. (See illustration below.) (Plate 13)

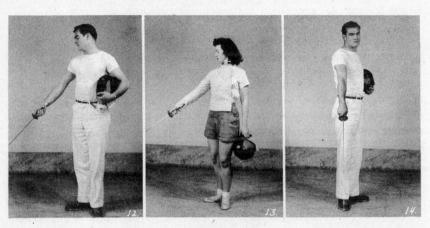

Face of Mask Toward Opponent. Slight Knee Flexion. Mask Hanging Down. Hand in Pronation.

2. Knees are flexed slightly rather than held straight.
3. The back of the hand holding the foil is sometimes turned upward, or the hand is held in full pronation. (Plate 14)
4. The tip of the foil is one to two inches from the floor, rather than the usual six inches.

ADVANTAGES

1. a. If the hand holds the head spring, rather than the bottom of the mask, it facilitates donning the mask for fencing.
   b. Mask held under the arm, gives the fencer a better appearance.
2. Holding the knees straight gives the fencer a better appearance, although there is very little, if any advantage over slightly flexed knees.
3. Semi-pronation, or the thumb up, seems easier, although the advantage over full pronation is negligible.
4. Holding the foil tip six inches from the floor, rather than one or two inches, makes a straight line from the shoulder to the foil tip easier to accomplish. If the foil tip is held lower, beginners have a tendency to lower the right shoulder.
5. The major advantage in an analysis of attention into specific steps lies in clarity of visualization for the learner.

SALUTE

The salute is a courteous acknowledgement of opponents, spectators, and judges. This precedes and ends each bout and lesson.

SKILL SUMMARY

Assume the position of attention. Bend the arm so that the foil and forearm are perpendicular to the floor, guard level with the chin, and the fingers toward the face. Lower the foil to shoulder height directly toward the opponent. The hand is in supination, fingernails up, thumb to the right. Return foil to the perpendicular position. Lower foil to the left,. shoulder height, arm and foil forming a straight line, hand in supination, fingernails up, and the head turns to the left to look at the spectators and judges. Return foil to the perpendicular position. Lower foil to the right, shoulder height, arm and foil in a straight line, hand in pronation, fingers down. Turn the head to the right to look directly at spectators and judges. Return the foil to the perpendicular position, and lower foil to the position of attention, and supinate the hand, fingernails up.

SKILL ANALYSIS AND ILLUSTRATION (Plate 15a, b, c, d, e, f)

Assume the position of attention.

Count 1. Raise foil perpendicular to fencing strip, guard level with chin, fingers toward the face, foil and forearm in a straight line.

Count 2. Lower foil shoulder height, fingers up, in a straight line toward opponent.

Count 3. Return to position described in Count 1.

Count 4. Lower foil shoulder height to left, finger-nails up, and foil and arm in straight line horizontal to fencing strip.

Count 5. Return to position described in Count 1.

Count 6. Lower foil to right, fingers down, foil and arm in straight line, shoulder height and horizontal to fencing strip.

Count 7. Return to position described in Count 1.

Count 8. Return to position of attention, supinate hand, fingernails up.

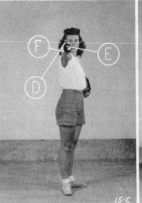

Assume Position of Attention. Count 1. Count 2. Count 4.

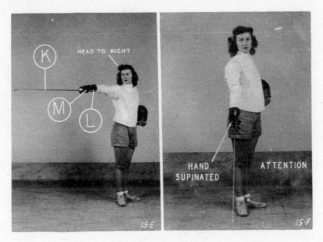

Count 6. Count 8.

GENERAL TEACHING AIDS

I. Explanation and demonstration by instructor. (Stress slight pause between movements in the SALUTE.)

II. Salute drills accompanying verbal instruction from instructor. (Plate 16)
(Use of chalk lines or regular gymnasium lines aid in checking the position of the feet.)

III. Salute drills to slow count. (See SKILL ANALYSIS count.)

IV. Salute drills in groups of four. Two fencers complete a salute, while two students check for, and correct, errors in performance. (Plates 17, 18, 19)

V. Salute drill disregarding counts, when salute is learned.

Salute Drill, Counts 1, 3, 5, 7, Are Shown. 'X' Denotes Error in Performance
Right Foot Out of Line. Salute Drill. (This May Also Be Performed with
Partners Facing Each Other.)

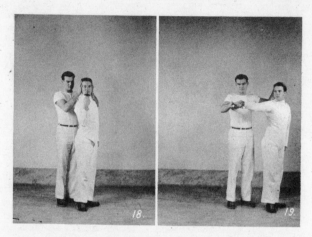

Physical Aid to Stop Forward and Back Head Movement. (*Count 1 of Salute Drill.*) Physical Aid for Horizontal Foil Position.

Verbal Teaching Aids

A. Foil and forearm in straight line perpendicular to floor, opposite right shoulder.
B. Fingers toward face.
C. Guard level with chin. (*Do not jut out chin to meet foil.*)
D. Foil and forearm in straight line, shoulder height.
E. Foil pointed toward opponent.
F. Fingernails up.
G. Foil pointing left toward audience and judges.
H. Arm and foil, shoulder height in straight line, horizontal to floor.
I. Fingernails up.
J. Head turned to left. (*Do not tip head.*)
K. Foil pointing right toward audience and judges.
L. Foil and arm, shoulder height in straight line horizontal to the floor.
M. Fingers down.
N. Position of attention, but hand supinated, fingernails up, thumb pointing toward the right.

Variations

1. Foil is first raised shoulder high toward opponent to begin the salute, rather than raised to perpendicular position from the position of attention.
2. The salute to the audience and judges on either side is sometimes omitted.
3. From the final phase of the salute when foil is held horizontally toward the right, the foil is moved in that same horizontal position to the left until it is pointing directly toward the opponent.

ADVANTAGES

1. It would seem unnecessary to add an additional movement of the foil to shoulder height toward the opponent since a salute begun from the attention position would accomplish this, and the first position of the salute, in one movement, and eliminate the pause necessary if the former is used.

2. The shorter salute is less time consuming; however the official salute affords more opportunity for handling the foil, as well as insuring correct performance in the total salute when the student is ready for official bouts.

3. There is little advantage in either moving the foil horizontally toward the opponent in the final phase of the salute or in returning the foil to a perpendicular position and thence to the position of attention. The type used would depend upon the method selected for performing the on guard position.

ON GUARD

The on guard position is the fundamental fencing position from which all fencing movements develop. If the on guard position is correct, the fencer is able to execute any movements of attack or defense, easily and quickly.

SKILL SUMMARY

Don the mask with the left hand, while holding the last position of the salute, and lower left hand to the side. Rotate the right hand to the left, thus turning the foil across the body until the tip can be grasped with the left hand, and the foil is parallel to the floor. Raise both hands above the head, the upper arms level with the shoulders, and the forearms perpendicular to the floor. Release the tip of the foil from the left hand, keeping the left arm in the same position as when holding the foil. Keep the right arm bent and lower the foil directly toward the opponent until the tip of the foil is level with the opponent's eyes and the hand and guard are breast high. Turn the fingers of the left hand toward the head, palm down forming a graceful arch in a relaxed hand and wrist. The right elbow is about 6 inches from the right hip, and the foil and forearm form a straight line. The hand is in supination, fingernails up. Advance the right foot forward approximately 2 foot-lengths. Bend the knees, keeping the trunk erect, until the right knee is above the instep of the right foot, and the left knee is directly above the toes of the left foot. The weight is distributed evenly on both feet, and the hips are tucked under.

SKILL ANALYSIS AND ILLUSTRATION (Plate 20a, b, c, d)

Count 1. Don mask, lower left arm, and maintain position of attention.

Count 2. Turn foil across body and grasp tip of foil with left hand.

Count 3. Raise both hands holding foil above head.

Count 4. Release foil tip with left hand and lower foil, arm bent, toward opponent.

Count 5. Turn left hand, palm down, fingers toward head.
Count 6. Advance 2 foot-lengths with right foot. Bend knees and distribute weight evenly.

Count 1. Count 2. Count 3. Counts 4, 5, 6.

GENERAL TEACHING AIDS

   I. Donning masks. (Plate 21a, b, c, d, e)
  II. Explain and demonstrate the position of on guard.
 III. On guard drills accompanying verbal instruction from instructor.
 IV. On guard drills to slow count.

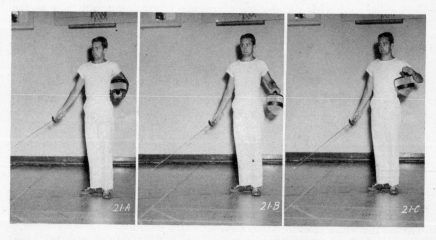

Mask Under Arm. Rotate Wrist to Left, Allowing Mask to Hang at Side, Thumb and Fingers Gripping Head Spring. Slip Index Finger on Top of Head Spring, and Thumb Underneath Allowing Rest of Fingers to Follow to Top of Head Spring.

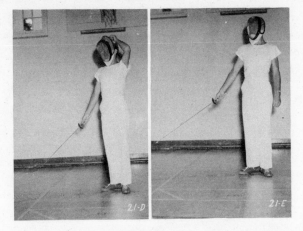

Raise Mask in Front of Face, Chin Pad Close to Chin, and Place Chin in Mask. Slip Head Spring Over Head, Check for Comfort and Lower Left Hand to Side.

V. On guard drills to count in groups of four. Two fencers on guard, two check for, and correct errors in performance. (Plate 22a, b, c, d)

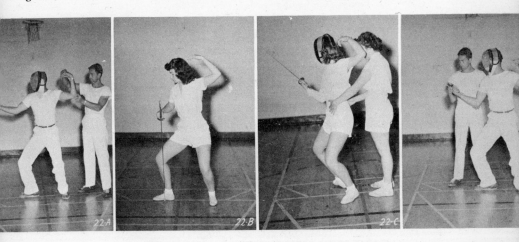

Aid for Arch in Left Hand. Aid for Right Knee Position. Aid for Hip and Trunk Positions. Aid for Arm and Foil Positions.

VI. Check weight distribution and balance by teaching the Appel or call. (Two quick stamps of the right foot while in the on guard position.) Explain that this action designates a desire to stop the bout. (Plate 23a, b, c, d, e)

VII. On guard movements without the foil, checking particularly on hip, feet, leg, and trunk positions.

VIII. Disregard verbal counts, when on guard is learned. The command "On Guard" should be sufficient.

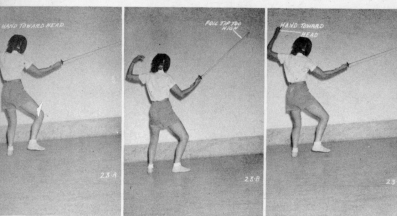

The Appel.

VERBAL TEACHING AIDS

A. Don mask with left hand, and maintain position of attention. (See TEACHING AID Number 1 for specific instructions.)

B. Lower left hand to side.

C. Rotate right hand to left, turning tip of foil across body.

D. Grasp tip of foil in left hand.

E. Foil held parallel to floor.

F. Raise both arms above head, upper arms parallel to floor.

G. Forearms are perpendicular to floor.

H. Foil is held parallel to floor.

I. Release tip of foil, keep left hand and arm in same position.

J. Keep right arm bent, and lower foil directly toward opponent. Right elbow six inches from right hip.

K. Tip of foil held level with opponent's eyes. (*Held lower leaves target unguarded.*)

L. Hand and guard are held breast high.

M. Turn fingers of left hand toward head, palm down.

N. Foil and forearm form a straight line.

O. Hand in supination, fingernails up.

P. Advance right foot forward 2 foot-lengths.

Q. Trunk erect, hips tucked under. (*Command to sit down between the heels will aid in keeping the hips tucked.*)

R. Right knee above instep of right foot.

S. Left knee directly above toes of left foot.

T. Right foot parallel with fencing strip.

U. Left foot horizontal to fencing strip.

V. Weight distributed evenly. (*Watch for "riding" or pronation, which causes painful ankle, and places knees out of line.*)

W. Body in profile, right shoulder toward opponent. (*Presents less target to opponent.*)

VARIATIONS

1. *WOMEN* may need a slight modification in the angle between the heels. Slightly less than the 90 degree angle may be necessary.

2. From the last position of the salute described in VARIATION No. 3, raise both arms shoulder height and horizontal to the floor. Bend the right arm until the elbow is 6 inches from the right hip, and the forearm and foil form a straight line, the tip of the foil about level with the opponent's eyes. (Plate 24a, b, c) Bend the

Count 1, Count 2, Count 3.

left arm at the elbow, and curve the hand and wrist toward the head, palm down, fingers pointing toward the head. Step toward the opponent 2 foot-lengths, with the right foot. Bend the knees, keeping the trunk erect, until the right knee is above the instep of the right foot, and the left knee is directly above the toes of the left foot. Keep the hips tucked under.

ADVANTAGES

1. Modification in the angle of the heels for some *WOMEN* fencers may be necessary due to weakness in the leg muscles, and a slightly less than 90 degree angle may increase agility and speed in the leg performance.

2. Less movements in the on guard position have the advantage of being less time consuming. More complicated methods of assuming the on guard position have the advantage, at least in the initial learning period, of affording students more opportunities to handle the foil and gain control of foil movements.

ADVANCE

The advance is made from the guard position, and its purpose is to approach within attacking distance of the opponent.

Skill Summary

Assume and maintain the on guard position. Step forward with the right foot, toes leading and landing first on the right heel. The left foot follows immediately and advances the same relative distance as the right foot. Thus the position of the feet and body retain the exact position of on guard.

Skill Analysis and Illustration (Plate 25a, b, c, d)

Assume the on guard position.

Count 1.   (a) Step forward with the right foot, toes leading.
            (b) Land on right foot, heel touching floor first.
Count 2.   (a) Immediately step forward with left foot, the same relative distance as the step made with the right foot.
            (b) Land flat-footed on left foot.

Count 1a. Count 1b. Count 2a. Count 2b.

General Teaching Aids

I. Explain and demonstrate the advance.

II. Drill in advance accompanied by verbal instruction.

III. Drill in advance to slow count of "one" for right foot, and "two" for left.

IV. Drill in advance to command by instructor. The command "advance" given for each complete step, or movement of both feet, should be sufficient. (i.e.: advance, advance, advance, etc.)

V. Teach the retreat. (See page 114.)

VI. Drill to single command "advance," allowing no more than 3 or 4 steps before the "retreat" command is given.

VII. Drill in advance and retreat in groups of four students. Two students advancing and retreating to commands, while two students check for, and correct errors in performance.

VIII. Stress the importance of maintaining the on guard position during the advance and retreat.

Verbal Teaching Aids

A. Assume on guard position, check possible points of error.
B. Step forward with right foot, toes leading.
C. Feet lifted but close to the floor. (*Higher step tends to raise body from crouch position.*)
D. Land first on right heel.
E. Right foot parallel with fencing strip.
F. Step forward with left foot, same relative distance covered by right foot. (*Longer step with left foot moves feet out of position and body off balance for on guard.*)
G. Use short steps. (*Do not allow side of left foot to lift from floor due to a too long step with the right foot.*)
H. Keep feet close to floor. (*Do not slide feet.*)
I. Land flat-footed.
J. Check position of feet at 90 degree angle.
K. Check position of knees in relation to feet. (*Same as on guard.*)
L. Erect trunk.
M. Hips tucked under. (*Sway back, less agility and more body strain. Especially harmful for women.*)
N. Smooth gliding motion, no movement above hips. Body must not jiggle or move up and down.

Variations

Variations in advance are generally a result of differences in body build, length of step, and strength of leg muscles. Actual differences in the advance itself are a direct result of the distance to be covered. The short distance may be covered by extending the arm, and no steps are necessary. The middle distance requires a lunge to reach the opponent. The long distance requires an advance of one to four steps (rarely more than four), to be in lunging distance of the opponent.

Advantages

Any advantage achieved through the advance is brought about by continued drill in the advance so that the individual is able to perform it quickly, easily, and with such smooth co-ordination that specific movements of the advance are scarcely apparent.

RETREAT

The retreat is the reverse of the regular advance; therefore its purpose is to get out of reach, or away from, the opponent. The retreat is also made from the on guard position.

SKILL SUMMARY

Assume and maintain the on guard position. Step backward with the left foot, landing flat-footed. Step backward immediately the same relative distance with the right foot, and land flat-footed. The position of the feet and body retain the on guard position throughout.

SKILL ANALYSIS AND ILLUSTRATION (Plate 26a, b, c, d)

Assume the on guard position.

Count 1. (a) Step backward with the left foot.

           (b) Land with the left foot flat.

Count 2. (a) Immediately step backward with the right foot the same distance as the step made with left foot.

           (b) Land with the right foot flat.

Count 1a. Count 1b. Count 2a. Count 2b.

GENERAL TEACHING AIDS

I. Explain and demonstrate the retreat.

II. Drill in retreat to verbal instruction.

III. Drill in retreat to slow count of "one" for left foot, and "two" for right foot. Several retreats should be made in quick succession.

IV. Drill in retreat to command by instructor. The command "retreat" given for each complete step or movement backward by both feet. (i.e.: retreat, retreat, retreat, etc.)

V. Drill to single command "retreat," allowing no more than four retreats before "advance" command is given.

VI. Drill in groups of four students. (See page 112, TEACHING AID Number VII.)

VII. *Always* check for errors in maintaining the on guard position.

Verbal Teaching Aids

A. Assume on guard, check possible points of error.
B. Step backward with left foot.
C. Make step short and close to floor. (*High step raises body from crouch.*)
D. Land flat-footed.
E. Immediately step back same relative distance with right foot.
F. Lift foot from floor but keep foot close to floor.
G. Land flat-footed.
H. Check angle of feet at 90 degrees.
I. Check knee positions for correct on guard position. (*No "riding" or ankle pronation. This causes painful ankles. Angle of left knee toward opponent, causes rotation of body and loss of profile.*)
J. Erect trunk.
K. Hips tucked under.
L. Smooth gliding motion, no movement above hips. (*Body movement up and down, and jiggling, should be stopped immediately.*)
M. Body in profile toward opponent. (*Presents less target.*)

Variations

Variations in the retreat are generally a result of differences in body build, length of step, and strength of leg muscles. The same distances must be covered by the retreat as are covered in the advance.

Advantages

Any advantage achieved through the retreat is brought about by continued drill in the retreat so that the individual is able to perform it quickly, easily, and with such smooth co-ordination that the specific movements of the retreat are scarcely apparent.

LUNGE AND RECOVERY

The lunge, executed from the guard position, is a projection of the body and foil toward the opponent in order to attempt a touch.

The recovery, as the term implies, is the method by which a fencer regains the on guard position after completing the lunge.

Skill Summary

Lunge: Assume the on guard position. Extend the right arm, shoulder high toward the opponent, foil and arm in a straight line, horizontal to the fencing strip, the fingernails up. Step forward rapidly with the right foot, toes leading, and landing first on the heel. Simultaneously extend the left leg vigorously without moving the left foot from the flat-footed position of on guard and straighten and lower the left arm, palm upward, parallel to the left leg.

Recovery: Bend the left knee and pull with the left leg. Push slightly with the right until the weight is on the left foot. Move the right foot back and simultaneously bend the right arm and raise the left to assume the original on guard position.

SKILL ANALYSIS AND ILLUSTRATION (Plate 27a, b, c, d)

Count 1. (a) Extend right arm toward opponent, foil and arm in straight line.

(b) Step forward with right foot, toes leading, landing heel first.

(c) Extend left leg, straighten and lower left arm parallel to the left leg, palm up.

Count 2. (a) Bend left knee and pull with left leg, and push slightly with right.

(b) Weight on left foot, move right foot back, bend right arm and raise left arm, assuming original on guard position.

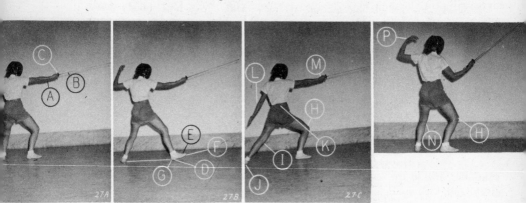

Count 1a. Count 1b. Count 1c. Count 2.

GENERAL TEACHING AIDS

I. Explain and demonstrate the lunge and recovery.

II. Drill in lunge and recovery to verbal instruction. (Chalk lines or regular gymnasium lines will aid in checking the position of the feet.)

III. Drill in lunge and recovery without foil, checking on feet position.

IV. Drill in lunge and recovery to slow count, holding lunge position on count of one, until count two is given for the recovery. Instructor checks for individual errors. (See VERBAL AIDS.) *Be sure complete arm extension is made before the lunge.*

V. Use commands "lunge" and "recover." Check for errors. Hold position until next command.

VI. Drill in lunge and recovery against wall targets, mats, or opponents' jackets. (Plate 28a, b, c)

On Guard. Arm Extension. Lunge.

Check positions and upward arch in foil at the touch. Four students may work together, two performing and two checking.

VII. Combine commands: "Advance-Retreat-Advance-Lunge-Recover." Students holding lunge or recovery, and continuing advance or retreat until a further command is given. Later allow students to work in partners using same commands. Designate one group to perform commands, their partners performing the opposite command.

Verbal Teaching Aids

Lunge:

A. Extend right arm shoulder height toward opponent. (*Preliminary to foot movement.*)

B. Arm and foil in straight line. (*If lunge is too long it places foil out of line.*)

C. Fingernails up. (*Hand in supination.*)

D. Step forward with the right foot toward the opponent, maintaining direct line with left heel. (*Fraction of a second after foil extension.*)

E. Toes leading. (*If outer border of foot is toward opponent, balance is poor.*)

F. Foot close to floor. (*High step raises body, slows lunge, and places foil out of line.*)

G. Land heel first, foot parallel to fencing strip. (*Foot not parallel causes loss of balance.*)

H. Right knee perpendicular above instep of right foot.

I. Fully extend left leg simultaneously with step of right foot.

J. Left foot remains flat on floor. (*Left foot rolled on inner border places too much weight on right foot making recovery slow. Rolling also caused by too long a step with right foot.*)

K. Trunk erect. (*Leaning forward rolls or lifts left foot.*)

L. Extend and drop left arm parallel to left leg. (*Movement made simultaneously with foot and leg movements, and aids in balance and recovery.*)

M. Palm up.

Recovery:

    N. Bend left knee, take weight on left foot. (*Not bent, right foot must push too hard.*)

    O. Pull with left leg and push with right. (*Do not throw body back with right foot, spare right foot as much as possible.*)

    P. Lift left arm to on guard position. (*This must be vigorous. It adds momentum to pulling the body back and takes much of the work of pushing from the right foot. This movement is made at the same time as the leg movements.*)

    Q. Bend right arm and assume on guard position. (*Simultaneous with leg movements.*)

    R. Check on guard position for errors and variations.

VARIATIONS

Lunge:

    1. Foil slightly lower, rather than level with the hand.
    2. Trunk inclined forward, rather than erect.
    3. Left hand horizontal to fencing strip, rather than parallel with the left leg.

Recovery:

    4. Left leg and arm recover without push from right foot.

ADVANTAGES

1. Since the lowering of the foil below the hand in the lunge is slight, the advantage would also seem slight. The horizontal position seems more logical, since a student's tendency in the lunge is to lower the point. Knowledge of a definite position for the foil makes concentration on foil position easier with less lowering of foil and sagging of right arm.

2. Inclination of the trunk forward has a distinct advantage if it happens to be the individual preference of an advanced fencer. Beginners should keep the trunk erect to avoid placing increased weight on the right foot with resulting loss in balance and slowness in recovery.

3. Parallel position of the left hand to the left leg has a distinct advantage over the horizontal, *especially for women,* for it adds more momentum to the recovery due to the increased arc in returning to position. This takes much of the pull from the leg muscles. In the lunge it seems easier to let the arm drop naturally than to have to concentrate upon halting the drop at the horizontal position.

4. In all cases the left leg and arm should perform most of the pull in the recovery. Allowing some of the aid from the right foot with a slight push or press in the recovery has a distinct advantage for individuals with weak leg muscles. Needless to say, the right leg should be spared as much work in the recovery as possible.

TARGET

The target is the area in which legal touches can be made, and is divided into four sections by an imaginary horizontal and perpendicular line.

SKILL SUMMARY

The four sections of the target are designated by the terms outside high, outside low, inside high, and inside low. These divisions have two guards each, through which a fencer, by hand and blade positions, may cover each portion of the target. Numbers one through eight denote the specific guards, for each section.

SKILL ANALYSIS AND ILLUSTRATION (Plate 29a, b)

OUTSIDE HIGH: The upper right quarter of the target area, guarded by 3rd and 6th.

OUTSIDE LOW: The lower right quarter of the target area, guarded by 2nd and 8th.

INSIDE HIGH: The upper left quarter of the target area, guarded by 1st and 4th.

INSIDE LOW: The lower right quarter of the target area, guarded by 5th and 7th.

NOTE: *Right* refers to that portion of *own* target area nearer *own* right arm, and *left* refers to the portion of *own* target area nearer *own* left arm.

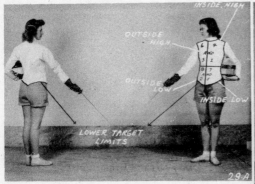 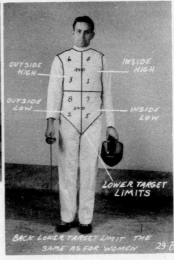

Target Area. (*Women*) Target Area. (*Men*)

HAND POSITIONS

The correct position of the hand in the various guard positions is necessary to successful performance. The following definitions and explanations should clarify much of the material to follow.

SUMMARIES

SUPINATION: The thumbnail points toward the right and the fingernails are up. Used in the guards and parries of 6th, 7th, and 8th.

NORMAL: The thumbnail is up, and the fingernails point toward the left. Used in guard and parry of 4th.

PRONATION: The thumb points toward the left, the fingernails down. Used in guards and parries of 2nd, 3rd, and 5th.

FIRST: The thumb points toward the floor and the back of the hand is toward the face. Used in guard and parry of 1st. (Plate 30a, b, c, d)

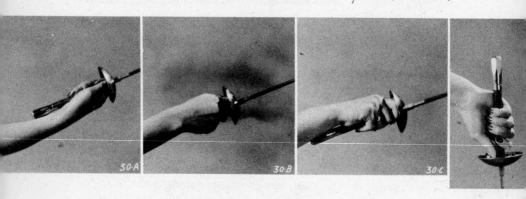

Supination. Normal. Pronation. First.

DEFINITIONS

1. *Guards:* Hand and foil positions which protect each portion of the target. These are numbered one through eight and are designated as: First guard position, second guard position, third guard position, etc.

2. *Parries:* Parries are movements of the foil *to the various guard positions,* in order to deflect the attacking point. These are designated by the numbers 1 to 8, and their hand and foil positions are identical to the guard positions.

3. *Line of Attack:* The line of attack is an imaginary line followed by the foil to reach the target. (Attack in fourth would be on the right of the opponent's blade, and directed at the inside high portion of the target area.)

4. *An Engagement:* An engagement is made by the crossing in contact of the two blades in any of the guard positions. Usually the weak part of the blades are crossed in long distance, and the middle of attacking blade against weak part of opponent's blade in the middle distance.

5. *Foils crossed on right:* Whenever the term, "foils crossed on the right" occurs, it denotes own right hand. In other words own blade is nearer right side of own body.

6. *Foils cross on left:* Denotes own left hand or side.

7. *Right of opponent's foil:* Same as No. 5 above, denotes own right hand.

8. *Left of opponent's foil:* Same as No. 6 above, denotes own left hand.

ENGAGEMENT IN FOURTH AND SIXTH

Fourth: Two blades crossed in contact in fourth guard position.

Sixth: Two blades crossed in contact in sixth guard position.

SKILL SUMMARY

Fourth: From the on guard position assume the guard of fourth by moving the hand to the left at breast height, the point of the foil directed toward the opponent's eyes, thumb up, finger-nails to the left in the "normal" position. The foils are crossed in contact on the right. In other words, each foil is on the side nearest the opponent's inside high area of the target.

Sixth: Assume the on guard position and cross foils on the left with the opponent. In other words, each foil is on the side nearest the opponent's outside high area of the target. The hand is in supination and the body position is identical with "on guard."

SKILL ANALYSIS AND ILLUSTRATION (Plate 31a, b, c, d)

Fourth:

Count 1. On guard position.

Count 2. Move hand to left at breast height, hand in normal position, foils crossed on right.

Sixth:

Count 1. Assume the on guard position. Cross foils on left, hand in supination.

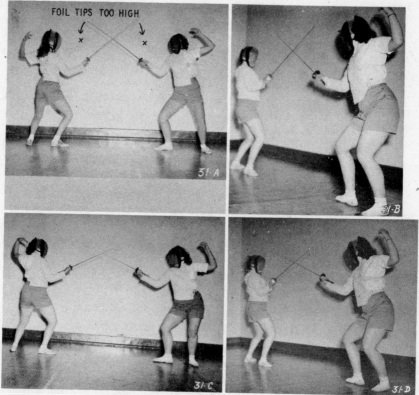

Fourth Guard Position. (*Front View*) Fourth Guard Position. (*Side View*)
Sixth Guard Position. (*Front View*) Sixth Guard Position. (*Side View*)

GENERAL TEACHING AIDS

I. Check general body positions from AIDS for on guard, page 108.

II. Assume these engagements at the command of the instructor until both fourth and sixth are thoroughly mastered.

VERBAL TEACHING AIDS

A. See VERBAL AIDS for on guard position.

B. Check hand position in fourth.

C. See PARRY AIDS for 4 and 6.

DIRECT THRUST IN FOURTH

A direct thrust in fourth is an extension of the foil and arm in the line of engagement, with or without a lunge, toward the opponent's inside high target area. This is made from an engagement or with the blades not touching.

Skill Summary

Without a lunge: Engage opponent in fourth position, close distance. Opponent continues to hold fourth guard position. Extend the arm and foil in the line of engagement, (on right of opponent's blade), and touch in fourth, inside high line. Foil is bent upward, and the hand is in normal position, slightly higher than the blade.

With a lunge: Engage opponent in fourth, middle distance. Opponent continues to hold fourth guard position. Extend the arm and foil in the line of engagement, lunge, and touch in fourth. The body position is the same as in the lunge (page 117), the foil is bent upward, and the hand is slightly higher than the shoulder, when the touch is made.

Skill Analysis and Illustration (Plate 32a, b, c)

Without a lunge:

> Count 1. Engage in fourth, close distance. (Not illustrated.)
> Count 2. Extend arm in line of engagement, and touch in fourth.
> Count 3. Recover to guard position. (Not illustrated.)

With a lunge:

> Count 1. Engage in fourth, middle distance. (Not illustrated.)
> Count 2. Extend arm in line of engagement.
> Count 3. Lunge and touch in fourth.
> Count 4. Recover to guard position. (Not illustrated.)

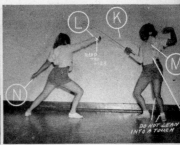

Count 2. (*Without a Lunge.*) Count 2. (*With a Lunge.*) Count 3.

General Teaching Aids

I. Explain and demonstrate:

(a) Fourth guard position; (b) close distance; (c) middle distance; (d) engagement in fourth; (e) direct thrust without a lunge and recovery; (f) direct thrust with a lunge and recovery; (g) touch in fourth without a lunge; (h) touch in fourth with a lunge.

II. Class drills in a; e; and f; above.

III. Couple drills in b; c; d; above.

IV. Divide class in couples. Students engage in fourth and alternate attempts at a touch in fourth at close distance without a lunge. Defense holds fourth guard position and checks form of offense. (Offense holds touch until partner gives command to recover.) Later touch in fourth and recover immediately.

MOVEMENT IS SMOOTH AND CONTINUOUS, BUT PERFORM FIRST TO SLOW COUNT OR COMMAND.

V. Couples engage in fourth and attempt alternate touches in fourth from middle distance, which necessitates a lunge. Defense holds fourth guard position and checks form of offense. Hold touch until opponent gives the command to recover. This allows time for checking body, foil, and hand positions.

VI. Same drill as number V, but recover immediately.

VII. *Couple Drill:* (1) attention; (2) salute; (3) on guard; (4) advance to middle distance; (5) engage in fourth; (6) alternate lunge and touch in fourth and recovery to guard position; (7) five touches each, retreat to starting position, and repeat drill.

VERBAL TEACHING AIDS

Without a lunge:
    A. Engage in fourth, close distance.
    B. Extend arm in line of engagement and touch in fourth.
    C. Arm fully extended. (*Bent arm, too close to opponent.*)
    D. Blade bent upward. (*Incorrect grip if not bent upward.*)
    E. Hand in normal position.
    F. Recover to guard position.

With a lunge:
    G. Engage in fourth, middle distance. (*Lunge required for touch.*)
    H. Foil and arm in straight line, shoulder height. (*Arm extension before lunge, gives right to attack.*)
    I. Hand in normal position.
    J. Lunge.
    K. Foil bent upwards.
    L. Hand slightly higher than shoulder. (*Keeps foil tip from slipping.*)
    M. Touch in fourth.
    N. Left arm parallel to left leg. (*Aids in balance and later in recovery.*)
    O. Recover to guard position after touch.

FOR VARIATIONS AND ADVANTAGES SEE THE LUNGE, PAGE 118.

DIRECT THRUST IN SIXTH

A direct thrust in sixth is an extension of the foil and arm in the line of engagement, with or without a lunge, toward the opponent's outside high target area. This is made from an engagement or with the blades not touching.

Skill Summary

Without a lunge: Engage opponent in sixth position, close distance. Opponent continues to hold sixth guard position. Extend arm and foil in the line of engagement, (on left of the opponent's blade), and touch in sixth, outside high line. Foil is bent upward, and the hand is slightly higher than the shoulder. Hand in supination.

With a lunge: Engage in sixth, middle distance. Opponent continues to hold sixth guard position. Extend the arm and foil in the line of engagement, lunge, and touch in sixth. The body position is the same as in the lunge, the foil is bent upward, and the hand is slightly higher than the shoulder when the touch is made. The hand is in supination.

Skill Analysis and Illustration (Plate 33a, b, c)

Without a lunge:
>Count 1. Engage in sixth, close distance.
>Count 2. Extend arm in line of engagement.
>Count 3. Recover to guard position. (Not illustrated.)

With a lunge:
>Count 1. Engage in sixth, middle distance.
>Count 2. Extend arm in line of engagement.
>Count 3. Lunge and touch in sixth, hand in supination.
>Count 4. Recover to guard position. (Not illustrated.)

Count 2. (*Without a Lunge.*) Count 2. (*With a Lunge.*) Count 3.

General Teaching Aids

>I. Review previous lessons.
>II. Review Couple Drill in Teaching Aid V, page 124.
>III. Explain and demonstrate:
>>(a) sixth guard position; (b) engagement in sixth; (c) direct thrust and touch in sixth; (d) thrust, lunge, and touch in sixth.
>IV. Class drill in sixth guard position, and engagement in sixth.
>V. Couples drill in alternate thrust and touch in sixth, close distance. Defense holds sixth guard position and checks form of offense. Hold

touch until partner gives command to recover. Later touch and recover immediately.

VI. Couples alternate touches at middle distance, with lunge. Defense holds sixth guard position and checks form of offense. Hold touch until partner gives command to recover.

VII. Same drill as above, but recover immediately.

VIII. *Couple Drill:* (1) attention; (2) salute; (3) on guard; (4) advance to middle distance; (5) engage in sixth; (6) alternate lunge and touch in sixth and recovery to guard position; (7) five touches each, retreat to starting position and repeat drill.

MOVEMENTS ARE SMOOTH AND CONTINUOUS, BUT PERFORM TO SLOW COUNT OR COMMAND UNTIL THOROUGHLY MASTERED. IF SMOOTHNESS IS LOST, WHEN SPEED IS TRIED, RETURN TO THE USE OF A SLOW COUNT.

VERBAL TEACHING AIDS

Without a lunge:

    A. Engage in sixth, close distance.
    B. Extend arm in line of engagement and touch in sixth.
    C. Arm fully extended.
    D. Blade bent upward. (*Firm touch.*)
    E. Hand in supination.
    F. Recover to guard position.

With a lunge:

    G. Engage in sixth, middle distance.
    H. Foil and arm in straight line, shoulder height. (*Gives right of attack.*)
    I. Hand in supination.
    J. Lunge.
    K. Foil bent upwards.
    L. Hand slightly higher than shoulder. (*Keeps point from slipping.*)
    M. Touch in sixth.
    N. Left arm parallel to left leg. (*Balance and recovery aid.*)
    O. Recover to guard position.

FOR VARIATIONS AND ADVANTAGES SEE THE LUNGE AND RECOVERY, AND ENGAGEMENT IN SIXTH.

OPPOSITION PARRY IN FOURTH

An opposition parry in fourth is a defensive move of the blade to the left at breast height with the hand in normal position, while maintaining contact with the opponent's blade.

SKILL SUMMARY

Engage opponent in fourth. *Offense:* thrust and lunge in the line of engagement in an attempt to make a touch in fourth, inside high line. *Defense:* Move the hand slightly to the left in the normal position. Maintain pressure on the attacking blade, thus diverting the foil tip from the target area. Keep the hand at breast height, and the point of the foil directed toward the opponent's eyes.

(*See* GENERAL TEACHING AID *Number VII for parry 4 from sixth guard position, which is a more usual position from which parry 4 is executed in actual bouts.*)

SKILL ANALYSIS AND ILLUSTRATION (Plate 34a, b, c)

Count 1. Engage in fourth. (Not illustrated.)

Count 2. Offense extends arm, and lunges in fourth.

Count 3. Defense executes parry 4 by moving hand slightly to the left. This movement is made with wrist and fingers only.

Count 4. Recover immediately to guard position. (Not illustrated.)

COUNTS ARE FOR ANALYSIS ONLY, THE MOVEMENTS ARE ALMOST SIMULTANEOUS WHEN EXECUTED CORRECTLY.

Count 1. Count 2. Count 3.

GENERAL TEACHING AIDS

I. Review previous lessons pertaining to guard and engagement positions in four, as well as the direct thrust in four with no opposition.

II. Explain and demonstrate parry 4 from engagement in four.

III. Line drill in parry 4.

IV. Divide class in couples, engage in four, close distance. Couples alternate thrust in four without lunge, and parry 4. Check errors.

V. Engage in four, middle distance, and alternate lunges and parries in 4. Partners check for errors in form.

VI. *Couple Drill, No. 1:* (1) attention; (2) salute; (3) on guard; (4) advance to middle distance; (5) engage in 4; (6) alternate lunge and parry in 4 with recovery to guard position; (7) five parries each, retreat to starting position. Repeat drill.

VII. *Couple Drill, No. 2:* Offense in *fourth guard position.* Defense in *sixth guard position,* (hand in supination). (Plate 35a, b) Blades do not touch. Offense extends arm and foil and lunges in fourth. Defense parries 4 from sixth position by moving hand to left and into fourth guard position. Hand moves from supination to normal position and from sixth to fourth guard position to parry lunge of offense. Couples change from offense to defense after three lunges. Partners should be changed after each individual has performed 3 parries.

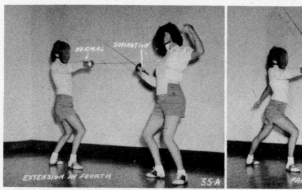

Offense in Fourth; Defense in Sixth, Offense Extends Arm in Fourth. Offense Lunges in Fourth. Defense Parries 4.

STRIVE FOR SMOOTH MOVEMENT BY PERFORMING THE DRILLS SLOWLY. DO NOT ATTEMPT SPEED UNTIL THE MOVEMENTS HAVE BEEN THOROUGHLY MASTERED.

VERBAL TEACHING AIDS

A. Engage in fourth.

B. Direct thrust and lunge in fourth.

C. Defense moves hand slightly to left. (*Wide movement leaves too large a portion of own target unguarded.*)

D. Blades in contact and crossed. (*Opposition parry.*)

E. Hand breast height. (*Low hand decreases strength of parry.*)

F. Point of foil toward opponent's eyes. (*Foil out of line, check position of point.*)

G. Hand in normal position. (*Slow recovery caused by pronation.*)

H. Elbow six inches from body. (*Cramped parry, arm too close to body; weak parry, arm too far away from body.*)

I. Recover to guard position immediately.

SEE BEAT PARRY FOR VARIATIONS AND ADVANTAGES.

OPPOSITION PARRY IN SIXTH

An opposition parry in sixth is a defensive move of the blade to the right at breast height with the hand in supination, while maintaining contact with the opponent's blade.

SKILL SUMMARY

Engage opponent in sixth. *Offense:* thrust and lunge in the line of engagement in an attempt to make a touch in sixth, outside high line. *Opposition:* Move hand slightly to the right in supination. Maintain pressure on the attacking blade, thus diverting the foil tip from the target area. Keep the hand at breast height, and the point of the foil directed toward the opponent's eyes.

(*See* GENERAL TEACHING AID *No. VII for Parry 6 from fourth guard position, which is a more usual position from which it is made in a bout.*)

Count 2. Count 3.

SKILL ANALYSIS AND ILLUSTRATION (Plate 36a, b)

Count 1. Engage in sixth. (Not illustrated.)
Count 2. Offense extends arm and foil, and lunges in sixth.
Count 3. Defense executes parry 4 by moving hand slightly to the right, hand in supination.
Count 4. Recover to guard position. (Not illustrated.)

GENERAL TEACHING AIDS

I. Review previous lessons pertaining to guard and engagement positions in sixth, as well as the direct thrust in sixth with no opposition.

II. Explain and demonstrate parry 6 from engagement in sixth.

III. Line drill in parry 6.

IV. Divide class in couples, engage in sixth, close distance. Couples alternate thrust in sixth without lunge and parry 6. Check errors.

V. Couples engage in sixth, middle distance. Alternate lunge in six with parry 6. First to slow command. Later speeded up when thoroughly learned.

VI. *Couple Drill No. 1:* (1) Attention; (2) salute; (3) on guard; (4) advance to middle distance; (5) engage in sixth; (6) alternate lunge and recover and parry 6; (7) five parries each, retreat to starting position. Repeat drill.

VII. *Couple Drill No. 2:* Offense in *sixth guard position*, hand in supination. Defense in *fourth guard position*, hand in normal position. (Plate 37a, b) Blades do not touch. Offense extends foil and lunges in sixth. Defense moves hand to right into sixth guard position, hand in supination, and parries lunge of offense. Couples change from offense to defense after three lunges. Change partners after 3 parries each.

Offense in sixth. Defense in Fourth. Offense Extends Arm and Foil in Sixth. Offense Lunges in Sixth, Defense Parries 6.

PERFORM ALL DRILLS SLOWLY AT FIRST. SPEED UP WHEN MOVEMENTS ARE MASTERED. SLOW DOWN IF SMOOTHNESS OF MOVEMENT IS LOST.

VERBAL TEACHING AIDS

A. Engage in sixth.
B. Direct thrust and lunge in sixth.
C. Defense moves hand slightly to right. (*Wide movement leaves target unguarded.*)
D. Blades in contact. (*Opposition parry.*)
E. Hand at breast height. (*Hand low, parry ineffective.*)
F. Point of foil toward opponent's eyes. (*Keeps foil in line.*)
G. Hand supinated.
H. Elbow six inches from body. (*Closer: cramped parry; Farther away: weak parry.*)
I. Recover to guard position.

SEE BEAT PARRY FOR VARIATIONS AND ADVANTAGES.

DISENGAGE FROM FOURTH TO SIXTH

A disengage from fourth to sixth, (high line), is an extension of the arm and blade in the line of engagement and the passing of the point *UNDER* the opponent's forearm in order to attempt an immediate lunge and touch in sixth, the opposite line of engagement.

SKILL SUMMARY

Engage in 4th, *Offense:* Extend the arm in the line of engagement. Use fingers and wrist only. Allow the foil tip to drop under the opponent's right forearm. Lunge and touch in 6th and recover. Keep the foil close to the opponent's blade, and the semicircle under the forearm small. Change the hand position from normal to supination.

SKILL ANALYSIS AND ILLUSTRATION (Plate 38a, b, c)

Count 1. Engage in fourth, middle distance. (Not illustrated.)

Count 2. Offense extends arm in line of engagement.

Count 3. Allow foil tip to drop below and under opponent's forearm to opposite line of engagement.

Count 4. Lunge and touch in sixth.

Count 5. Recover to guard position. (Not illustrated.)

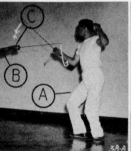

Count 2. Count 3. Count 4.

STRIVE FOR SMOOTHNESS OF MOVEMENT, COUNTS ARE FOR ANALYSIS ONLY.

GENERAL TEACHING AIDS

I. Review direct thrusts and lunges in fourth and sixth.

II. Explain and demonstrate the disengage from fourth to sixth.

III. Divide class into couples. Engage in four. Alternate drill in arm extension in four, and allow foil tip to fall below and under forearm of opponent. Check individuals for complete arm extension, and use of fingers and wrist in changing line of engagement, as well as foil position close to opponent's blade. Couples also act as critics.

PERFORM MOVEMENTS SLOWLY. STRIVE FOR ACCURACY.

IV. Drill as in III above, and add immediate lunge in six.

V. Slow drill to command or count, as above, but add parry 6.

VI. *Couple Drill:* (1) attention; (2) salute; (3) on guard; (4) advance to middle distance; (5) engage in fourth; (6) alternate disengage from four to six with parry 6; (7) five disengages each, retreat to starting position, and repeat drill.

VERBAL TEACHING AIDS

A. Engage in fourth.

B. Extend arm in line of engagement. (*If semicircle is made before this extension, it is easily parried.*)

C. Hand in normal position.

D. Tip of foil passes under opponent's forearm. (*Foil passes under opponent's forearm in all disengages in the high lines.*)

E. Keep foil close to opponent's blade. (*Small semicircle, greater accuracy and speed.*)

F. Fingers and wrist control foil. (*Control lost, look for upward or sideward movement of arm. Target unguarded, look for dropping of arm.*)

G. Lunge. (*Immediately follows disengage in a continuous movement.*)

H. Hand in supination. (*In Counts 3 and 4 above, student has not done this.*)

I. Recover to guard position. (*Protects own target.*) (Not illustrated.)

DISENGAGE FROM SIXTH TO FOURTH

A disengage from sixth to fourth, high line, is an extension of the arm and foil in the line of engagement, and the passing of the point of the blade *UNDER* the opponent's forearm in order to attempt an immediate lunge and touch in fourth, the opposite line of engagement.

SKILL SUMMARY

Engage in sixth. *Offense:* Extend the arm in the line of engagement. Use fingers and wrist only. Allow foil tip to drop below and under opponent's right forearm. Lunge in four, and recover. Keep the foil close to the opponent's blade, and the semicircle under the forearm small. Change hand position from supination to normal.

SKILL ANALYSIS AND ILLUSTRATION (Plate 39a, b, c)

Count 1. Engage in sixth, middle distance. (Not illustrated.)

Count 2. Offense extends arm in line of engagement.

Count 3. Allow foil tip to drop below and under opponent's forearm to opposite line of engagement.

Count 4. Lunge and touch in fourth.

Count 5. Recover to guard position. (Not illustrated.)

Count 2. Count 3. Count 4.

COUNTS DESIGNATE STEPS WITHIN THE SKILL AND ARE FOR ANALYSIS OF ACTION ONLY. STRIVE FOR SMOOTH ACTION. WORK FOR RHYTHM.

GENERAL TEACHING AIDS

I. Review direct thrusts and lunges in fourth and sixth.

II. Explain and demonstrate the disengage from sixth to fourth.

III. Divide class into couples. Engage in sixth. Alternate drill in arm extension in six, and allow foil tip to fall below and under forearm of opponent. Check individuals for complete arm extension, as well as foil position close to opponent's blade. Couples also act as critics.

IV. Drill as in III above, and add immediate lunge in four. Couples alternate disengage and defense positions.

V. Slow drill to command or count, as above, but add opposition parry in four.

VI. *Couple Drill:* (1) attention; (2) salute; (3) on guard; (4) advance to middle distance; (5) engage in sixth; (6) alternate disengage from six to four with parry 4; (7) five disengages each, retreat to starting position, and repeat drill.

VII. Allow short bout, stressing slow movements, and the use of skills previously learned. Conduct as in the couple drill above; however (5), (6), and (7) above would be replaced by use of skill desired by each individual, and offense and defense alternated by each individual. (i.e.: Fencer A engages in fourth; lunges and attempts touch in four. Fencer B parries 4. Fencer B engages in sixth; lunges and attempts touch in six; Fencer A parries 6, etc.) Students may be divided in groups of four. Two engaged in the bout, and two acting as judges and critics, with power to stop the bout, when either fencer has made a touch or has used an incorrect form in the performance of a skill.

VERBAL TEACHING AIDS

A. Engage in sixth.

B. Extend arm in line of engagement.

C. Hand in supination. (*Sixth.*)

D. Tip of foil passes under opponent's forearm. (*For all high lines.*)

E. Keep foil close to opponent's blade. (*Speed and accuracy aid.*)

F. Fingers and wrist control foil. (*Do not drop hand or move arm sideward or up and down.*)

G. Lunge.

H. Hand in normal position. (*Fourth.*)

I. Recover to guard position. (*Protection.*)

VARIATIONS

1. PARRIES may also be executed as beat parries, see page 147 for discussion of beat as an attack on the blade. Teach the beat parries after the beat has been learned.

2. Variations in parries and disengages result from length of fingers and strength of wrist.

Such individual differences require compensations such as more movement from the wrist to aid weak fingers, while strong fingers may easily execute the parries and disengages with the fingers alone.

A strong wrist aids in accuracy and firmness in parries and touches.

ADVANTAGES

1. Beat parries are used with greatest success against a weak attack. Firm, strong attacks require the opposition parries to divert opponent's attack. The beat parries are made with fingers and wrist, with the least possible use of the forearm.

2. Individual compensations if made, should conform as closely as possible to the accepted technique of performance; however they should be allowed provided they increase, rather than decrease the performance level of that individual.

ENGAGEMENT IN SEVENTH AND SECOND

Seventh: Two blades crossed in contact in the seventh guard position.

Second: Two blades crossed in contact in the second guard position.

SKILL SUMMARY

Seventh: From the on guard position, assume the guard position of seventh by moving the hand to the left and lowering it directly toward the floor until the arm is only slightly bent. The elbow is six inches from the hip, and the tip of the foil is lowered until it is directed at the opponent's knee. The pommel is thus raised above the wrist. The foil is on the right of the opponent or on the side nearer opponent's inside low line. The general body position is the same as in the on guard position. The hand is in supination.

Second: From the on guard position, assume the guard of second by moving the hand from supination to pronation and lowering it directly toward the floor until the arm is only slightly bent. The elbow is about six inches from the hip and the tip of the foil is lowered until it is directed at the opponent's knee. The pommel extends to the right of the hand and wrist. The foil is on the left of the opponent, or on the side nearer opponent's outside low line. The general body position is the same as in the on guard position.

SKILL ANALYSIS AND ILLUSTRATION (Plate 40a, b, c, d)

Seventh:

Count 1. On guard position.

Count 2. Move hand in supination to left. Lower hand until right arm is slightly bent. Direct tip of foil at opponent's knee. Foils crossed on the right.

Second:

Count 1. On guard position.

Count 2. Pronate hand. Lower hand until right arm is slightly bent. Direct tip of foil at opponent's knee. Foils crossed on the left.

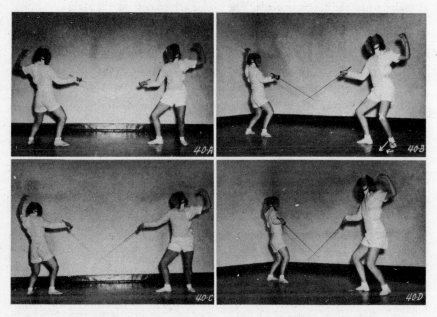

Seventh Guard Position. Front View. Seventh Guard Position. Side View. Second Guard Position. Front View. Second Guard Position. Side View.

GENERAL TEACHING AIDS

I. Check general body position from AIDS for on guard. Assume these engagements at the command of instructor until both second and seventh are learned.

II. Assume engagements of fourth, sixth, seventh, and second on command.

VERBAL TEACHING AIDS

See VERBAL AIDS for on guard. Check hand positions of 7th and 2nd. See parry aids 2 and 7.

DIRECT THRUST IN SEVENTH

A direct thrust in seventh is an extension of the foil and arm in the line of engagement, with or without a lunge, toward the opponent's inside low target area. This is made from an engagement, or with the blades not touching.

SKILL SUMMARY

Engage opponent in seventh, middle distance. Opponent continues to hold seventh guard position. Extend the arm and foil in the line of engagement, lunge and touch in seventh. The body position is the same as in the lunge, the foil is bent upward, the hand is in supination, and slightly higher than the shoulder when the touch is made. The blades are crossed on the right.

SKILL ANALYSIS AND ILLUSTRATION (Plate 41a, b)

Count 1. Engage in seventh, middle distance. (Not illustrated.)
Count 2. Extend arm and foil in line of engagement.
Count 3. Lunge and touch in seventh.
Count 4. Recover to guard position. (Not illustrated.)

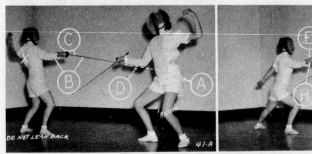

Count 2. Count 3.

GENERAL TEACHING AIDS

I. Review of previous lessons, with special emphasis on the lunge.
II. Explain and demonstrate:

(a) Seventh guard position; (b) engagement in seventh; (c) direct thrust and touch in seventh without a lunge; (d) direct thrust and touch in seventh with a lunge.

III. Class drills in seventh guard position.
IV. Couple drills in b; c; and d; above.
V. Divide class in couples. Students engage in seventh and alternate

attempts at a touch in seventh, close distance without a lunge. Defense holds seventh guard position and checks form of offense. Offense holds touch until partner gives the command to recover. Later touch and recover immediately.

VI. Couples engage in seventh and attempt alternate touches in seventh from middle distance, which necessitates a lunge. Defense holds seventh guard position and checks form of offense. Offense holds touch until partner gives a command to recover. This allows time for checking body, foil, and hand positions.

VII. *Couple Drill:* (1) attention; (2) salute; (3) on guard; (4) advance to middle distance; (5) engage in seventh; (6) alternate lunge and touch in seventh and recovery to guard position; (7) five touches each, retreat to starting position. Repeat drill.

VIII. Short bout including all offense and defense tactics learned with the exception of seventh, as conducted in TEACHING AID VII, page 133.

VERBAL TEACHING AIDS

A. Engage in seventh, middle distance.
B. Extend arm and foil in line of engagement. (*Right of opponent's blade.*)
C. Arm and foil in straight line. (*Hand slightly lower than 4th.*)
D. Tip of foil directed toward inside low target area.
E. Hand in supination.
F. Lunge in seventh.
G. Foil bent upward on touch.
H. Hand slightly higher than shoulder on touch.
I. Recover to guard position.

DIRECT THRUST IN SECOND

A direct thrust in second is an extension of the foil and arm in the line of engagement, with or without a lunge, toward the opponent's outside low line. This is made from an engagement or with the blades not touching.

SKILL SUMMARY

Engage opponent in second position, middle distance. Opponent continues to hold second guard position. Extend the arm and foil in the line of engagement, lunge and touch in second. The body position is the same as in the lunge, the foil is bent upward, the hand is in pronation, and slightly higher than the shoulder when the touch is made. The blades are crossed on the left.

SKILL ANALYSIS AND ILLUSTRATION (Plate 42a, b)

Count 1. Engage in second, middle distance. (Not illustrated.)
Count 2. Extend arm and foil in line of engagement.
Count 3. Lunge and touch in second.
Count 4. Recover to guard position. (Not illustrated.)

Count 2. Count 3.

GENERAL TEACHING AIDS

I. Review previous lessons, particular emphasis on lunge.

II. Explain and demonstrate:

(a) second guard position; (b) engagement in second; (c) direct thrust and touch in second, without a lunge; (d) direct thrust and touch in second with a lunge.

III. Class drill in second guard position.

IV. Couple drills in b; c; d; above.

V. Divide class in couples. Students engage in second, and alternate attempts at a touch in second, close distance without a lunge. Defense holds second guard position and checks form of offense. Offense holds touch until partner gives command to recover. Later touch and recover immediately.

VI. Couples engaged in second and attempt alternate touches in second from middle distance, which necessitates a lunge. Defense holds second guard position and checks form of offense. Offense holds touch until partner gives command to recover. This allows time for checking body, foil, and hand positions.

VII. *Couple Drill:* (1) attention; (2) salute; (3) on guard; (4) advance to middle distance; (5) engage in second; (6) alternate lunge and touch in second with recovery to guard position; (7) five touches each, retreat to starting position. Repeat drill.

VIII. Short bout, including all offense and defense tactics learned with the exception of seventh and second, as conducted in TEACHING AID VII, page 133.

VERBAL TEACHING AIDS

A. Engage in second, middle distance.

B. Extend arm and foil in line of engagement. (*Left of opponent's blade.*)

C. Arm and foil in straight line. (*Hand slightly lower than sixth.*)

D. Tip of foil directed toward 2nd. (*Outside low line.*)

E. Hand in pronation.

F. Lunge in second.

G. Foil bent upward on touch.

H. Hand slightly higher than shoulder on touch. (*Hold point firm.*)

I. Recover to guard position. (Not illustrated.)

OPPOSITION PARRY IN SEVENTH

An opposition parry in seventh is a defensive movement of the blade and hand until the hand is slightly lower than the hand position of the fourth guard, and the point of the blade is directed at the opponent's knee. The hand is in supination. Contact with the opponent's blade is maintained throughout.

SKILL SUMMARY

Engage opponent in seventh. *Offense:* Thrust and lunge in the line of engagement, and attempt to make a touch in seventh, outside low line. *Defense:* Describe a small semicircle clockwise with the tip of the foil, hand in supination, and maintain pressure on the attacking blade. The hand is slightly lower than the fourth guard position. The tip of the foil is directed toward the opponent's knee.

(*See Teaching Aid Number VII for parry 7 from the fourth guard position.*)

SKILL ANALYSIS AND ILLUSTRATION (Plate 43a, b)

Count 1. Engage in seventh. (Not illustrated.)

Count 2. Offense extends arm in seventh.

Count 3. Offense lunges in seventh; defense executes parry 7 by describing small semicircle clockwise with the tip of the foil. Hand in supination.

Count 4. Recover immediately to guard position. (Not illustrated.)

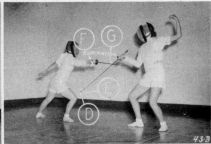

Count 2. Count 3.

MOVEMENTS ARE CONTINUOUS. USE COUNTS FOR ANALYSIS AND APPROXIMATE TIME ELEMENTS OR RHYTHM.

GENERAL TEACHING AIDS

I. Review previous lessons pertaining to guard and engagement positions in seventh, as well as the direct thrust in seventh with no opposition.

II. Explain and demonstrate parry 7 from engagement in seven.

III. Line drill in parry 7.

IV. Divide class in couples, engage in seventh, close distance. Couples alternate thrust in seventh, without lunge, and parry 7. Check for errors.

V. Couples engage in seventh, middle distance, and alternate lunges and parries in seventh. Partners check for errors in form.

VI. *Couple Drill No. 1:* (1) attention; (2) salute; (3) on guard; (4) advance to middle distance; (5) engage in seven; (6) alternate lunge and recovery to guard position with parry 7; (7) five parries each, retreat to starting position. Repeat drill.

VII. *Couple Drill No. 2:* Offense in seventh guard position. Defense in fouth guard position. Blades do not touch. Offense extends arm and foil, and lunges in seventh. Defense parries in seventh from fourth guard position by slightly lowering the hand and moving the point of the foil clockwise in a semicircle until it reaches the height of the opponent's knee. The hand position changes from normal to supination as the parry is executed. The guard position changes from fourth to seventh. Couples change from offense to defense after 3 lunges. Partners should be changed after each individual has performed 3 parries.

VERBAL TEACHING AIDS

A. Engage in seventh.

B. Direct thrust and lunge in seventh.

C. Hand lowered. (*Slightly lower than fourth.*)

D. Clockwise semicircle. (*Use fingers and wrist only.*)

E. Point of foil toward opponent's knee.

F. Hand in supination. (*Do not move hand up or down, forward or back in parry.*)

G. Blades in contact and crossed. (*Opposition parry.*)

H. Recovery.

OPPOSITION PARRY IN SECOND

An opposition parry in second is a defensive movement of the blade and hand until the hand is slightly lower than the hand position of the sixth guard, and the point of the foil is directed at the opponent's knee. The hand is in pronation. Contact with the opponent's blade is maintained throughout.

SKILL SUMMARY

Engage opponent in second. *Offense:* Thrust and lunge in the line of engagement in an attempt to make a touch in second, outside low line. *Defense:* Describe a small semicircle counter-clockwise with the tip of the foil, hand in pronation and slightly lower than the sixth guard position. The tip of the foil is directed toward the opponent's knee.

(*See Teaching Aids No. VII for parry 2 from the sixth guard position.*)

SKILL ANALYSIS AND ILLUSTRATION (Plate 44a, b)

Count 1. Engage in second. (Not illustrated.)

Count 2. Offense extends arm in second.

Count 3. Offense lunges in second; defense parries 2 by describing a small semicircle counter-clockwise with the tip of the foil. Hand is in pronation, movement made with wrist and fingers only.

Count 4. Recover immediately to guard position. (Not illustrated.)

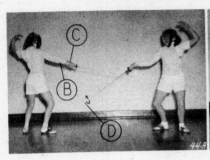 

Count 2. Count 3.

RHYTHM. SMOOTH MOVEMENT. CONTROL.

GENERAL TEACHING AIDS

I. Review previous lessons pertaining to guard and engagement positions in second, as well as the direct thrust in second with no opposition.

II. Explain and demonstrate parry 2 from engagement in 2.

III. Line drill in parry 2.

IV. Divide class in couples, engage in 2nd, close distance, and couples alternate thrust in second, without lunge, and parry 2. Check for errors.

V. Couples engage in second, middle distance, and alternate lunges and parries in two. Partners check for errors in form.

VI. *Couple Drill No. 1:* (1) attention; (2) salute; (3) on guard; (4) advance to middle distance; (5) engage in second; (6) alternate lunge and recovery to guard position with parry 2; (7) five parries each, retreat to starting position. Repeat drill.

VII. *Couple Drill No. 2:* Defense in sixth guard position. Offense in second guard position. (Plate 45a, b, c) Blades do not touch. Offense extends foil and lunges in second. Defense parries in second from sixth guard position by slightly lowering the hand and moving the point of the foil counter-clockwise in a semicircle until it reaches the height of the opponent's knee. The hand position changes from supination to pronation as the parry is executed. The guard position changes from sixth to second. Couples change from offense to defense after 3 lunges. Partners should be changed after each individual has performed 3 parries.

Defense Sixth, Offense Second. Offense Extends Arm and Foil in Second. Lunges in Second.

VERBAL TEACHING AIDS

A. Engage in second.
B. Direct thrust and lunge in second.
C. Hand lowered. (*Slightly lower than sixth.*)
D. Point of foil toward opponent's knee.
E. Semicircle counter-clockwise. (*Use fingers and wrist only.*)
F. Hand in pronation. (*Only movement left and right in actual parry, after guard position has been reached.*)
G. Blades in contact and crossed. (*Opposition parry.*)
H. Recover to guard position.

SMOOTH RHYTHMIC MOVEMENT . . . ACCURACY . . . SPEED WHEN RHYTHM AND ACCURACY OF MOVEMENT HAVE BEEN MASTERED.

DISENGAGE FROM SEVENTH TO SECOND

A disengage from seventh to second (low line), is an extension of the arm or blade in the line of engagement and the passing of the point of the blade OVER the opponent's forearm in order to attempt an immediate lunge and touch in second, the opposite line of engagement.

SKILL SUMMARY

Engage in seventh. *Offense:* Extend the arm in the line of engagement. Use the fingers and wrist only, and raise the foil tip up and over the opponent's forearm. Lunge and touch in second, and recover. The foil is kept close to the opponent's blade, and the semicircle over the arm is small. The hand position changes from supination to pronation.

SKILL ANALYSIS AND ILLUSTRATION (Plate 46a, b, c, d)

Count 1. Engage in seventh, middle distance.

Count 2. Offense extends arm in line of engagement.

Count 3. Raise tip of foil up and over opponent's forearm to opposite line of engagement.

Count 4. Lunge and touch in second.

Count 5. Recover to guard position. (Not illustrated.)

Count 1. Count 2.

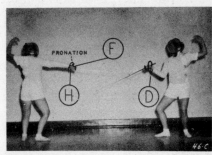 

Count 3. Count 4.

GENERAL TEACHING AIDS

I. Review direct thrusts and lunges in second and seventh.

II. Explain and demonstrate the disengage from seventh to second.

III. Divide class into couples. Engage in seventh. Alternate drill in arm extension in seventh, and raising of foil tip up and over forearm of opponent. Check individuals for complete arm extension, as well as foil position close to opponent's blade. Couples also act as critics.

PERFORM MOVEMENTS SLOWLY, BUT WITH RHYTHM AND RELAXATION.

STRIVE FOR ACCURACY AS RELAXATION DEVELOPS.

IV. Drill as in III above, and add immediate lunge in second.

V. Slow, rhythmic drill to command or count, as above, but add opposition parry in second.

VI. *Couple Drill:* (1) attention; (2) salute; (3) on guard; (4) advance to middle distance; (5) engage in seventh; (6) alternate disengage from seventh to second with parry 2; (7) five disengages each, retreat to starting position, and repeat drill.

VERBAL TEACHING AIDS

A. Engage in seventh.
B. Extend arm in line of engagement. (*Precedes semicircle.*)
C. Hand in supination.
D. Tip of foil passes over opponent's forearm counter-clockwise.
E. Foil close to opponent's blade.
F. Fingers and wrist control foil.
G. Lunge.
H. Hand in pronation.
I. Recover to guard position. (*Protection.*)

RELAX! LET THE FOIL DO THE WORK!

DISENGAGE FROM SECOND TO SEVENTH

A disengage from second to seventh, (low line), is an extension of the arm and blade in the line of engagement and the passing of the point of the blade *OVER* the opponent's forearm in order to attempt an immediate lunge and touch in seventh, the opposite line of engagement.

SKILL SUMMARY

Engage in second. *Offense:* Extend the arm in the line of engagement. Use the fingers and wrist only. Raise the foil tip up and over the opponent's right forearm, lunge, and touch in seventh, and recover. The foil is kept close to the opponent's blade, and the semicircle over the arm is small. The hand position changes from pronation to supination.

SKILL ANALYSIS AND ILLUSTRATION (Plate 47a, b, c, d)

Count 1. Engage in second, middle distance.
Count 2. Offense extends arm in line of engagement.

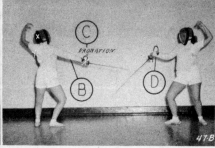

Count 1. Count 2.

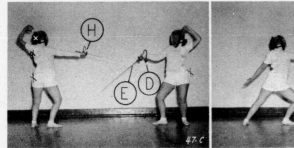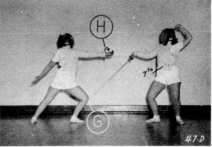

Count 3. Count 4.

Count 3. Raise the tip of the foil up and over opponent's forearm to opposite line of engagement.

Count 4. Lunge and touch in seventh.

Count 5. Recover to guard position. (Not illustrated.)

General Teaching Aids

I. Review direct thrusts and lunges in seventh and second.

II. Explain and demonstrate the disengage from second to seventh.

III. Divide class into couples. Engage in second. Alternate drill in arm extension in second and raising of foil tip up and over forearm of opponent. Check individuals for complete arm extension, and use of fingers and wrist only in changing line of engagement, as well as foil position close to opponent's blade. Couples also act as critics.

IV. Drill as in III above, and add immediate lunge in seventh.

V. Slow rhythmic drill to command or count, as above, but add opposion parry in seventh.

VI. *Couple Drill:* (1) attention; (2) salute; (3) on guard; (4) advance to middle distance; (5) engage in 2nd; (6) alternate disengage from second to seventh with parry 7; (7) five disengages each, retreat to starting position. Repeat drill.

VII. Short bout as described in Teaching Aid No. VII page 133, using all offense and defense tactics learned in previous lessons.

Verbal Teaching Aids

A. Engage in second.

B. Extend arm in line of engagement. (*Precedes semicircle.*)

C. Hand in pronation.

D. Tip of foil passes over opponent's forearm. (*Clockwise.*)

E. Foil close to opponent's blade.

F. Fingers and wrist control foil.

G. Lunge.

H. Hand in supination.

I. Recover to guard position.

The Material Presented in Every Group of Teaching Aids Covers Much More Than One or Two Lessons.

DISENGAGE FROM SIXTH TO SEVENTH

A. Allow foil tip to drop below and under oponents's arm.
B. Line changes from sixth to seventh. (High to low line.)
    Exercise: (1) Engage in sixth; (2) Disengage to seventh; (3) Lunge in seventh; (4) Recover.

DISENGAGE FROM SEVENTH TO SIXTH

A. Raise foil tip up and over opponent's forearm.
B. Line changes from seventh to sixth. (Low to high.)
    Exercise: (1) Engage in seventh; (2) Disengage to sixth; (3) Lunge in sixth; (4) Recover.

DISENGAGE FROM FOURTH TO SECOND

A. Allow foil tip to drop below and under opponent's forearm.
B. Line changes from fourth to second. (High to low.)
    Exercise: (1) Engage in fourth; (2) Disengage to second; (3) Lunge in fourth; (4) Recover.

DISENGAGE FROM SECOND TO FOURTH

A. Raise foil tip up and over opponent's forearm.
B. Line changes from second to fourth. (Low to high.)
    Exercise: (1) Engage in second; (2) Disengage to fourth; (3) Lunge in fourth; (4) Recover.

USE THE SAME TYPE OF TEACHING AIDS AS IN PREVIOUS DISENGAGE LESSONS.

ANALYZE ACTIONS AND FORMULATE OWN GENERAL AND VERBAL TEACHING AIDS.

DOUBLE DISENGAGE

A double disengage is a compound attack, consisting of two or more foil movements in making two disengages in the opposite directions.

SKILL SUMMARY

Engage in sixth. Extend arm in line of engagement and disengage to fourth, returning immediately by a second disengage to sixth, lunge and touch in sixth, the original line of engagement.

SKILL ANALYSIS AND ILLUSTRATION (Plate 48a, b, c, d, e)

Count 1. Engage in sixth.
Count 2. Extend arm in sixth.
Count 3. Disengage to fourth.
Count 4. Disengage from fourth to sixth.
Count 5. Lunge and touch in sixth.
Count 6. Recover to guard position. (Not illustrated.)

Count 1. Count 2. Count 3.

Count 4. Count 5.

Use the Same Type of Teaching Aids for Double Disengage as for Disengages Discussed Previously.

NOTE: A triple disengage consists of three disengages. Using the SKILL ANALYSIS of a double disengage, counts 1, 2, 3, and 4 would remain the same. Count 5 would change to: disengage from six to four. Count 6 would change to: lunge and touch in fourth. Count 7 would be added for the recovery.

THE BEAT

The beat is an attack on the blade by means of a quick, sharp blow with the middle of the blade against the weak or middle part of the opponent's blade. This is used to open the way for an attack, as a feint, or as an invitation to the opponent to attack. The beat may be made from an engaged or an unengaged position.

Skill Summary

Engage in fourth. *Offense:* Give opponent's blade a quick, sharp blow with the middle of the blade. The hand is in the guard position, and the blow is made with the fingers only. The arm is bent as the beat is made, and the arm extension, lunge, touch, and recovery in fourth, follow immediately in the order named.

SKILL ANALYSIS AND ILLUSTRATION (Plate 49a, b, c)

Count 1. Engage in fourth. (Not illustrated.)
Count 2. Beat to open line of fourth.
Count 3. Extend arm in line of fourth.
Count 4. Lunge and touch in fourth.
Count 5. Recover to guard position. (Not illustrated.)

Count 2. Count 3. Count 4.

GENERAL TEACHING AIDS

I. Review previously learned skills as thought necessary by the instructor.

II. Explain and demonstrate the beat.

III. Divide class into couples. Couples alternate beat, using fingers only. Check for errors.

IV. Couples alternate beat and direct thrust in open line. Attempt in all lines.

THE BEATS USED HERE ARE HEAVY BEATS.

V. Couples alternate attempts at a beat, disengage, thrust, lunge, and touch in opposite line. USE LIGHT BEAT. (i.e.: engage in fourth. Offense performs light beat on opponent's blade, extends arm, and as defense returns to position, offense disengages, lunges, and touches in fourth, and recovers to guard position.)

PERFORM IN ALL DISENGAGES.

VI. Review opposition parries in four, six, seven, and two.

VII. Couple drill in parries in four, six, seven, and two, using beat parry.

VERBAL TEACHING AIDS

A. Engage in fourth.
B. Beat. (*Sharp and heavy.*)
C. Middle of blades hit. (*Middle of blade of offense against weak or middle of defense blade.*)

D. Hand in guard position. (*On beat attacks in any line.*)

E. Use fingers only.

F. Keep arm bent. (*Straight arm detracts from surprise element of beat.*)

G. Foil moves from left to right. (*Moved to right by thumb and forefinger, and to left by snap of fingers toward palm.*)

H. Foil stops in line. (*In this instance, in 4th line.*)

I. Extend arm.

J. Lunge and touch in fourth.

K. Recover.

VARIATIONS

1. The beat may be made in any line.

2. *Change Beat:* Engage in fourth. With a circular movement of foil arrive on other side of opponent's blade and by means of a beat, *further* open sixth, which is already the open line, lunge, and touch in sixth, and recover to guard position. Action of foil to other side of opponent's blade, denotes the change beat.

THE TEACHING AIDS COVER A NUMBER OF LESSONS, AND CANNOT BE COVERED IN ONE LESSON. DO NOT TRY TO FORCE STUDENT PROGRESS.

CUTOVER

The cutover is a disengage in the high lines, when pressure is being exerted on the blade, in order to lunge in the opposite line of engagement. The foil is raised up and over the point of the opponent's blade in executing the cutover.

SKILL SUMMARY

Engage in sixth. *Defense:* Apply pressure on blade of offense. *Offense:* Raise the point of the foil with wrist, fingers, and slight use of forearm, up and over the point of the opponent's blade. Immediately extending the arm smoothly, and attack in fourth with a direct thrust and lunge.

SKILL ANALYSIS AND ILLUSTRATION (Plate 50a, b, c, d)

Count 1. Engage in sixth, middle distance. Defense applies pressure on blade of offense.

Count 2. Offense raises blade over tip of opponent's foil.

Count 3. Extend arm and foil in fourth.

Count 4. Lunge and touch in fourth.

Count 5. Recover to guard position. (Not illustrated.)

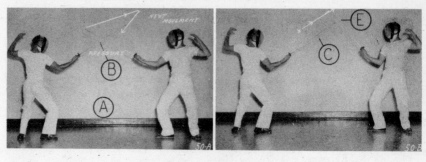

Count 1. Count 2.

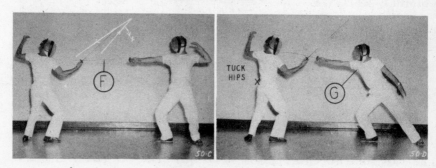

Count 3. Count 4.

GENERAL TEACHING AIDS

I. Review skills as desired.

II. Explain and demonstrate cutover.

III. *Couple Drill:* Defense holds sixth guard position in engagement in sixth. Offense attempts cutover without following with a lunge. Alternate attempts with checking for errors.

IV. Same drill as III above, adding direct thrust, lunge, and touch in fourth.

V. Same drill from fourth engagement with lunge and touch in sixth.

VI. Repeat drills IV and V adding parries 4 and 6.

VII. Repeat drill IV with lunge in second; lunge in seventh; adding parries of 2 and 7.

VIII. Short bout, instructor designating offense. Change to defense on command from instructor. (Short periods.)

VERBAL TEACHING AIDS

A. Engage in sixth.

B. Defense applies pressure on the blade.

C. Raise foil with fingers and wrist. (*Loss of control due to use of only thumb and index finger.*)

D. Keep point in line. (*Use of forearm takes point out of line.*)

OPPOSITION PARRIES IN EIGHT, FIVE, THREE, AND ONE

Opposition parries in 8, 5, 3, and 1, correspond to the defense of the same target areas guarded by 2, 7, 6, and 4, respectively. These may also be executed as beat parries.

OPPOSITION PARRY IN EIGHTH

Defends lower outside target area.
1. Engage in sixth.
2. *Offense:* Lunge in eight. (2)
3. *Defense:* Parry 8. (Plate 52a, b)

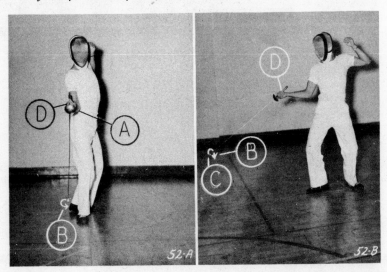

Opposition Parry Eighth. Front View. Opposition Parry Eighth. Side View.

    A. Lower hand.
    B. Move point in semicircle clockwise.
    C. Foil directed at opponent's knee.
    D. Hand remains in supination.

Not as strong as a parry in second.

OPPOSITION PARRY IN FIVE

Defends lower inside target area.
1. Engage in sixth.
2. *Offense:* Disengage and lunge in five. (7)
3. *Defense:* Parry 5. (Plate 53a, b)
    A. Move foil to left.
    B. Hand changes to pronation.
    C. Hand 4 inches below breast.
    D. Point of blade higher than hand.

Seldom used, leaves target exposed and point too far out of line.

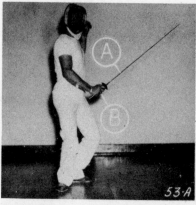

Opposition Parry Fifth. Front View. Opposition Parry Fifth. Side View.

OPPOSITION PARRY IN THREE

Defends upper inside target area.
1. Engage in fourth.
2. *Offense:* Disengage and lunge in three. (6)
3. *Defense:* Parry 5 (Plate 54a, b)

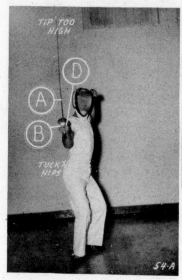

Opposition Parry Third. Front View. Opposition Parry Third. Side View.

   A. Foil to right.
   B. Hand at breast height.
   C. Point of blade toward opponent's eyes.
   D. Hand in pronation.
More awkward than sixth.

OPPOSITION PARRY IN FIRST

Defends upper inside target area.
1. Engage in sixth.
2. *Offense:* Disengage and lunge in 1. (4)
3. *Defense:* Parry 1. (Plate 55a, b)

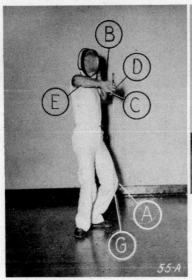

Opposition Parry First. Front View. Opposition Parry First. Side View.

A. Lower point of blade.
B. Turn hand to left.
C. Thumb down.
D. Fingernails to right.
E. Forearm horizontal to floor.
F. Wrist slightly higher than chin line.
G. Point of foil directed at opponent's foot.

Point too far out of line, leaves target unguarded.

TEACHING AIDS

If used for intermediate and advanced fencers, conduct learning periods as discussed under parries 6, 4, 2, and 7.

ADVANTAGES

The advantages are in parries 2, 7, 6, and 4. The disadvantages of parries 8, 3, 5, and 1 are listed below each parry.

COUNTER PARRIES

There is a counter parry for each parry, although only one is visualized. A counter parry is used against simple attacks. These differ from simple parries since the action not only diverts the attacking blade, but changes the line of engagement.

1. Engage in sixth.
2. *Offense:* Disengage and lunge in four.
3. Counter parry of 6. (Plate 56a, b, c)

Count 2. Count 3. Count 4.

A. Follow opponent's blade around.
B. Defensive foil makes small circle around opponent's blade.
C. Circle starts *under* opponent's blade. (*All high lines.*) (Circle started over opponent's blade is all low lines.)
D. Use fingers only.
4. Follow counter parry with direct thrust, touch in sixth and recover.

ALLOW STUDENTS TO DISCOVER AND DEMONSTRATE OTHER COUNTER PARRIES.

PRESS

The press is made slowly and is controlled by the fingers. Offense exerts continual pressure on the blade for the same purpose for which the beat is used. The press should be heavy when a direct thrust is intended, and light and quick when followed by a disengage. The press may also be preceded by a change as in the change beat.

1. Engage in sixth.
2. Offense executes press. (Moves blade aside.) (Plate 57a, b, c)
   A. Arm in normal guard position. No bend or extension.
   B. Middle or weak part of blade used.
   C. Use fingers only.
3. Lunge in opening made by press.
4. Recover to guard position.

Count 1. Count 2. Count 3.

TEACHING AIDS

USE SAME TYPE OF TEACHING AIDS AS USED IN ELEMENTARY
FENCING SKILLS.

AUTHOR'S NOTE

Further skills in fencing include the following:

Attacks on the Blade:
Pressure glide.
Glide.
Bind.
Envelopment.

Counter Attacks:
Time thrust.
Stop thrust.

Parries:
Variations.

Retaking Attacks:
Redouble.
Replacement.

Returns:
Compound reposte.
Delayed reposte.
Counter reposte.

Fencing skills include many variations of each skill listed above, as
well as those inadvertently omitted from the list.

These may be generally classified as intermediate and advanced
fencing skills. No attempt was made to include their analyses in this
volume, since it was felt that each instructor could better classify them

according to the needs and progress of student personnel. A thorough understanding of the preceding material should insure complete comprehension of the terms used in the reference material, as well as the general procedure necessary in skill analysis and efficient instruction.

OFFICIAL BOUTS

Recommendations for participation in short periods of combat in official bouts of short duration have been purposely omitted. Such periods can be more advantageously and correctly placed in the learning progression by the individual instructor.

STRATEGY FOR BEGINNERS

Introduction. Since the periods of combat in official bouts are few for beginners, and the actual number is left to the judgement of individual instructors, a discussion of strategy must necessarily be quite general. No attempt has been made to cover the problem of strategy completely, since the course of action arises from the preceding attack or parry; however the few examples given may aid the instructor in further explanations of the subject to the students.

In nearly every fencing class, an instructor will find three types; the overly-aggressive, the average, and the timid fencers. The same principles of strategy may be applied for each group; however the overly-aggressive fencer must learn to fence with precision rather than with a continuous series of attacks, while the timid fencer must learn to attack rather than perform a series of ineffectual parries. The average fencer is usually quite methodical, both in practice and combat, and the general rules of strategy are easily applied, while the others require individual attention, before strategy can be practiced.

Essentials. Lessons should afford the student practice in the fundamentals basic to fencing. Until parries, direct thrusts in all four lines, disengages, and fundamental positions have become natural movements, combat is wasteful.

Purpose. The purpose of a bout is to reach the target without receiving a touch.

Positions. There are two possible positions for a *beginner* in starting a bout. The first is an engagement with foils in contact. The second is open invitation with the point off the target, and the foils not touching.

Elementary Strategy. The engagement offers an opportunity for a disengage and feint or lunge in the opposite line. Another course of action is the press, or to exert pressure on the opponent's blade in order to secure an opening, although this would not be used in *initial* trials at combat. A beat is a dangerous attack when in an engagement.

The open invitation offers only one opportunity as the best course of action. A feint at the target in the open line is always in order, for an attack on the blade would throw the foil too far out of line. If the opponent parries, the opportunity arises for a disengage, and a lunge in the opposite line. If he declines to parry, the feint is continued, and a try made for a touch in the open line. Use all lines when engaged in combat.

Further strategy. As the fencers progress, the beat, the cutover, the press, the reposte, the double and triple disengages, and the counter parries may be used. In all cases the instructor should be quite explicit about possible courses of action, both for the attack and the defense. The advantages and possible disadvantages of each course of action should be explained clearly, accompanied by the explanation that the *actual* course of action arises from the preceding attack or parry.

The Teaching Aids for each skill offer specific items suggested for use in the general activities listed below.

SUGGESTED CLASS ORGANIZATION
(60 *minutes*)

Initial lessons   SUGGESTED ACTIVITY

		APPROXIMATE TIME
1st three weeks.		
Arrive and Dress		10 minutes
(Spontaneous activity if dressed in less time.)		
Roll Call and Preliminaries		3 minutes
Warm Up Drills (teacher initiated and led)		7 minutes
Review		10 minutes
Explanation and Demonstration of New Material		5 minutes
Class Drills (line and target)		5 minutes
Couple Drills		5 minutes
Individual Couple Activity		5 minutes
Shower and Dress (longer period of couple activity if less time is needed to dress)		10 minutes
4th through 8th week.		
Arrive and Dress (student activity if dressed in less time)		10 minutes
Roll Call and Preliminaries		3 minutes
Warm Ups (student led if desired)		5 minutes

Review .... 3 minutes
> (This may be led by student unless teacher
> wishes to accomplish a specific purpose by
> the review.)

Explanation and Demonstration of New Material .... 4 minutes
Class Drills .... 5 minutes
Couple Drills .... 5 minutes
Individual Couple Activity (student initiated, teacher
advised) .... 15 minutes
Shower and Dress .... 10 minutes

10th through 12th week.

Arrive and Dress .... 10 minutes
Roll Call and Preliminaries .... 3 minutes
Warm Ups (may be student led) .... 5 minutes
Review .... 4 minutes
Explanation and Demonstration of New Material .... 3 minutes
Individual Couple Drills .... 5 minutes
Individual Couple Activity: Demonstration of Dis-
coveries Made in New Disengages, and Uses of
Skills Previously Learned in Attack and Defense 20 minutes
Shower and Dress .... 10 minutes

NOTE: Modified or actual bouts may be substituted as desired or thought advisable. Some modified competition, fencing films, demonstrations, etc., prove good motivation factors.

FURTHER REFERENCES

1. Ainsworth, Dorothy S.; Broer, Marion R.; Goss, Alice G.; Goss, Gertrude; Jennings, Evelyn; Pitkin, Bertha A.; Ryder, Florence: *Individual Sports for Women,* W. B. Saunders and Company, Philadelphia and London, 1943, 392 pages.

2. Barbasetti, Luigi: *The Art of the Foil.* E. P. Dutton and Company, New York, 1932, 275 pages.

3. Castello, J. M.: *Theory and Practice of Fencing.* Charles Scribner's Sons, New York, 1933, 269 pages.

4. Hett, G. V.: *Fencing.* Pitman Publishing Corporation, New York, 1939, 131 pages.

5. National Section on Women's Athletics: *Individual Sports Guide.* Official Sports Library for Women, A. S. Barnes and Company, Publishers, New York, 1945-46.

6. Vince, Joseph: *Fencing,* Barnes Dollar Sports Library, A. S. Barnes and Company, Publishers, New York, 1937, 59 pages.

VI

GOLF

TEACHING PREMISE

THE teaching progression in golf instruction seems to vary with
each instructor, because the usual logical order of simple to complex is interpreted differently. Authorities are quite generally agreed
that the grip and stance are necessary first steps in any teaching progression. General agreement is also apparent on the classification of
putting as a simple skill, and the order of instruction in the approach
shots from the quarter to the half, to the three quarter swing.

Disagreement occurs on the order of instruction in putting, approaches, and wood shots. A few examples of these variations, and
their justification as teaching progressions, are listed below.

1. SHORT APPROACHES, LONG APPROACHES, WOOD SHOTS, PUTT-
   ING.

   A. Justification:
      (a) Simple to complex in actual golf swing.
      (b) Swing remains constant throughout use of any club,
          and this progression gradually progresses to the most
          difficult skill, the wood shot.
      (c) Putting is placed last, even though it is a simple skill,
          because of its dissimilarity to the golf swing.
      (d) Putting does not confuse the student if placed last in
          the teaching progression.

2. WOOD SHOTS, LONG APPROACHES, SHORT APPROACHES, PUTT-
   ING.

   A. Justification:
      (a) Actual order used in play.
      (b) Students want to swing the woods first. (Motivation
          factor.)

161

3. PUTTING, SHORT APPROACHES, LONG APPROACHES, WOOD SHOTS.

   A. Justification:
   (a) Putting first, because it is 50% of the game or strokes included in par.
   (b) More truly simple to complex.
   (c) Students who seriously want to learn golf, or improve their game, will not mind serious practice on putting.

4. PUTTING, WOOD SHOTS, LONG APPROACHES, SHORT APPROACHES.

   A. Justification:
   (a) Putting is most easily learned; ready success is good motivation factor.
   (b) Wood shots before approaches. Based on the belief that the full swing, once learned, may be carried over to the approach shots.

The following analyses of skills in golf are presented from the simple to the complex, and do not necessarily represent a rigid teaching progression. The analysis of putting concludes the series of skills, and its place in the actual teaching progression would be determined by each instructor. The actual order of instruction chosen as a complete course in golf instruction, is influenced by student personnel, necessity of motivation, equipment, facilities, weather conditions, and desired teacher-student outcomes.

A BRIEF HISTORY OF GOLF

Credit for the early development and widespread growth of golf, belongs to Scotland, and minimizes the importance of the controversy concerning its origin. Both Scotland and Holland claim this origin, although there is some historical evidence that the Ancient Romans knew the game, and called it Paganica.

In 1457 and again in 1491, the Scotch parliament legislated against golf, because it interfered with the practice of archery, which at that time was the means of national defense. King James IV of Scotland was probably the first king to participate in golf, although King William IV, was considered the first Royal Patron of the game. The equipment for the game consisted of balls made of leather and stuffed with feathers, and a few clubs, which the caddy carried like sticks in his arms.

The granddaughter of King James IV, Mary Queen of Scots, was probably the first woman golfer. She became quite adept at the sport, but received much criticism and ridicule for playing it.

As early as 1552, the St. Andrews course was known, but the formal organization of the well-known St. Andrews Club was culminated in 1754.

In 1608, five Scotchmen were imprisoned and fined nearly $100 each for playing golf on Sunday, while others were rebuked for playing without proper uniforms. From 1754 to 1893, golf courses, and golfers, increased, and the gutta-percha ball came into use. This ball was called the gutty ball, and was made from a gum compound derived from the Gutta tree of the Malay Archipelago, and the Percha tree of South Africa.

Golf came to America via the Scotch, English, and Dutch immigrants to the United States. The first golf club in America was established in 1795 at Charleston, South Carolina, on Harleston Green. In 1894, the United States Golf Association was founded, rules were established, and the first Amateur Tournament was held at Newport. The following year, the American Open and Amateur Championships were established.

The first rubber cored ball, bound with rubber bands was introduced by Haskell in 1898, and introduced into Great Britain in 1902.

From 1907 to 1931, scientifically constructed golf equipment, standardization of rules, beautifying of golf courses, and the study of golf techniques, were the major developments. These developments included steel shafted clubs, larger and lighter balls, vulcanized balls with different types of centers, balanced clubs, golf shoes, golf bags, inexpensive tees, and reduction of equipment cost. Care and beautification of golf courses became a science, and the popularity of golf increased, while the stigma of "sissy or dude" game practically vanished.

From 1931 until the present time, the popularity of golf has increased; high speed photography has made analyses of the golf swings possible; and further scientific research in kinds of equipment has continued to present the public with all of the advantages of its discoveries.

Golf has become an international form of recreation, and such champions as Bobby Jones, Gene Sarazen, Lawson Little, Sam Snead, Patty Berg, Jimmie Thompson, Helen Hicks, Walter Hagen, Ralph Gudahl, Dick Metz, Byron Nelson, and many others, have not only added to the popularity of the game, but deserve additional recognition for their work in establishing types of play, analyses of golf techniques, and demonstration of the sportmanship, and courtesy inherent in the game of golf.

THE GAME

Golf is usually played in foursomes, (four players), or twosomes, (two players), although one person may play alone, or a threesome, (three players), may participate in a game. It is possible for more than four people to play together, although it is seldom done, because of the time element involved in completing the game, and as a courtesy to players who may be following.

The game itself involves hitting the ball from the tees, approaching the greens, and putting the ball into the cup in the fewest possible strokes. An explanation for the beginner may be more easily understood if a practical example is given.

A mixed twosome, (man and woman), arrive at the first tee, which is the area behind which a ball must be played, and is the place which designates the beginning or starting point of each hole. The man, as a courtesy, allows the woman to drive first, since it is the first hole, and no honors are given. An honor is the opportunity to drive first from the tee, and is usually won by placing first, in the last hole played. The woman places her ball behind the markers, and uses a tee to elevate her ball. Tee has two meanings, the one mentioned previously, and the small wooden, or other material, peg which elevates the ball for teeing off at the beginning of each hole. Using a driver, No. 1 wood club with a flat face, or a brassie, a No. 2 wood club with a slanted face, she hits the ball down the fairway. The fairway is the closely cut area between the tee and the green, and is usually bounded laterally by areas called rough. Rough is usually uncut or wooded areas. The woman drives the ball approximately 160 yards. The man now tees off from the same area and drives the ball approximately 225 yards. (See Plate 1.)

The twosome, the drives finished, walk toward their balls. Ball No. 1, the woman's is reached first; therefore she plays her ball first. Using a brassie, or a spoon, a No. 3 wood club with a greater face slant than a brassie, and *without* a tee, she hits the ball approximately 100 yards. She now has made two strokes. The man, who is 140 yards from the green decides to approach with a No. 5 iron. An approach is an attempt to reach the green. The green is the very closely cropped area within which the cup is placed. His shot falls just short of the green, and his second stroke is completed.

Again the woman's ball is reached first, and her third shot, an approach of 105 yards is played with a No. 7 iron, and lands at the edge of the green. The man now attempts a short approach with an 8 or a 9 iron, and the ball lands just short of the cup, the hole into which the ball must be played. The iron clubs by the way, have various names; however the modern terminology designates them as 1 to 9 and No.10 as the putter. The slant of the face, or hitting area of the club, increases as the number of the club increases; therefore the loft of the ball is likewise increased, while the distance which the ball is carried forward is decreased.

Both balls are now on the green. The flag is removed from the cup, and both flag and golf bags are laid *off* the green, while the putts are attempted. The woman, who is the greatest distance *away* from the cup, putts first, using a No. 10 iron, or putter. She putts toward the hole, but the ball, although directed correctly, is still farther away from the cup than the man's ball; therefore she must putt again. This time the ball lands in the cup, and her score for that hole is five, 3 strokes and 2 putts. She is one over par and enters the number 5, opposite hole No. 1 on the score card. The man sinks his putt in one stroke; therefore his score is three strokes and one putt, making a total of 4 to be entered below his name, and opposite hole No. 1 on the score card. Par designates a perfectly played hole. In other words, the number of strokes taken are equal to the usual standard set for a 365 yard hole.

The flag is then replaced, and the players proceed to the second tee, and so on through 9 or 18 holes. The man is accorded the honors, or the privilege of driving first from the second tee. If the score had tied at 4 strokes each, the same order of play would have occurred at the second hole, with the woman, or the first player of the preceding hole, accorded the honors. When a very short hole is reached, the first strokes made are with the appropriate iron for that distance, rather than with a wood club. A tee to elevate the ball may be used if desired, although some players prefer not to use them with iron shots even though they are allowed on any initial stroke that begins play on a new hole.

The total score for each hole is added for the final score. The low score wins the game. (Plate 1)

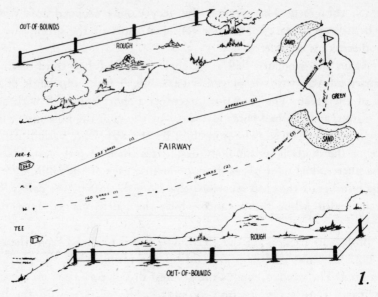

Game Explanation.

The above diagram does not illustrate all of the hazards of play from sand traps, water, knolls, in wooded areas, behind trees, etc., that might occur in an actual game. Some of these require special shots, or are governed by special rules. These were purposely omitted in the example given, since it was felt that the general aspect of the game was sufficient, and further information might confuse the student. Such rules and shots are more easily learned and understood when they appear in the general learning process, practice on the course, or an actual practice game situation.

Rules should be discussed and studied by the students, and problems pertaining to them discussed with the instructor. Official golfing rules may be obtained through the United States Golf Association, 73 East 57th Street, New York City, or from most Sporting Goods Companies.

Away: Ball farthest away from the hole. Ball to be played first.

Par: Standard number of strokes set according to yardage for a perfectly played hole.

Birdie: One stroke under par designated for a particular hole.

Eagle: Two strokes under the par designated for a particular hole.

Dodo: Three strokes under the par designated for a particular hole.

Bogey: (Commonly referred to as Colonel.) An imaginary player, who is given a certain number of strokes for each hole. A player may play against that score.

Bunker: Usually a sand trap. May refer to grassy knolls or rough ground.

Caddie: A person who carries bag and clubs for a player, and is usually familiar with the course and clubs to be used for certain distances.

Course: Grounds within the boundaries of the total number of holes available for play.

Green: Short, clipped grass around cup. Used for putting only.

Foursome: A match in which two players compete against two others.

SELECTION, CARE, AND REPAIR OF EQUIPMENT

CLUBS

Selection. The selection of golf clubs has been considerably simplified due to the scientifically designed clubs for men and women that have been developed in the past decade. Any professional golfer, or reputable sporting goods store, can recommend suitable clubs that will provide for factors such as body build, quality of clubs desired, weight and length of clubs, and shaft tensions. Both the quality of clubs and the shaft tensions vary with the ability of the golfer. The actual make or endorsement of the clubs, matters little in the selection of the club, after weight, length, balance, shaft tensions, etc., have been ascertained, for the "feel" of the club to each individual should govern the final selection. Many women, because of height and body build, prefer men's clubs, while some men have preferred to use women's clubs. The main difference again is in the points mentioned previously and in the "feel" of the clubs when swung.

The illustrations which follow were made from one of a number of sets of equipment, and the choice for visualization does not necessarily imply preference for, or a recommendation of, the particular make or type of equipment. Many students learn the fundamentals of golf with "hand-me-down" clubs, or clubs donated to a physical education department. Selection oftentimes follows the learning of the fundamentals. If golf equipment is not furnished, or cannot be borrowed, a student can learn with the use of a minimum set of inexpensive clubs, and the purchase of a full set of clubs can await the initial learning.

Brassie (No. 2. wood)		Driver (No. 1 wood)
No. 2 iron		Spoon (No. 3 wood)
No. 5 iron	OR	No. 3 iron
No. 7 iron		No. 5 iron
Putter (No. 10)		No. 8 iron
		Putter

The average golfer's set includes the driver, brassie, and spoon in the wood clubs, the numbers 2, 3, 4, 5, 6, 7, and 8 irons, and the putter. A full set includes such valuable clubs as the No. 9 iron, the No. 4 wood, and the No. 1 driving iron. These and others are omitted from the illustration, since, with the possible exception of the No. 9 iron, they are not generally found in the average golfer's set of clubs. (Plate 2)

Matched Set of Golf Clubs.

Care. All defects of clubs should be repaired or replaced immediately. Clubs should be cleaned and wiped after each use, and waxed at the end of each season's play. Waxing is sometimes done twice during the season, as well as at the end of the season's play. Mittens should be placed on the wood clubs at all times, and removed only when the club is in actual use. The hood should be placed on the clubs whenever they are transported by vehicle. It should also be used in inclement weather.

Repair. To prevent warping, clubs and bag should be laid flat on a shelf, with the club heads placed over the edge. See the club storage at any golf course for an example.

Repair. The most common damage to equipment, and the suggested repairs are as follows:

> *Unwinding of shaft threads.* (Usually on wood clubs.)—Re-wind club if method is known, or have it re-wound by the club professional or a sporting goods repair shop.
>
> *Nicks in Wood Clubs*—Filled with plastic wood, and re-shellacked.
>
> *Scarred Wood Clubs*—Deep scratches filled with plastic wood, and re-painted.
>
> *Loosened Grip*—Re-wound or replaced. Tape substitutes temporarily, but is not satisfactory for continued use.
>
> *Cracked Club Head*—Replacement best.

MITTENS

Selection. Selection of club mittens may be made as desired. These merely protect the wood clubs from mars and scratches. (Plate 3)

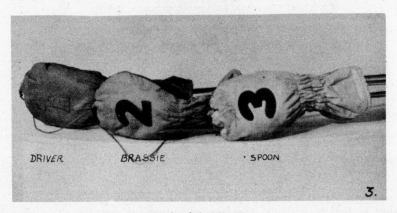

DRIVER   BRASSIE   · SPOON

3.

Wood Club Mittens.

Care. Mittens should be slowly and thoroughly dried when damp or wet. Specific care varies with the material used in the mittens. A string through the mittens will prevent loss.

GOLF BAGS

Selection. Selection of a golf bag depends entirely upon the taste of the individual, the additional amount of weight added to the load to be carried, and the amount of money the golfer wishes to put into the purchase. In general, a bag should have a carrying strap, a handle,

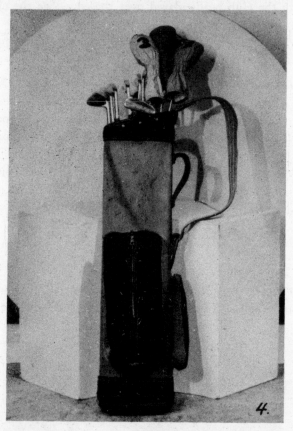

Golf Bag.

a pocket for tees and balls, and a hood for covering the clubs when not in use. This hood may also be used for a shoe pocket, if the bag does not include one. Weight is an important item for women, for unless a caddy is used exclusively, the fatigue caused by carrying the clubs and bags, will impair the calibre of the golf played. (Plate 4)

Care. Handle golf bags carefully and avoid throwing bag forcefully to the ground. Brushing, cleaning, oiling, etc., depending upon the material of the bag, will lengthen the period of use. Wire frames are now on the market that will allow the bag to remain in an upright position while a stroke is being played. The use of this frame will increase the life of the bag immeasurably for the greatest wear is from dropping the bag to the ground as each stroke is played. "Kaddy-Karts" are now available at most golf courses and are gaining widespread popularity, particularly with women golfers.

Repair.

> *Broken Strap on Bag*—Replace strap or mend with leather and rivets.
>
> *Handle Pulled Loose*—Mend with leather and rivets.

GOLF SHOES

Selection. Flat-heeled shoes are a "must" in golf, for shoes with heels are not allowed on the greens. This is not a problem for the men,

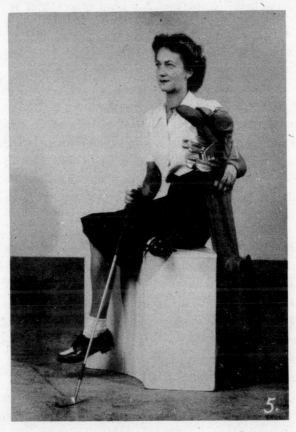

Golf Equipment.

and the majority of women students solve it by selecting the well-known saddle-shoes. If golf shoes are purchased, they should be selected for comfort and a size chosen that will allow the wearing of two pair of stockings, or one heavy pair of anklet type socks. (Plate 5)

Care and Repair. Oiling prevents leaking and cracking of shoe leather, as well as insuring the player against possible wet feet. Cleaning after use, and the daily use of shoe trees will make golf shoes last longer. Re-soling, and re-cleating cost less than replacement, and insure a comfortable pair of shoes that need no "breaking-in" period.

BALLS

    Selection.

        Practice balls—Fluff balls, Sponge rubber balls old re-painted balls.

        Game balls—6 to 12 of any good make. Price as desired.

    Care. Place name on each ball, and wash after each period of use. Frequent washing between holes will save on the cost of replacing lost balls, for the whiter the ball, the more easily it is found.

    Repair. Re-paint old balls for practice balls. Replace balls used for practice with new balls, to keep up initial supply.

    If repair is impossible, replacement may be made at any sporting goods store. In case of a matched set of clubs, or a specific make of equipment, consult the appropriate sporting goods store handling that make of equipment. Care of equipment insures protection of initial investment, and reduces materially the cost of the game, because replacements are relatively few.

TEES, GOLF GLOVES, COSTUME, AND TEACHING EQUIPMENT

    Any type of tees desired, may be purchased. Wooden tees usually give the best satisfaction for the least cost.

    Usually left-hand gloves are more generally used, although both left and right are worn by some golfers. This is not a necessary part of the equipment; however women find them valuable in protecting the hands. Selections should be based entirely upon the correct fit for ease of movement.

    Sports clothing generally accepted as correct in the area in which the golf is to be played should be worn. Costumes vary in different sections of the country.

Since teaching equipment is used for specific practice and learning situations, it is preferable to present it in the TEACHING AIDS for each skill, rather than with the general golf equipment used in actual play.

Halved: When each side takes the same number of strokes to "hole out."

Hole Out: Final stroke into cup.

Cup: Hole or receptacle into which the ball is played to end the counting of strokes on a hole.

Hazard: General term for sand, rough, water, or difficult terrain between the tee and the hole.

THE OVERLAPPING GRIP

The overlapping grip is the manner of holding the club, in which the little finger of the right hand overlaps the forefinger of the left.

GRIP SUMMARY

Place the left hand on the club handle, palm down, so that the "V" made by the thumb and forefinger points to the right shoulder. The thumb is slightly to the right of the top of the shaft. The right hand closes over the handle so that the left thumb is in the palm of the right hand, and the palm faces the direction in which the shot is to be made. The first, second, and third fingers close around the shaft, while the little finger overlaps the index finger of the left hand. The right thumb is placed slightly to the left of the top of the shaft, and the "V" made by the thumb and forefinger also points toward the right shoulder.

GRIP ANALYSIS AND ILLUSTRATION (Plate 6a, b, c, d)

Top View: "V's" made by forefingers and thumbs point to the right. Forefinger forms a hook around club handle. Right thumb slightly to left of top of shaft.

Right Side View: Base of handle at heel of left hand. Forefinger spread comfortably. Club handle diagonal to fingers. Back of right hand in full view.

Left Side View: Right palm faces direction in which shot is to be played. Left thumb in palm of right hand. Club handle diagonal to fingers. Back of left hand in full view.

Bottom View: Hands in opposition. Little finger overlapped. Base of club at heel of left hand. Forefinger spread comfortably. Hands close together. Firm grip by anchor fingers, last three fingers of left hand.

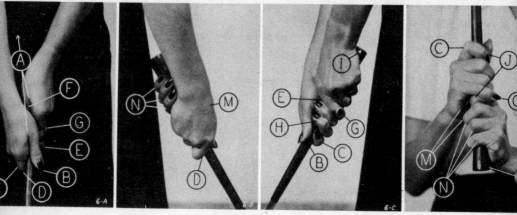

Top View. Right Side View. Left Side View. Bottom View.

GENERAL TEACHING AIDS

I. Explain and demonstrate the overlapping grip.
II. How to obtain the overlapping grip: (Plate 7a, b, c, d)

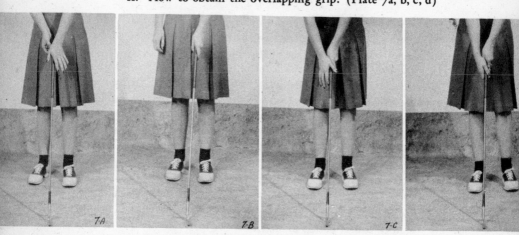

Step Two. Step Three. Step Four. Step Six.

(1) Rest club base on ground, handle toward body, and within easy reach of the hands.

(2) Place left hand on club, palm down, base of handle at heel of hand. Line made by forefinger points toward right shoulder. Handle is diagonal to fingers.

(3) Place fingers of left hand comfortably around shaft. Two to three knuckles should be visible to student. Place thumb slightly to right of top of shaft. "V" points toward right shoulder. "Anchor fingers" (last three) grip handle firmly.

(4) Place palm of right hand directly over left thumb and in direction in which shot is to be played.

(5) Place 1st, 2nd, and 3rd fingers around club shaft. Place thumb slightly to right of top of shaft. "V" points toward right shoulder. Spread forefinger to form hook around the shaft and check to be certain the base of the forefinger is on the back (right) of the shaft.

(6) Place little finger over left forefinger for the completion of the overlapping grip. Grip club with fingers.

III. Check individuals for errors.

IV. Demonstrate checking points for correct grip.

Verbal Teaching Aids

A. "V's" point toward right shoulder.

B. Right thumb slightly to left of top of shaft.

C. Right forefinger hooks around shaft. (*Aids control.*)

D. Base of forefinger on right side of shaft. (*Placed under shaft causes loss of power.*)

E. Right palm faces direction in which shot is to be played.

F. Left thumb in palm of right hand.

G. Right little finger overlaps left forefinger.

H. Club gripped in fingers. (*Speed and control.*)

I. Base of handle at heel of left hand.

J. Forefingers spread comfortably. (*To form hook.*)

K. Club handle diagonal to fingers.

L. Back of right hand away from direction in which shot is to be played.

M. Hands in opposition, and close together.

N. Firm grip by "anchor" fingers. (*Last three fingers of left hand.*)

Allow for Individual Variations in Grip.

Variations

1. Interlocking Grip (Plate 8)

    A. Right little finger and left forefinger interlock, rather than overlap.

    B. Other aspects identical with overlapping grip.

Advantages:

The overlapping grip is preferable to the interlocking grip, because it allows for more sensitive finger control of the club. The interlocking grip lessens sensitivity of finger control, and the right hand has a tendency to overpower or control the left hand, with consequent loss of power, rhythm, and accuracy in the swing.

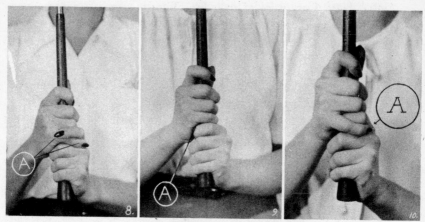

Bottom View. Bottom View. Overlapping Grip Variation.

2. NATURAL GRIP (Plain or Baseball Grip) (Plate 9)

A. Hands held as closely together as possible, with no overlapping or interlocking of fingers.

B. Other aspects of grip conform to checking points listed for the overlapping grip.

Advantages:

The natural grip is sometimes advantageously used by players with very small fingers, or with a physical handicap such as loss of one or more fingers, provided the other aspects of the overlapping grip are adhered to as closely as possible. Control of club is usually lost in the upper part of the swing, with the natural grip.

3. VARIATIONS OF OVERLAPPING (Plate 10)

A. Wider spread of left forefinger, little finger of right hand placed between 1st and 2nd fingers of left hand.

B. Individual variations due to size of hand, length of fingers, physical handicaps, etc.

Advantages:

Individuals should be allowed variations in the overlapping and other grips, provided firm, accurate control of the club can be maintained, and that such variations increase, rather than decrease, the effectiveness of the individual's performance of golf skills.

Honor: The right to play first from the tee. Won by low score on the previous hole.

Lie: Position of ball, whether good or bad.

Loft: To elevate the ball.

Match Play: Competition by holes. Highest number of holes won, wins the match.

Medal Play: Competition by strokes. Lowest number of strokes taken, regardless of holes won, wins the match.

AUTHOR'S NOTE

For purposes of clarity, the short approaches have been divided into three types which describe the approximate amount of backswing used. These types are: the quarter, the half, and the three quarter swings.

The amount of backswing necessary for each shot, and the club selected, depends upon the distance each individual can obtain from a particular iron. In general, short approaches are made with the short irons.

As a beginner's skill increases, these distances change; therefore it is necessary in practice and play, to stress the importance of accurately judging the distances that can be expected from shots played with specific irons.

SHORT APPROACHES

Iron shots, made from distances ranging from one to sixty yards from the green, in an attempt to place the ball on the green and as close to the flag as possible, are usually called short approach shots.

ADDRESS POSITIONS FOR SHORT APPROACHES

QUARTER SWING OR CHIP SHOT (Plate 11)

    A. Grip the club firmly with an overlapping grip, about half way down the leather grip.

    B. Place the feet close together, heels almost touching, toes out, and stance open (left foot slightly farther back than the right).

    C. Feet close to the ball, weight on the heels.

    D. Eyes almost over the ball.

    E. Knees relaxed.

    F. Body as erect as possible; yet crouched naturally to reach the ball.

    G. Ball out from inside of right heel.

HALF SWING OR PITCH SHOT (Plate 12)

    A. Open stance, firm overlapping grip.

    B. Allow club head to rest naturally behind the ball, not on the heel or toe of the club.

    C. Feet slightly farther apart than in the chip shot (approximately 12 inches).

    D. Weight on the heels.

    E. Ball out from right heel, or nearly centered between the feet. (Beginners should use the former ball position.)

Address Positions for Chip Shot. Pitch Shot. High Pitch Shot.

F. Body as erect as possible; yet crouched enough to comfortably reach the ball.

G. Hands hang naturally at center of body, and opposite the ball.

THREE QUARTER SWING OR HIGH PITCH SHOT (Plate 13)

A. Open stance, firm overlapping grip.

B. Allow club head to rest naturally behind ball.

C. Feet farther apart than in chip shot, approximately 12 to 16 inches.

D. Weight on heels.

E. Ball out from right heel, or centered between feet. (Beginners should use the former ball position.)

F. Erect as possible, crouched comfortably to reach ball.

G. Hands hang naturally at center of body, and opposite ball.

HIGH PITCH SHOTS MAY ALSO BE MADE WITH A FULL SWING.

GENERAL TEACHING AIDS

I. Teach the address for each approach as the stroke is learned. DO NOT CONFUSE THE STUDENTS WITH DIFFERENCES IN THE ADDRESS POSITIONS UNTIL EACH STROKE IS PRESENTED.

II. Allow for individual variations, provided such variations increase the effectiveness of the address for the individuals attempting them.

III. PERFORM THE WHOLE SKILL EACH TIME. CONCENTRATE UPON ONE TECHNIQUE AT A TIME.

USE OF VERBAL AIDS

I. Use verbal aids sparingly at first. Golf, perhaps more than any other sport, can be made confusing to students by the constant use of many verbal aids.

II. Such verbal aids as: "Keep the left arm straight," "relax," "head down," and "swing the club head through," will be about the maximum a beginner can use and assimilate in the initial learning periods. The other verbal aids are presented for the use of the instructor in improving the analysis of each stroke, and for later use in correcting students who have built up a vocabulary of familiar golf terms.

III. As the student acquires a mental conception of the correct swing, additional verbal aids may be used to correct errors; however the student should be cautioned to concentrate upon one technique at a time, allowing the rest of the swing to take care of itself.

Variations and Advantages

1. *Distance from the ball.* Many instructions have been devised to place the student the proper distance from the ball. In general, they serve the purpose for which they are intended; however body build, length of club used, and many other factors influence this distance. Usually if the club rests naturally on the ground behind the ball so that the handle can be reached comfortably with the left hand hanging straight down from the shoulders and far enough away from the body to insure a free swing, the distance away from the ball is sufficient.

2. *Ball positions in relation to the feet.* In general, the wood shots are played opposite the left heel, and as the irons are used, the ball moves toward a point opposite the right heel, as the length of the clubs decrease. Short irons, played off the right heel, may make the stroke seem cramped for players who have already mastered the golf swing; however beginners should be advised to use this ball position in the initial learning period for it will aid materially in insuring a down-stroke on the forward swing, and use of the club face to obtain ball elevation.

CHIP SHOT

(Quarter Swing)

The chip shot is a short approach made from a distance of one to thirty yards from the green, in an attempt to place the ball as close to the flag as possible, or in the cup. A club with considerable loft is usually selected, although it may be played with any iron desired.

Skill Summary

Assume the stance and address for a chip shot. Keep the hands low and at the center of the body. Take the club back on a straight line from the ball, and slightly inside the line of proposed flight. Raise the club with the wrists and hands only, until the club head is approximately two feet from the ground. The club does not quite reach a horizontal position. Bring the club head down and into the ball in a flat arc, just clipping the grass and meeting the ball squarely. *After the ball is hit*, move the hands away from the body, toward the line of flight. Transfer the weight naturally to the left leg, and flex the right knee a little more. The finish of the swing brings the club to the same approximate height in front of the body as was reached in the backswing. The hands point toward the hole, and the right hand finishes palm up. There is no head or body motion, or weight transfer until the follow through is nearly completed. The hit is crisp and decisive, although the ball is not hit hard.

SKILL ANALYSIS AND ILLUSTRATION (Plate 14a, b, c, d)

Count 1.   Address for chip shot and low backswing.

Count 2.   Slight pause at end of backswing, and hit down into the ball.

Count 3.   Ball is crisply hit and hands and club begin follow through toward line of flight.

Count 4.   Head raised slightly, hands toward line of flight, right palm up, and slight weight transfer to left leg as right knee flexes and body turns slightly toward line of flight.

Count 1. Count 2. Count 3. Count 4.

THE TERM "QUARTER SWING" IS USED ONLY AS DEFINED IN AUTHOR'S NOTE.

THE LENGTH OF THE BACKSWING WILL VARY SLIGHTLY DEPENDING UPON THE DISTANCE TO THE HOLE.

GENERAL TEACHING AIDS

I.   Explain and demonstrate the position of address for the chip shot.

II.   Check address position for errors.

III.   Explain and demonstrate the chip shot.

     IV. Perform the chip shot slowly and allow students to imitate the demonstration.

     V. Student drill to verbal explanation, without the use of a ball. Check for errors.

     VI. Practice with fluff balls indoors, or official ball in golf cages or outside. Check for errors.

     VII. As success in the swing of the chip shot is attained, divide the group into fours and have them chip to waste baskets, small boxes, sticks or pegs in the ground, until a degree of accuracy is attained.

     VIII. Pitch shots should be played naturally, without attempt at top spin or overspin. If weather permits, practice chip shots to an official green. The use of golf course facilities aids in student interest, motivation, and encourages individual practice.

PLAY THE SHOT SLOWLY AND SMOOTHLY. DO NOT JAB.

VERBAL TEACHING AIDS

A. Assume the stance and address for the chip shot.
B. Keep hands low. (*At level of address until follow through.*)
C. Take club back with hands and wrists only.
D. Backswing is straight back from ball, and just inside of ball flight.
E. Top of backswing brings club head about two feet from ground, and not quite horizontal to ground. (*Varies with distance desired.*)
F. Arch of backswing is flat. (*Pause slightly at top of backswing.*)
G. Forward swing made with wrists and hands only.
H. Forward swing follows same arc as backswing.
I. Let the left hand dominate the swing. (*Hit ball crisply but not hard.*)
J. Grass is clipped as ball is met.
K. Hands move away from body after ball is hit.
L. Hands follow line of ball flight.
M. Weight transfers to left leg. (*Natural because of reach toward ball.*)
N. Right knee flexes a little more than knee flexion in address.
O. Head down in address position.
P. No body pivot, weight still on heels. (*Heels remain in contact with ground throughout stroke.*)
Q. Finish of follow through allows head to turn toward line of flight.
R. Club points face up toward hole.
S. Right palm faces upward.
T. Height of club head corresponds to height of club head on backswing.
U. Body turns slightly toward line of flight.

ENTHUSIASM FOR DRILL VARIES IN DIRECT RATIO TO STUDENT'S EAGERNESS TO LEARN. INDIVIDUALS DIFFER IN THEIR RESPONSE TO DRILL.

PITCH SHOT · (HALF SWING)

The pitch shot with a half swing is a short semi-lofted approach from a distance of thirty to fifty yards from the green, in an attempt to place the ball as close to the flag as possible. Any short iron desired may be used.

SKILL SUMMARY

Assume the stance and address for a pitch shot. Start the backswing slowly and accurately in direct line with the ball, without bending the wrists until the hands pass the right foot. Allow the wrists to begin cocking at this point. Keep the left arm straight, and the right arm close to the body. Continue the backswing until the club head is three to four feet from the ground. This will place the club head on an approximate line out from the right shoulder, or slightly lower. There has been no hip pivot, although the shoulders turn slightly on the last part of the backswing. Without uncocking the wrists, pull the club handle down until the hands are near the center of the body. As this position is approached, uncock the hands. Keep the left leg straight, and allow the right to turn in a little. Continue to uncock the wrists, and swing the club head down and into the ball. Hit the ball first, and take a shallow divot after the impact. Let the club and hands follow the line of ball flight until they pass the left foot. Roll the wrists naturally and raise the club to approximately shoulder height. Keep the right arm straight, and let the left arm bend to allow the club to be raised. Raise the head slightly, after the follow through is almost completed.

SKILL ANALYSIS AND ILLUSTRATION (Plate 15a, b, c, d, e)

Count 1.   Address for pitch shot and begin backswing.
Count 2.   Reach height of backswing and pause momentarily.
Count 3.   Start forward swing, uncock wrists, and meet ball in address position.
Count 4.   Take divot and begin follow through.
Count 5.   Finish follow through.

Count 1. Count 2. Count 3. Count 4. Count 5.

Do Not Hurry This Stroke: Smoothness, Rhythm, Accuracy, and Deliberateness are Essential to Successful Execution of This Shot.

The Term "Half-Swing" is Used Only as Defined in the Preceding Author's Note.

General Teaching Aids

I. Explain and demonstrate the address position for the pitch shot.

II. Check address position for errors.

III. Explain and demonstrate the pitch shot.

IV. Perform the pitch shot slowly and allow students to imitate the demonstration.

V. Student drill to verbal explanation, without use of ball.

VI. Individual practice without balls. Check for errors.

VII. Student drill with fluff, knitted, or practice balls.

VIII. Practice with official ball in golf cages, or against a canvas drop. Specially marked areas or pockets in the canvas drop aid students in achieving accuracy of direction and distance in pitch shot practice.

IX. As soon as possible allow students to pitch to regulation green.

X. Use verbal aids sparingly. Do not confuse the students with too many verbal directions.

Swing the Club Head Down Into, and Through, the Ball.

Verbal Teaching Aids

A. Assume stance and address for pitch shot.

B. Start backswing slowly and in line with the ball.

C. Wrists do not bend at the beginning of the backswing.

D. Keep club close to ground until hands pass right foot.

E. Cock wrists and raise club in upright arc.

F. Club head approximately shoulder height. (*Pause at end of backswing.*)

G. Left arm straight and dominates the swing.

H. Right arm bent, and close to body.

I. Shoulders turned very slightly. (*No hip pivot.*)

J. Weight back on heels. (*Heels remain flat on ground throughout stroke.*)

K. Wrists remain cocked as hands pull club handle down.

L. Uncock wrists as hands pass right foot.

M. Transfer weight to left leg.

N. Ball hit when back in address position.

O. Ball hit first with a downswing.

P. Divot taken after ball is hit.

Q. Club and hands follow line of flight until they pass left foot.

R. Wrists roll naturally.

S. Club raised approximately shoulder height in an upright arc.

T. Right arm straight.

U. Left arm bent.

V. Right knee rolls in slightly.

W. Head lifts as follow through is completed.

THE SIX, SEVEN, AND EIGHT IRONS ARE GENERALLY CONSIDERED THE SHORT IRONS.

BACKSWINGS VARY WITH THE DISTANCE DESIRED, AND THE AMOUNT OF DISTANCE AN INDIVIDUAL CAN OBTAIN FROM A CLUB.

HIGH PITCH SHOT

(THREE QUARTER SWING)

The high pitch shot with the three quarter swing is a short high approach from a distance of thirty to sixty yards from the green, in an attempt to place the ball as close to the flag as possible. Any short iron may be used, and as in the backswing, the selection varies with the distance desired.

SKILL SUMMARY

Assume the stance and address for a high pitch shot. This is the same as for the pitch shot. The backswing is identical with that used in the pitch shot with the quarter swing; however the top of the backswing is higher. When the height of the quarter backswing is reached, continue the movement by raising the arms and hands waist high, allowing the shoulders to turn a little more, and cocking the wrists until the club is perpendicular to the ground, the toe of the club pointing toward the hole. Pull the hands down, without uncocking the wrists, until the hands pass the right foot. Transfer the weight, meet the ball, and follow through as in the pitch shot; however finish the follow through with the club in a perpendicular position, rather than at shouder height.

SKILL ANALYSIS AND ILLUSTRATION (Plate 16a, b, c, d, e, f)

Count 1. Address for high pitch shot and begin backswing.

Count 2. Reach height of backswing and pause momentarily.

Count 3. Start forward swing by pulling hands down toward ball.

Count 4. Uncock wrists and meet ball in address position.

Count 5. Take divot and begin follow through.

Count 6. Finish follow through.

"THREE-QUARTER" SWING USED ONLY AS DEFINED IN AUTHOR'S NOTE.

Press: Attempting to hit harder in order to recover lost ground. This is never advisable, since it usually causes errors in play due to tension developed in the muscles.

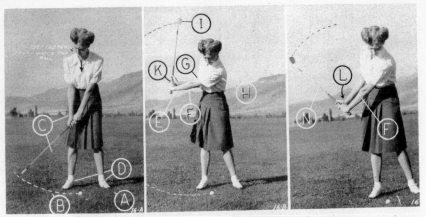

Count 1. Count 2. Count 3.

Count 4. (*Contact Point Missed in Plate.*) Count 5. Count 6.

Rough: Long grass on either side of fairway.

Stroke: Hitting ball with club, or swinging in an attempt to do so.

GENERAL TEACHING AIDS

    I. Review address position for pitch shots. Check errors.

    II. Explain and demonstrate the high pitch shot.

    III. Student drill imitating slow demonstration by instructor.

    IV. Drill to verbal explanation; to count. Check errors.

    V. Practice with fluff balls; with regulation balls.

    VI. Golf cage or outdoor practice.

    VII. Practice high pitch shots to golf green.

    VIII. Physical aid for leaving feet flat on ground. (Plate 17)

Physical Aid for Keeping Feet on Ground.

NOTE: As the swing more nearly approaches a full swing, the heels may raise slightly.

VERBAL TEACHING AIDS

A. Address for pitch shot.
B. Start backswing slowly and in line with the ball.
C. Cock wrists as hands pass right foot. (*Upright swing.*)
D. Weight on heels.
E. Wrists cocked.
F. Left arm straight.
G. Right arm close to body.
H. Shoulders turned slightly. (*No hip pivot.*)
I. Club perpendicular at top of backswing. (*Pause slightly.*)
J. Toe of club pointing towards hole.
K. Hands approximately waist high.
L. Pull hands down leaving wrists cocked. (*Left hand dominates swing.*)
M. Head position remains fixed.
N. Same arc for forward swing as for backswing.

O. Uncock wrists as hands pass right foot. (*Smooth, quick motion.*)

P. Transfer weight slightly to straight left leg.

Q. Right knee flexes a little. (*Rolls in, no hip pivot.*)

R. Ball met with body in address position. (*Hit down into ball.*)

S. Take divot after ball is hit. (*Hit through ball.*)

T. Arms reach out toward ball flight until they reach left foot.

U. Roll arms naturally as club is raised.

V. Arms and hands approximately waist high.

W. Club perpendicular to ground. (*Same height as on backswing.*)

X. Right arm straight.

Y. Left arm flexed.

Z. Head and body turn slightly toward line of ball flight.

SWING THE CLUB HEAD DOWN INTO AND THROUGH THE BALL. LENGTH OF BACKSWING VARIES WITH DISTANCE FROM GREEN.

Stymie: When a player's ball lies in line of another player's putt.

FULL SWING WITH A SHORT IRON

A short approach shot with a full swing is often necessary when greater distance or loft is required.

SKILL SUMMARY

Assume a stance and address for the pitch shot. The backswing is identical with that used in the three quarter swing; however the top of the backswing brings the club almost to a horizontal position above the shoulders, and the hands are approximately opposite the right ear. The weight transfer to the right leg is more clearly seen, and the left heel may raise slightly from the ground as the top of the backswing is reached. The shoulders turn a little more than in the three quarter swing, although the hip pivot is still not used. The hands pull the club head down as in the three quarter swing; however the wrists begin to uncock before they quite reach the right knee. The impact with the ball, and the follow through are the same as in the three quarter swing, although the follow through continues to nearly a horizontal position of the club, with the hands raising higher at the end of the follow through. The body turns more toward the line of ball flight, and the right heel raises from the ground as the follow through is completed.

SKILL ANALYSIS AND ILLUSTRATION (Plate 18a, b, c, d, e, f)

Count 1. Address for pitch shot. Start of slow backswing.

Count 2. Height of backswing is reached and pause made.

Count 3. Pull hands down toward ball, wrists cocked.

Count 4. Uncock wrists and meet ball in approximate address position.

Count 5. Take divot and begin follow through.

Count 6. Finish follow through.

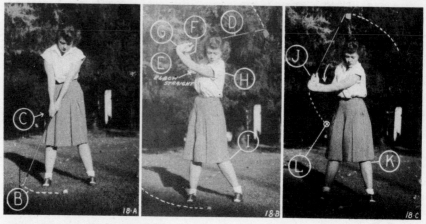

Count 1. Count 2. Count 3.

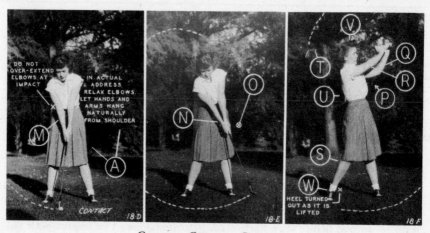

Count 4. Count 5. Count 6.

MANY TEACHING AIDS VALUABLE IN TEACHING THE FULL SWING
WITH THE WOOD CLUBS, CAN BE MORE ADVANTAGEOUSLY EMPLOYED
IF USED FIRST WITH A FULL SHORT IRON SWING.

Down: Number of holes or strokes a player is behind an opponent.
(1 down, 2 down, 3 down, etc.)

Up: Number of strokes a player is ahead of an opponent. (2 up;
2 strokes ahead, etc.)

GENERAL TEACHING AIDS

I. Review address for pitch shots. Check for errors.
II. Review short approach with three quarter swing.

III. Explain and demonstrate a full swing with a short iron.

IV. Demonstrate differences and similarities between a full swing and a three quarter swing with a short iron.

V. Student drill imitating slow demonstration by instructor.

VI. Student drill to verbal instruction.

VII. Individual drill without balls. Check for errors.

VIII. Practice with fluff balls; practice balls; on golf greens.

IX. Physical aid for keeping head down. (Plate 19)

X. Physical aid for top of backswing. (Plate 20)

XI. Drill for control of swing by left hand and arm. (Plate 21)

Physical Aid for Keeping Head Down. Top of Backswing.

Address and Contact. Backswing.

Verbal Teaching Aids

A. Address for pitch shot.
B. Start backswing slowly in line with the ball.
C. Wrists begin cocking as hands pass right foot.
D. Club almost horizontal.
E. Left arm straight.
F. Right arm bent and away from body.
G. Hands opposite right ear.
H. Shoulders turned.
I. Left knee rolled in. (*Weight on right leg.*)
J. Pull hands down. (*Transfers weight to left leg.*)
K. Left leg straight.
L. Wrists begin uncocking just before hands reach right knee.
M. Arms straight at impact. (*Hit ball first, then take turf.*)
N. Reach out after ball.
O. Roll wrists naturally as hands pass left foot. (*Do not stress this movement, it is a natural one.*)
P. Raise arms and hands and cock wrists to raise club.
Q. Left arm bent.
R. Right arm straight.
S. Right knee rolled in.
T. Club approximately horizontal above shoulders.
U. Body turns toward line of ball flight.
V. Head raises at end of follow through.
W. Raise right heel slightly from ground.

Use Verbal Aids Understood by Students. Do Not Confuse Them With Terms They Do Not Understand. This Causes Body Tension. Note Additional Verbal Aids From Pitch Shots That Will Aid in the Stroke Analysis of a Full Swing.

LONG APPROACHES

Iron shots played with the long irons, made from distances ranging from sixty to one hundred and fifty yards from the green, in an attempt to place the ball as close to the flag as possible, are generally termed long approach shots. The number one and two irons are long driving irons, and the three and four irons may also be classified as long irons; however they are slightly shorter than the number one and two irons. The number one iron is seldom found in the average golfer's set of clubs, and usually is made to order at the request of the individual golfer.

Address Position for Long Approaches (Plate 22a, b)

A. Rest sole of club naturally on ground.
B. Stand close enough to the ball so that the left hand reaches the

Front View. Side View.

handle of the club while the left arm hangs comfortably down from the shoulder.

C. Place the ball about three inches inside a point opposite the left heel.

D. Weight on both heels.

E. Arms hang naturally from shoulders.

F. Hands at center of body.

G. Feet spread comfortably at less than shoulder width.

H. Stance slightly open.

I. Relaxed position, no tenseness.

J. Head down.

K. Body as erect as possible; yet within comfortable reach of the club in position B above.

WOMEN, BECAUSE THEY CANNOT OBTAIN GREAT DISTANCE WITH WOOD SHOTS, SHOULD UNDERSTAND CLEARLY THE VALUE OF THE SHORT AND LONG APPROACHES TO THEIR SUCCESS IN GOLF.

Flag: Pennant mounted on a pole, and placed in the cup to show the position of the hole. The pennant number denotes the hole number.

TEACHING AIDS

I. Explain and demonstrate the address position for the long approaches.

II. Individuals assume address position and are checked for errors.

III. Review of previously taught address positions.

IV. Comparison and explanation of differences.

V. Instruction in long iron approaches.

USE OF VERBAL AIDS

1. Use verbal aids sparingly until students have learned the fundamentals necessary to a comprehension of the terms used in verbal aids.
2. Use the list of verbal aids for each skill to aid analysis of strokes and locating individual's errors.
3. Explain clearly the cause of student's error, and choose one technique that needs correction. Advise the student to perform the total skill, but to concentrate upon that particular technique, allowing the remainder of the swing to take care of itself.
4. Allow for individual variations.
5. The distances obtained on the iron shots will vary with each golfer.

ACCURACY IS THE KEYNOTE OF VALUE IN IRON SHOTS.

Handicap: Strokes or holes given by a player to another player of less ability, to equalize the score and make better competition.

Hole-in-One: From tee into cup on one stroke.

Divot: Piece of grass and dirt lifted from the ground when a shot is made. These should be replaced immediately and stepped down.

THE LONG APPROACH

A long approach is a stroke played as close to the flag as possible with the use of a long iron. Distances attempted vary considerably, depending upon each individual's skill in the long approach.

SKILL SUMMARY

Assume address position for long approaches. Let the hands, arms straight, take the club head straight back from the ball and close to the ground, until they reach the full limit of their arc, (arm's reach). The wrists do not bend. From this position, begin to cock the wrists. This raises the club head, moves the right hip to the rear, and starts the left shoulder turn. Continue this movement until the left shoulder points at the ball, the weight moves to the right foot, and the left knee turns in toward the center of the body. Continue to cock the wrists, keeping a firm grip on the club with both hands, left arm straight, until the club is horizontal and the left heel raises slightly from the ground. Pause momentarily at the top of the backswing. Start the forward swing by pulling the hands down toward the ball, wrists still cocked. This throws the weight to a straightened left leg, heel flat on the ground. As the club reaches a horizontal position with the hands approximately waist high and near the starting position, uncock the wrists smoothly and quickly. This brings the club head into the same position as at address, and the ball is hit squarely. Reach the hands and club out toward the intended line of flight as if hitting a second ball placed in front of the first. Both arms are still fully extended as in impact, and as the forward arc, arm's reach, is attained, the wrists roll naturally, and the arms carry the body around toward the line of flight, the head still down. The hands carry the club up by the cocking of the wrists, flexion of the left arm, and straight right arm. The finish is high with the club slightly higher than horizontal. The head raises and turns toward the line of flight, and the right heel raises as the follow through is completed.

SKILL ANALYSIS AND ILLUSTRATION (Plate 23a, b, c, d, e)

Count 1. Address for long approach. Begin backswing.
Count 2. Complete backswing and pause.
Count 3. Downward pull of hands. Wrists cocked.
Count 4. Divot taken, begin follow through.
Count 5. Complete follow through.

Count 1. Count 2. Count 3.

Count 4. Count 5.

FIT THE SWING TO THE INDIVIDUAL . . . NOT THE INDIVIDUAL TO THE SWING.

General Teaching Aids

I. Review address for long irons.

II. Explain and demonstrate the long approach.

III. Review three quarter swing using the long iron.

IV. Point out necessary differences between three quarter and full swings using a long iron.

V. Slow demonstration by instructor; imitation by students.

VI. Slow drill to verbal commands; to counts. Check errors.

VII. Individual practice without balls; with fluff balls; with regulation balls. Check errors.

VIII. Practice in golf cage or against canvas drop. Check for individual variations.

IX. Practice long approaches to golf green. Check errors and variations. Stress rhythm of swing.

Teaching Aids Used for Wood Shots, Approaches, and Address Positions May Be of Value in the Long Iron Instruction Also. Check Them.

Verbal Teaching Aids

A. Address position for long approaches.

B. Keep backswing close to ground and straight back from ball.

C. Take club back with wrists and arms straight until they attain arm's reach.

D. Weight moves to left foot.

E. Begin cocking wrists to raise club head.

F. Right hip moves back. (*Body pivot begins.*)

G. Left shoulder turns in toward ball. (*Result of body pivot.*)

H. Right knee flexes and turns in.

I. Club horizontal to ground. (*Left arm straight.*)

J. Left heel raises slightly from ground. (*Pause at top of backswing.*)

K. Pull hands down toward ball, wrists cocked.

L. Weight moves to straight left leg.

M. Left heel on ground.

N. Hands waist high and almost body center, reach hitting area.

O. Uncock wrists smoothly and quickly to hit ball.

P. Both arms straight at impact.

Q. Reach toward line of flight, both arms straight until arm's reach is attained.

R. Wrists roll naturally.

S. Cock wrists to raise club high.

T. Club finishes higher than horizontal.

U. Left arm bent.

V. Right arm straight.

W. Head raises at end of follow through.

X. Right heel raises slightly from ground.

ALLOW FOR INDIVIDUAL VARIATIONS IF THEY AID IN THE PER-
FORMANCE OF A RHYTHMIC SWING. STRESS RHYTHM AND ACCURACY
IN EVERY TYPE OF SWING.

ADDRESS FOR WOOD SHOTS

The address for the wood shot is the position assumed by the
player in order to get into position to play the ball.

SKILL SUMMARY

Stand with the heels parallel to the line of flight of the ball, feet
spread about shoulder width, and the toes slightly turned out. The weight is
on the heels, and slightly more on the left than on the right. The ball is
opposite the inside of the left heel, and the club head is at right angles to the
ball. The handle of the club is grasped in the overlapping grip. The hands hang
naturally, directly below the chin. The right arm reaches a little farther than
the left; the eyes are on the ball; the body is slightly forward from the waist;
and the knees are flexed just enough to be comfortable.

SKILL ANALYSIS AND ILLUSTRATION (Plate 24a, b)

Count 1. Grasp club in overlapping grip, place feet parallel to the
line of intended ball flight, ball opposite left heel.

Count 2. Flex knees slightly and settle weight comfortably on the
heels. Let the hands hang comfortably at the center of the
body.

Count 3. Bend forward slightly from the waist.

Front View. Side View.

BE COMFORTABLE. RELAX.

Dog-Leg: Sharp turn in the fairway.

GENERAL TEACHING AIDS

I. Explain and demonstrate the stance and manner of addressing the ball for the wood shots.

II. Check errors in stance and address from verbal aids.

III. Physical aid for getting weight back on heels. (Plate 25a, b, c)

Club Behind Hips. Sit on Club Weight on Heels. Remove Club.

Checking. Position.

IV. Distance from ball. (Plate 26)

V. Full swing taught immediately.

VERBAL TEACHING AIDS

A. Hands directly at center of body.

B. Ball opposite inside of left heel. (*Facilitates sweeping blow.*)

C. Toes out, feet spread shoulder width. (*Greater spread restricts pivot.*)

D. Heels parallel to line of flight.

E. Weight back on heels, left carries slightly greater part of weight.

F. Right arm reaches farther than left. (*Due to position on handle.*)

G. Club head at right angles to intended flight of ball.

H. Hands hang naturally. (*If reach is necessary, ball is too far away.*)

I. Body slightly forward from waist. (*Do not crouch.*)

J. Hands below chin. (*Hands at center of body.*)

K. Eyes on ball, head down.

L. Knees flexed comfortably. (*Stiff legs, lock knee points for pivot.*)

Playing Through: Passing ahead of a group of players. Play through only at the invitation of players ahead.

WOOD SHOTS

Wood shots are those strokes played with a driver, brassie, or spoon, from the fairway or tee, and which require a full swing.

SKILL SUMMARY

Address the ball for a wood shot. Move the club straight back from the ball, without bending the arms or wrists, until the hands attain the extent of their reach without raising the club from near the ground. The left knee will begin to flex slightly as this movement is made. Keep the left arm straight, and raise the club head up and toward the rear, by cocking the wrists. Continue this movement until the club reaches the top of the backswing. As this position is reached, the club is in a horizontal, or slightly lower position; hands are head high; the left shoulder is pointing toward the ball; hips, shoulders, and knees have made a right angle turn; the left arm is straight; weight is on the right foot; the left heel is raised, and the head has remained in the same position as the address. Pause momentarily and then bring the hands down in a quick, smooth, deliberate movement, wrists cocked, until they reach the hitting area which is approximately hip high. The weight transfers simultaneously to a straight left leg. From this position allow the wrists to uncock rapidly to the address position as impact with the ball is made. Club and hands follow the flight of the ball as far as possible, and wrists rotate naturally. Keep the right arm straight, and bend the left while cocking the wrists, to raise the club to horizontal position and complete the follow through. Keep the head down until the extent of the reach toward the line of ball flight is attained, and then it may be turned toward the line of flight as the body turns to follow the ball. As the follow through is completed the right heel raises from the ground.

SKILL ANALYSIS AND ILLUSTRATION (Plate 27a, b, c, d, e, f)

Count 1. Grip, address, and begin backswing in line with ball.
Count 2. Cock wrists and pause at top of backswing.
Count 3. Begin forward swing and reach hitting area.
Count 4. Uncock wrists and meet ball.
Count 5. Reach toward ball, and roll wrists.
Count 6. Finish pivot and follow through.

Count 1. Count 2. Count 3.

Count 4. Count 5. Count. 6.

WATCH FOR ERRORS IN ADDRESS. DO NOT ATTEMPT DISTANCE.

GENERAL TEACHING AIDS

I. Explain and demonstrate the full swing with the wood club.
II. Allow students to attempt the full swing.
III. Demonstrate slowly, giving verbal instruction at the same time, while students imitate movements.

   IV. Drill to verbal command; to slow count; to smooth, rapid count. Check for errors.

   V. Individual practice, instructor checking for errors and variations.

   VI. Practice with fluff balls. Check for errors.

   VII. Practice in cage or on driving range with official balls.

   VIII. Practice on golf course fairway.

   IX. Physical aid for "swinging through." (Plate 28)

Swing Through as if to Hit a Second Ball.

NOTE: Missing the ball entirely handicaps the initial learning of some beginners. Replacing the golf ball with an old tennis ball until it can be hit regularly has been found successful. The transfer to the golf ball is easily made.

VERBAL TEACHING AIDS

A. Overlapping grip and square stance. (*May use variations.*)

B. Move club straight back from ball. (*Watch for curved backswing and lifting of club.*)

C. Arms and wrists straight. (*Left arm and hand in control.*)

D. Left knee flexes slightly. (*Watch for too much weight to right foot caused by knee over right toe instead of turned in toward body.*)

E. Head down, eyes on ball. (*Watch for lifting of head too soon.*)

F. Cock wrists to raise club from ground. (*Watch for curved backswing caused by cocking wrists before arm's reach is attained, and by too tight a grip by the left hand, or palm gripping.*)

G. Left arm straight. (*Throughout swing, until follow through.*)

H. Pivot right finished, ball seen over left shoulder. (*Watch for straightened body, showing omission of pivot.*)

I. Weight on right foot, left knee flexed.

J. Left heel raises slightly from ground. (*Watch for balance and tenseness.*)

K. Left arm leads, hands remain cocked until hip level is reached.

L. Weight transfers to straight left leg as forward swing is started.

M. Uncock wrists and swing club head through ball. (*No sudden burst of speed.*)

N. Both arms straight at impact. (*Right arm close to side.*)

O. Arms reach out toward line of intended ball flight, wrists roll naturally.

P. Both arms straight until maximum forward reach is attained.

Q. Head raises at end of follow through.

R. Right heel raises slightly at end of pivot left.

S. Left arm bends to raise club, right arm straight.

T. Club horizontal or lower at end of follow through.

OTHER VERBAL AIDS MAY BE FORMULATED. THE LISTS ARE NOT COMPLETE.

VARIATIONS

Fit the swing to the student, not the student to the swing. Change the swing to fit the lie. Variations are necessary.

Count 1. Count 2.

Downhill Lie (Plate 29a, b)

A. Ball played back toward right foot.
B. Left leg straight.
C. Right leg relaxed.
D. Follow ground contour with club head. (*Backswing more upright.*)
E. Use a lofted club.
F. Slightly open stance.
G. Swing *easily*.
H. Club follows downhill line on follow through.

Count 1. Count 2.

Uphill Lie (Plate 30a, b)

A. Left leg flexed.
B. Right leg straight.
C. Left leg carries most of weight. (*Keeps weight from staying on right leg.*)
D. Aim slightly to right of objective. (*Prevents hooking.*)
E. Use a number 2 iron or brassie.
F. Slightly closed stance.
G. Stand closer to the ball.
H. Backswing lower and flatter.
I. Follow through in contour of hill.

SPOON SHOTS

The spoon shot is made in the same manner as the other wood shots; however the feeling of hitting down into and through the ball should be apparent to the player. Because of the lofted face of the spoon, the downswing gives the player much the same feeling as a full swing with an iron.

Note: In general, tall people seem to favor a more upright swing, while short people favor a slightly flat swing. A person of average height can more easily acquire a full circular swing.

SIDE HILL LIE WITH BALL BELOW FEET (Plate 31)

Side Hill Lie, Ball Below Feet.

A. Open stance.
B. Weight on toes.
C. Upright swing.
D. Aim to left of objective. (*Overcomes natural tendency to slice.*)
E. Maintain balance and pivot less to the left.
F. Use a long club.

Side Hill Lie With Ball Above Feet (Plate 32)

Side Hill Lie, Ball Above Feet.

A. Flat swing.
B. Keep hands low.
C. Use short club.
D. Slow short swing.
E. Be accurate. (*Do not try for distance.*)

Winter Rules: Regulations made by local clubs to allow players to improve lie of ball during period when weather hinders care of the course.

PUTTING GRIP

The putting grip is generally the reverse of the overlapping grip, and refers to the position of the hands on the club handle.

Grip Summary

Assume the overlapping grip, placing the thumbs on top of the shaft. Change the index finger of the left hand and the little finger of the right hand so that the index finger overlaps the little finger of the right hand, in the reverse of the overlapping grip.

NOTE: Many golfers find it advantageous to place the index finger of the right hand directly down the right (*player's right*) side of the shaft, rather than hooked around the shaft as in the overlapping grip. This is recommended for beginners.

Grip Analysis and Illustration (Plate 33a, b, c, d)

Top View: Palms of hands face opposite directions. Right thumb on top of shaft. Left thumb in palm of right hand.

Right Side View: Right forefinger hooked around shaft, (or extended down right side of shaft). Fingers spread comfortably.

Left Side View: Palm of right hand toward objective. Left index finger overlaps right little finger. Grip with the fingers.

Bottom View: Left index finger overlaps right little finger. Firm grip, but not rigid.

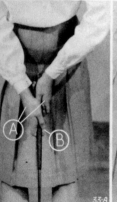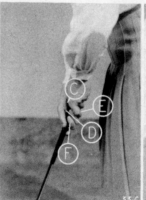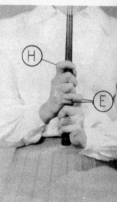

Top View. Right Side View. Left Side View. Bottom View.

GRIPS SHOWN ABOVE DO NOT INCLUDE SUGGESTION OF RIGHT FOREFINGER PLACEMENT FOR BEGINNERS. SEE NOTE ABOVE.

General Teaching Aids

    I. Explain and demonstrate putting grip.

    II. Point out reasons for differences in putting grip from previous grips used.

    III. How to obtain the putting grip. (Plate 34a, b, c, d)

Club Diagonal to Fingers, Left Forefinger Spread. Place Little Finger of Right Hand Between First and Second Finger of Left Hand. Place Right Thumb Just to Left of Top of Shaft or on Top of Handle, and Place Forefinger Down Back of Right Side of Shaft. Reverse Positions of Left Forefinger, and Right Little Finger.

    IV. Check grips for errors.

    V. Students change from reverse to overlapping to reverse, etc., until the change becomes familiar.

    VI. Teach putting address.

Verbal Teaching Aids

    A. Palms of hands face opposite directions.

    B. Right thumb on, or just to the left of, the top of the handle.

    C. Left thumb in pocket made by right palm.

    D. Right palm toward objective.

    E. Left index finger overlaps right little finger.

    F. Grip with fingers.

    G. Fingers spread comfortably.

    H. Right index finger hooked around shaft. (*See variations below.*)

    I. Firm grip, but not tight or rigid. (*No tension.*)

VARIATIONS (Plate 35)

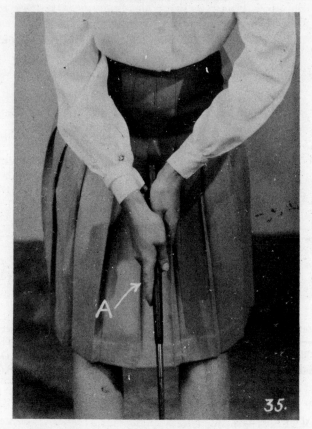

Top View.

A. Right forefinger down right side of shaft.
B. Aids accuracy in beginners and assures control of right hand in forward swing.

OBSERVE THE GREEN RULES. DO NOT PLACE BAGS ON GREEN.

PUTTING ADDRESS

The address in putting is the position assumed by the player to facilitate stroking the ball into the cup.

SKILL SUMMARY

With the club held in the reverse overlapping grip, assume a stance with the feet 8 to 10 inches apart, and at right angles to the line of the putt. Stand so that the ball may be played anywhere between the center of the stance and inside the left heel. Keep the eyes directly over the ball, relax the knees comfortably, weight on the heels, and greater portion of weight on left foot. Rest the right elbow against the right hip. Point the left elbow toward the cup. Hold the club lightly but firmly in the fingers, with the face of the putter at right angles to the line of the putt. Stand as erect as possible; yet allowing the knees to relax, and keeping the eyes over the ball.

Skill Analysis and Illustration (Plate 36a, b)

Count 1. Line up the putt. (See Teaching Aids.)
Count 2. Place putter directly behind ball, and assume putting grip.
Count 3. Place feet at right angles to line of putt.
Count 4. Address position. (Front and side view below.)

Front View. Side View.

Putting is a Game in Itself. Putts Comprise 50% of All Golf Strokes.

Variations Are More Common in Putting Than in Any Other Golf Skill. If the Ball is Consistently "Holed-Out," Allow Any and All Variations.

Do Not Talk or Move When a Player is Making a Shot. Stand, if Possible to the Right of, and a Little in Front of the Player Making the Shot.

General Teaching Aids

I. Check putting grips for errors.
II. Explain and demonstrate the putting address.
III. How to obtain the putting address. (May be used as a class drill.) (Plate 37)

Place Putter in Line with the Cup.

IV. Explain reasons for lining up putt.

V. Check for errors and variations in putting address. (Variations will appear as putting is practiced. Intermediate and advanced students will show variations immediately.)

VI. Proceed to instruction in putting stroke.

KEEP THE HEAD DOWN.

VERBAL TEACHING AIDS

A. Reverse of overlapping grip.

B. Feet comfortably close together. (*8 to 10 inches apart. "Rocking" caused by too wide a stance; loss of balance by narrow stance.*)

C. Feet at right angles to line of putt. Weight on heels.

D. More weight on left leg. (*Do not lean.*)

E. Face of putter at right angles to line of putt.

F. Right elbow rests against right hip. (*Eliminates tendency to move arms, and aids in steadiness and control of club.*)

G. Left elbow points toward cup. (*Increases accuracy.*)

H. Ball played from inside left heel. (*Beginners advised to use this ball position.*)

I. Knees relaxed.
J. Eyes over ball.
K. Body as erect as possible.
L. Firm, relaxed grip with fingers.
M. Palm of right hand and back of left toward cup.

DO NOT SHOOT UNTIL PLAYERS AHEAD ARE OUT OF RANGE.
SIGNAL PLAYERS BEHIND TO "GO THROUGH" IF THEY ARE BEING
HELD UP BY SLOW PLAYING, OR LOST BALLS.

VARIATIONS

1. OPEN STANCE (Plate 38)

Open Stance.

A. Left foot slightly back of line of putt.
B. *Advantage:*
   Moves left leg out of way of follow through.

2. FEET TOWARD CUP (Plate 39)

Feet Toward Cup.

A. Feet pointing toward cup.
B. Ball played from right foot.
C. Right hand does putting.
D. *Advantage:*
> Easier to line up ball and club with cup.

3. OVERLAPPING GRIP
A. Same as skill analyzed using overlapping grip.
B. *Advantage:*
> Less confusing to beginners than to have to learn a change of grips.

4. LOW CROUCH
A. Low crouch, knees bent.
B. Body leaning over ball.
C. *Advantage:*
> Players using this form believe greater relaxation is possible.

5. USE OF ARMS IN PUTTING
   A. Both arms bent.
   B. Elbows out from body.
   C. *Advantage:*
         More freedom of movement. Used for putting
   with arm motion.

6. STRAIGHT LEFT LEG
   A. Weight on straight left leg.
   B. Right leg relaxed.
   C. Weight on left foot and inside of right foot.
   D. *Advantage:*
         Keeps backswing short, and allows for a freer
   follow through.

NOTE: The advantages listed are not the opinions of the authors nor
are these variations recommended. However if a student can putt
consistently with any of these variations, or any devised by the student, allow the variation.

PUTTING

Putting is the action of the wrists in stroking the ball from the
green, toward and into the cup. This stroke is made with a putter,
usually number 10 in the majority of sets, although it is also numbered
9 in others. It is the shortest club in the set and has a flat face.

SKILL SUMMARY

Assume the grip and address for putting. Move the club back in a
straight line from the ball by flexing the left wrist until the desired backswing
is reached. This will vary with the length of the putt. Keep the club head
close to the green. As the top of the backswing is reached, push the club straight
toward the ball by a flexion of the right wrist. Impact with the ball is made in
exactly the same position as that of address, and the club head is held firm.
Allow the club head to follow the ball, which moves the hands past the center
of the body and out of the address position for the first time in the stroke.
Make the top of the follow through only slightly higher than the top of the
backswing. The right palm faces the cup at the end of the follow through.
Keep the head down until the ball drops into the cup, or the follow through
has been completed.

SKILL ANALYSIS AND ILLUSTRATION (Plate 40a, b, c, d)

Count 1. Address position and backswing.
Count 2. Ball contact.
Count 3. Begin follow through.
Count 4. Complete follow through.

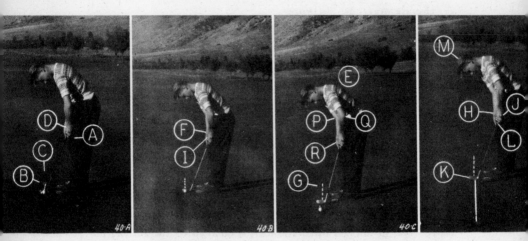

Count 1. Count 2. Count 3. Count 4.

Do Not Make an Approach to the Green Until Players Ahead Have "Holed-Out" and Replaced the Flag.

General Teaching Aids

I. Check grip and address positions for errors.

II. Explain and demonstrate putting stroke.

III. Slow demonstration, student imitation. Verbal instruction by instructor during action.

IV. Physical Aids. (Plate 41a, b)

Hand Aid for Putting Swing.

V. Lining up a putt. (Plate 42)

Lining Up Putt.

Verbal Teaching Aids

A. Assume putting grip and address.

B. Keep club head close to the green.

C. Backswing in direct line with the ball.

D. Left hand and wrist control backswing.

E. No body movement.

F. Push club forward with right wrist flexion.

G. Sweep the ball. (*Do not hit.*)

H. Follow ball toward cup by flexing right wrist. (*Meet ball squarely.*)

I. Hands still at center of body.

J. As hands continue follow through, they move past body center.

K. Club head finishes slightly higher than at top of backswing.

L. Right palm toward cup.

M. Keep head down until stroke is complete.

N. Relax.

O. Hands alone do putting.

P. Keep right elbow against right hip.

Q. Keep left elbow pointed toward cup.

R. Right hand controls forward swing.

THERE ARE ALMOST AS MANY PUTTING VARIATIONS AS THERE
ARE GOLFERS. CONSISTENT PUTTING IS THE OBJECTIVE. MOST VARIA-
TIONS OCCUR IN ADDRESS. THE SWEEPING MOTION, AND SLOW DE-
LIBERATE STROKE ARE COMMON TO ALL.

VARIATIONS

The term variations as used here, denotes variation from the form
previously analyzed. Since putting styles differ with almost every individual,
its general use would be incorrect.

FEET TOWARD CUP

Differences:

A. In address.

B. Right hand controls stroke.

ELBOWS OUT AWAY FROM BODY

Differences:

A. In address.

B. Arm movement added to stroke.

C. Stroke comes from shoulders rather than wrists.

STRAIGHT LEFT LEG

Differences:

A. In address.

ADVANTAGES

Variations in putting are as numerous as golfers. Each individual
seems to find a style particularly suited to his or her physical and mental re-
quirements for accurate putting. Actually no style or form can be set up as
the perfect style, guaranteeing accurate and consistent putting. It follows
logically then, that any advantages or disadvantages that might be stated by
golfers would be prejudiced against any style different from the one personally
favored. In general, individual variations should be allowed, provided accurate,
consistent putting can be achieved with such variations.

The style chosen for analysis seems to be more readily learned by
beginners, and embodies the basic fundamentals of nearly all types of putting.
Variations develop later, and usually have little effect upon the fundamentals
learned; however their value lies in the confidence acquired by the individual
in the variation adopted. Faith in some slight variation seems to create a mental
attitude favorable to relaxation and confidence, with consequent greater
accuracy in putting.

ADDRESS POSITION FOR AN EXPLOSION SHOT

The address for an explosion shot is the position assumed by the
player in order to play the ball from a sand trap.

Skill Summary

Grip the club firmly in the overlapping grip, about three inches from the end of the handle. Place the feet about four to five inches apart at the heels, with the toes turned out, and the stance open. The ball should be played just to the left of the center spot between the feet. Move the feet around in the sand to get the "feel" of the sand, and to assure a firm basis for the feet. Stand close to the ball so that the hands are near the body, and the knees are relaxed. Hold the club *ABOVE* the sand and behind the ball at the spot where the sand is to be hit, the face of the club open. Use a number 8 or 9 iron.

Skill Analysis and Illustration (Plate 43)

Count 1. Assume the overlapping grip, place feet, and obtain a firm stance.

Count 2. Hold the club, face open over the spot where contact with the sand is to be made.

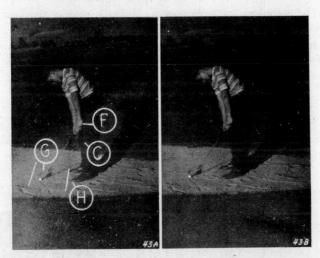

Side View.

It is Illegal to Touch the Club to the Sand When Addressing the Ball in a Sand Trap.

Smooth Out Tracks and Holes Before Leaving Sand Trap.

General Teaching Aids

I. Check overlapping grip for errors.

II. Explain and demonstrate the address position for explosion shots.

III. Practice in sand traps. Stress sand trap rules and regulations.

Verbal Teaching Aids

A. Feet close together.
B. Toes out.
C. Knees relaxed.
D. Club above sand where sand is to be hit, and behind ball.
E. Ball just to left of center between feet.
F. Hands close to body and centered.
G. Club face open.
H. Stance open.

EXPLOSION SHOTS

Explosion shots are strokes played to get the ball out of sand traps. They are made with an 8 or 9 iron, or a specially designed sand iron.

Skill Summary

The technique of performance in the explosion shot resembles in many respects the three quarter swing with the short iron. The main differences lie in the following factors: (1) the sand is hit first, and the cushion of sand plus the follow through of the club, take the ball out of the trap; (2) the club face is open, or nearly flat; (3) the swing is made distinctly from the inside out, and the cushion of sand taken by the club, keeps the ball from slicing; (4) the club goes down into and through the sand, and the ball starts on its flight while the club is still in the sand; and (5) the hands finish waist high at the end of the follow through, with the wrists slightly rolled, and the club pointing toward the line of flight.

Skill Analysis and Illustration (Plate 44a, b, c, d)

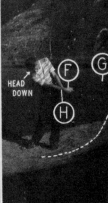

Count 1. Count 2. Count 3. Count 4.

Count 1. Address and begin backswing.
Count 2. Top of backswing, and pause.
Count 3. Impact with sand. Club goes through sand.
Count 4. Follow through.

NOTE: Refer to the three quarter swing with the short iron for additional material on summary and analysis, being sure to note the differences discussed in the above SKILL SUMMARY.

COVER FOOTPRINTS AND SMOOTH OUT SAND TRAP BEFORE PLAYING NEXT SHOT.

GENERAL TEACHING AIDS

I. Explain and demonstrate the explosion shot.

II. Check for errors in grip and address.

III. Explain the differences between the three quarter swing with the short iron on the fairway and an explosion shot in the sand.

IV. Practice in sand, attempting shorter distances first, and gradually working toward the longer shots from the larger sand traps.

V. Encourage practice from traps with different kinds of sand, and different playing conditions existing in the traps.

VERBAL TEACHING AIDS

SEE ALSO VERBAL AIDS AND TEACHING AIDS FOR SHORT IRONS WITH THE THREE QUARTER SWING.

A. Hands near body.
B. Club face open. (*Nearly flat.*)
C. Sand hit first. (*Cushion of sand raises ball.*)
D. Club must follow through sand. (*Do not stop when ball rises.*)
E. Swing from inside out. (*Sand keeps ball from slicing.*)
F. Hands are waist high at end of follow through.
G. Club points toward line of intended ball flight.
H. Wrists slightly rolled.
I. Allow for ball roll after it reaches the green.

VARIATIONS

EXPLOSION SHOTS WITH A CLEAN LIE

Take just enough sand to get under the ball.

EXPLOSION SHOTS IN DEEP SAND, OR WHEN BALL IS BURIED IN SAND

Take more sand than usual and hit harder than in a clean lie. Allow for a roll, and be sure to follow through. Do not stop until the swing is finished.

CHIP SHOTS FROM SAND TRAPS

The ball is played out from the right heel. The ball is hit first, and then the sand. Hit down into and through the ball, not across.

CHIP SHOTS FROM SAND TRAPS MAY BE MADE WHEN THE SAND IS PACKED AND THE BALL IN A FAVORABLE LIE; HOWEVER AN EXPLOSION SHOT IS GENERALLY THE SAFEST AND THE BEST. A CHIP SHOT FROM SAND HAS TO BE MADE PERFECTLY AND ALLOWS FOR LITTLE IF ANY ERROR, WHILE THE EXPLOSION SHOT ALLOWS FOR MORE ERROR THAN ANY OTHER GOLF STROKE.

ADDRESS POSITION FOR SLICING

The address position for slicing is the position assumed by the player in order to slice the ball, or send it from left to right.

COMPARISON: Between address position for straight fairway shot and a slice. (Plate 45a, b)

Address Position, Drive. Front View. Address Position, Slice. Front View.

| A. Open stance. | A. Left foot back of line of flight. |
| B. Body slightly to left. | B. Club ready for backswing *outside* line of flight. |

SLICING

A ball hit so that its flight starts to the left, or straight, and turns right near the end of the flight, is known as a slice.

COMPARISON: Between normal shot and slice.

Differences in slice:
A. Backswing moves outside line of flight.
B. Forward swing from outside to inside.
C. Less body pivot left.
D. Club head cuts across ball from right to left.
E. Ball takes clockwise spin, and flight moves from left to right.

THE AMOUNT OF SLICE VARIES WITH THE CUT THE BALL RE-CEIVES AT IMPACT.

ADDRESS POSITION FOR HOOKING

The address for hooking is the position assumed by a player in order to hook the ball, or send it from right to left.

COMPARISON: Between address position for normal shot and hook. Plate 46a, b)

Address Position, Drive. Front View. Address Position, Hook. Front View.

A. Body slightly to right.
B. Right hand slightly un-der shaft.
C. Club head square. (Closed club head smothers hook.)

A. Closed stance, right foot back from line of ball flight.
B. Club ready for backswing, inside line of ball flight.

HOOKING

A ball hit so that its flight starts to the right or straight, and turns left near the end of the ball flight, is a hook.

COMPARISON: Between a normal shot and a hook.

Differences in hook:

A. Backswing moves inside line of flight.
B. Forward swing inside to outside.
C. More pivot left.
D. Ball flight moves from right to left.

SUGGESTIONS FOR SHOTS FROM THE ROUGH

ROUGH: Ball under low hanging branches of tree.

A. Use club with little loft. (No. 1 or 2 iron.)
B. Hit from inside line out.
C. Right hand rolls over left as club meets ball.
D. Right shoulder stays higher than usual.

SHORT ROUGH

A. Stance open.
B. Backswing upright.
C. Finish upright as in a sand trap.

HEAVY DEEP ROUGH

A. Stance open.
B. Club face open.
C. Swing more upright than usual.
D. Hit down into the ball.
E. Keep swing moving. (*Do not stop when ball is hit.*)

PERFECT CONTROL OF CLUB HEAD IS NECESSARY WHEN PLAYING FROM THE ROUGH. DISTANCE CAN BE ATTEMPTED FROM SHORT ROUGH. DEEP ROUGH REQUIRES AN ATTEMPT TO GET OUT TO THE FAIRWAY BY THE SHORTEST POSSIBLE ROUTE. DO NOT TRY FOR DISTANCE FROM DEEP ROUGH.

CALL "FORE" IF BALL GOES NEAR ANOTHER PLAYER.

GENERAL TEACHING AIDS

I. As in learning the explosion shots, practice of so-called trouble shots, requires actual playing conditions; therefore, students should be afforded opportunities to attempt getting balls out of different types of rough.

II. Hooking and slicing are often acquired unconsciously while attempting the straight wood shots. If this happens, allow the student to perfect the hook or slice, before learning the original skill attempted, namely: the straight or normal wood shot.

III. Use the same GENERAL TEACHING AIDS as in the iron and wood shots; however, differences in the hook, slice, and rough shots should be considered, and allowances made for these differences in verbal instruction and in demonstration.

IV. Allow variations if the performance level of the individual is increased by such variations.

V. Swing the club head through. Never try to stop the swing, or any part of it, once it has been started.

RECORD SCORE AFTER LEAVING GREEN. KEEP SHADOW OUT OF LINE OF OPPONENT'S SHOT ON FAIRWAY AND GREENS, AS WELL AS AWAY FROM THE CUP.

HINTS FOR BEGINNERS

Introduction. Golf instruction in a class situation must of necessity use group instruction as a basis for teaching; therefore, individual attention from the instructor is generally a minimum of that needed for speedy learning. The alert beginner may counteract this disadvantage in two ways: (1) by close attention to explanations and demonstrations, and keeping in mind the techniques of performance presented, and (2) by participating in class drills and attempting to perform these drills as perfectly as possible. These, plus individual practice outside the class period, should materially increase the performance level of the individual, provided each practice stroke is made with as much precision as possible.

On the Course. As each skill in golf is learned, students should practice that skill on a golf course, and as soon as wood shots, irons, and putting have been presented, a full round should be attempted. Shots from the rough and sand might be lifted to the fairway until instruction has been received in these skills. Learn to judge the distances that can be obtained from each iron, and use the correct club for each shot, regardless of any possible greater proficiency with another. Learn the etiquette and rules of golf and abide by them.

Instruction in All Skills Received. Play as much golf as possible after instruction in all of the skills has been received. Play each shot with as much precision as possible. Try not to imagine where the ball might go. Choose the correct club for each shot, and play each shot from where it lands, unless course rules allow it to be moved. If consistent errors in strokes are noted, consult the instructor for individual aid and instruction on such strokes.

Concentration. The mental side of golf is as important to good golf as the physical aspect. Concentration is perhaps a common misuse of a term designating the correct mental set of a golfer, for that word used by an instructor may of itself, cause tension in the player. If an error is made, however, think of correcting just one technique of performance within the total skill, and allow the rest of the swing to take care of itself.

Relax. Another term that sometimes creates tension is the term "relax." Beginners react better to thinking in terms of standing naturally and comfortably, and swinging easily and rhythmically.

Scoring. Count each stroke. This includes each miss. Practice putting and the short irons, and the golf score will improve.

The Teaching Aids for each skill offer specific items suggested for use in the general activities listed below.

SUGGESTED CLASS ORGANIZATION
(60 *minutes*)

SUGGESTED ACTIVITY

	APPROXIMATE TIME
Initial lessons	
1st three weeks.	
Arrive and change shoes	5 minutes
Roll Call and Preliminaries	2 minutes
General Information	8 minutes
(History, rules, etiquette, care of equipment, etc.)	
Review	10 minutes
Explanation and Demonstration of New Material	5 minutes
Class Drills	10 minutes
Individual Activity and Practice	15 minutes
Shower and dress or change shoes	5 minutes
4th through 8th week.	
Arrive and change shoes and practice	5 minutes
Roll Call and Preliminaries	2 minutes
General Information	5 minutes
Review	10 minutes
Explanation and Demonstration of New Material	5 minutes
Class Drills	10 minutes
Individual Activity and Practice	23 minutes
(Individual attention from instructor.)	

9th through 12th week.

Arrive and change shoes and practice	5 minutes
Roll Call and Preliminaries	2 minutes
General Information	3 minutes
Review	6 minutes
Explanation and Demonstration of New Material	5 minutes
Class Drills	4 minutes
Individual Activity and Practice	35 minutes

(Individual attention from instructor.)

NOTE: In general, the use of a golf course for instructional periods, weather permitting, increases interest and lessens the motivation necessary for learning.

If gymnasiums, cages, etc., are used exclusively, introduce competitive activities in the seventh week, and allow time in the daily class periods for these activities. In all cases, an attempt should be made to create conditions as close to actual playing conditions as possible.

FURTHER REFERENCES

1. Ainsworth, Dorothy S.; Broer, Marion R.; Goss, Alice G.; Goss, Gertrude; Jennings, Evelyn; Pitkin, Bertha A.; Ryder, Florence: *Individual Sports for Women.* W. B. Saunders and Company, Philadelphia and London, 1943, 392 pages.
2. Berg, Patty, and Dypwich, Otis: *Golf.* A. S. Barnes and Company, Publishers, New York, 1941, 81 pages.
3. Jones, Ernest, and Brown, Innis: *Swinging Into Golf.* Whittlesey House, McGraw-Hill Book Co., Inc., New York, 1937, 150 pages.
4. Jones, Robert T., Jr., and Lowe, Howard E.: *Group Golf Instruction.* American Sports Publishing Company, New York, 1939, 63 pages.
5. Metz, Dick: *The Secret to Par Golf.* The Macmillan Co., Chicago, Illinois, 1940, 66 pages.
6. National Section on Women's Athletics: *Individual Sports Guide.* Official Sports Library for Women, A. S. Barnes and Company, Publishers, New York, 1945-46.
7. Schleman, Helen B., and Hayes, Virginia: *Group Golf Instruction.* A. S. Barnes and Company, Publishers, New York, 1934, 80 pages.
8. Snead, Sam: *A Quick Way To Better Golf.* The Sun Dial Press, 1938.
9. Thompson, Ben: *How To Play Golf.* Prentice-Hall, Inc., New York, 1939, 65 pages.

VII

TENNIS

TEACHING PREMISE

TENNIS skills, as presented in the following pages of this volume, are analyzed in the same order as skills in sports presented previously, namely: from the simple to the complex. This order designates a general teaching progression; however many of the skills are more advantageously taught, and more successfully learned, if presented together. One example of this is the forehand and backhand drives.

There is perhaps less conflicting thought in the teaching progression of tennis skills than in most sports; however methods of instruction vary with each individual instructor, class size, student personnel, weather conditions, facilities, equipment, etc.

The technique, or manner, of performance selected for the SKILL ILLUSTRATIONS does not attempt to follow any particular style successfully used by ranking players. In general the performance technique illustrated is an attempt to visualize both for the student and the teacher, the rhythmic steps or pattern of each skill as performed by the average player.

Each skill is presented in the style most commonly used, although each individual will vary this according to personal needs and abilities. Some variations are discussed and illustrated, although the two-handed method of stroking the ball is not discussed. Because of the additional power and resulting increase in speed, some players have used the two-handed stroke successfully.

Variations in stroking from the supposedly orthodox technique of performance should be allowed once the basic fundamentals of a skill are learned, provided they increase the skill performance for that individual attempting their use.

A BRIEF HISTORY OF TENNIS

Tennis, like "Topsy, jest growed," but its growth makes a fascinating story. To trace the game of tennis in chronological order is a job for an historian, and not one to be attempted in a condensation that purports merely to create interest in further individual research on the subject, and to serve in the capacity of an introduction to the techniques in teaching tennis. For this purpose an outline of the progress made in the various components of tennis as we know it today would seem sufficient.

Tennis had its origin in Ancient Greece under the guise of handball, and developed in the Middle Ages into a form of tennis as we know it today, in which two opponents hit the ball back and forth between them. "The Greeks may have had a word for it," but authorities agree that the term tennis actually originated from the French word "tenez," meaning "take" or "ready," although the French term previously used was "la paume."

The first balls used, were leather covered, and stuffed with hair. The French balls were black in color. As improvements were made in the game, its equipment and facilities, so the balls had to improve. Thus rubber came into use, until finally wool-covered balls, vacuum sealed, true bouncing, and fully tested, came into popular use. Reclaimed rubber, and the first synthetic rubber balls made during the second World War, marked the only exceptions in this steady progress.

Tennis in its original form made no use of racquets. Gloves were worn to protect the hand when the ball was hit. Later the gloves were corded for still greater protection. As the speed of the game increased and changes in the court were made, paddles were used. Finally the paddles were corded and progression made to the first top-heavy, large-handled racquets. Experiments were conducted along scientific lines, and the present streamlined racquets evolved. Simultaneously cord was discarded for stringing the racquets, and experiments gradually brought forth graded gut strings, silk strings, and nylon strings. It is now a matter of personal preference which type of stringing is chosen. Likewise it is a matter of preference, size of hand, and body build, which type of racquet is preferred.

Court surfacing and markings also changed with the improvement of equipment, and were sometimes instrumental in bringing about such improvement. No boundary lines graced the first tennis areas, and the net was an earthen mound. The first attempt at court marking resulted in a court the shape of an hourglass, with a net across the narrow center portion. As skill in the game increased, the court was made rectangular in shape, and so to the present dimensions. The first tennis was played on any level area; however lawns later became popular, and finally clay, asphalt, and cement courts were universally used. (Plate 1)

The scoring in the early form of tennis was too intricate for the common people. One historian suggests that 15 denoted 15 chases or separate plays, thus giving a player 1 point. Thirty chases gave a player 2 points and so on until 4 points were made. Thus our present scoring consists of 15-30-40-Game and may have evolved from this early form. Love referred to "playing for the love of the game, or for nothing"; hence love still means nothing or "no score," in tennis.

After many generations tennis made its way to America. Beginning with the ancient Greek handball players, the game was passed on to each generation through the Middle Ages, constantly changing as the popularity of, and skill in the game increased. The English nobility eventually participated in the game, and thus was it transferred to the wealthy people of England and France. Tennis was an expensive sport by this time, and only the wealthy could afford the luxury of playing it. From England and France, tennis made its way to Bermuda, only to be brought to American lawns via Staten Island by Mary Outerbridge in 1875. The Eastern Cricket Clubs soon became enthusiastic, about this sport, and tennis was on its way to becoming a popular American sport. In 1881, The United States Lawn Tennis Association assumed control of the rules and regulations governing tennis, and spread its popularity over the entire United States.

As skill in tennis increased, so individual interest increased in vying with friends for the winning of a match. Clubs formed tournaments. Communities held tournaments. So competition kept pace with, and sometimes led, the progress of tennis. State, Sectional, and National Tournaments were held under the sponsorship of the United States Lawn Tennis Association. International competition arose with the Davis Cup matches for men, and the Wightman Cup matches for women, the latter only between England and the United States. (National tournaments are usually open to players from other nations than the one sponsoring the tournament.)

From Ancient Greece to world-wide acclaim is quite a record for

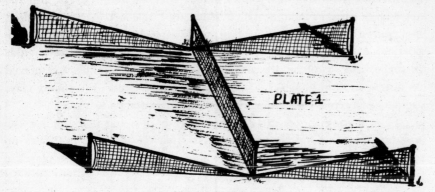

Ancient 'Hour-Glass' Court.

PLATE 1.

any sport, especially for one started as the handball of Ancient Greece. To play it, is to love it; to teach it, is a privilege.

THE GAME

A beginner, with no knowledge of tennis terminology, may find the game of tennis confusing, both in its scoring and court boundaries. A simple, concise explanation of the game is a necessary preface to tennis instruction. The following explanation attempts to present such a preface, although some of the points discussed, such as the doubles boundaries, deuce scoring, matches, etc., may be omitted in the initial explanation, and discussed later when the situation occurs in the class instructional periods.

The game of tennis is a racquet sport for two or four players: the former number of players, a singles game; the latter a doubles game. The object of the game is to gain a minimum of four points by keeping the ball in play within the court boundary lines, and over the net, until the opponent is forced to make at least four errors such as missing a shot, hitting the ball out of bounds, or placing the ball into the net.

Equipment will be discussed in detail later in this chapter; however, the minimum playing equipment consists of two balls, and a racquet for each player. The singles and doubles courts are usually lined on one court as illustrated in Plate 2 below. Areas in the court have been clearly marked to clarify the explanation of the game. The doubles court differs from the singles court only in the extension of the side boundary lines the full length of the court, but does not affect the size of the service court. (Plate 2)

Court.   PLATE 2.

Consecutive Order of Steps in Scoring in a Tennis Game.

1. Designation of Initial Server. (3 types.)
   A. Coin toss.
   B. Rally for service.

The players hit the ball back and forth over the net and within the boundary lines until one player misses the ball, hits the ball outside the boundaries, or places the ball in the net. The player making the error, loses the right to be the initial server.

   C. Spinning the racquet.

The choice of server is determined by placing the racquet vertical to the court, the top of the racquet head in contact with the court. The handle is twirled and released, allowing the racquet to spin to the court. As in the coin toss, the players call the side they believe will be up. The call in the racquet spin is "rough" or "smooth," rather than "heads" or "tails" as in the coin toss. The rough side is determined by the looped side of the racquet trim used at the top and bottom of the racquet strings. The smooth side shows no loops in the trim, merely a flat expanse of trim is apparent.

2. Service.
   A. The winner of the initial service, serves the entire first game, and has two trials to place the ball in the proper court, each time a point is made.
   B. The service begins in the right court, behind the baseline,

and at any point between the center mark and the side boundary line.

C. Service from the right court is made to the opponent's right service court and within its boundaries.

D. The next service is made from the left court; the next from the right, etc., until the end of the game.

E. Opponent serves entire next game. The service alternates by games.

3. Points.

A. A score of zero, or nothing, is designated "love."

B. First point: scores 15.

C. Second point: scores 30.

D. Third point: scores 40.

E. Fourth point: scores "Game."

F. The server's score is always called first, thus if the server had made two points, and the receiver none, the score would be called as: 30-love.

The following tabulation may aid the beginner in learning to score. Remember the server's score is always called first.

LOVE GAME		SERVER—2 Points RECEIVER—Game		SERVER—Game RECEIVER—1 Point	
Server	Receiver	Server	Receiver	Server	Receiver
15	love	love	15	15	love
30	love	15	15 (15 all)	30	love
40	love	15	30	40	love
Game	*	30	30 (30 all)	40	15
		30	40	Game	*
		*	Game		

* Have students attempt to determine where points were made, and by whom.

4. The Deuce Game.

A. In the event a game score reaches 40-40, or in other words both players acquire three points each, the score is 40-all or deuce.

B. The game is won by one player winning two points in succession, the first point is called "advantage," the second, if won immediately after the advantage point, is game.

C. If one player gains the advantage point, and loses the next point, the score reverts to deuce. If the server gains the advantage point it is called "advantage server," or in common usage, "ad-in." If the receiver gains the advantage point it is called "advantage receiver," or in common usage, "ad-out." These common terms are often used in recreational play; however the official terms should be used exclusively when officiating tennis play.

5. Set.

A. A set is composed of 6 games. Each set must be won by a margin of at least two games. Set scores may range from 6-love to any number such as 7-5, 8-10, 12-10, etc., depending upon how many games had to be played for one player to gain the margin of two games.

6. Match.

Women's Play: 2 out of 3 sets.

Men's Play: 3 out of 5 sets. This is sometimes modified arbitrarily to 2 out of 3 for intramural games, recreational tournaments, etc. It is not modified in championship matches.

7. Service Courts.

A. Service for each game begins in the right court. Score at the end of the service is odd; therefore 15-love score would denote the next service in the left court; 30-40 from the left court, etc.

B. Even scores are made in the left court; therefore a deuce score, (40-40), would denote service in the right court. The same for 15-15, 30-30, etc.

SELECTION, CARE, AND REPAIR OF EQUIPMENT

The type of equipment selected varies slightly according to the skill of the player. Beginners usually prefer to buy equipment within the medium price range. The cost of average equipment for a class in tennis, costs little more than the usual academic course equipment consisting of textbooks and laboratory fees. From the standpoint of use and durability, cheap equipment eventually proves more costly than equipment in the medium or top price range.

RACQUET (Plate 3a, b)

Selection. The racquet should be well-balanced and have a good "feel" to the individual player using it. The circumference of the racquet

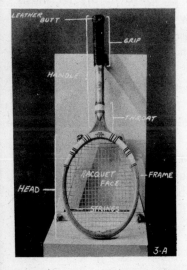

The Racquet. Storage.

handle should be 4½ inches for women; 5 inches for men. The weight of the racquet for women should be a maximum of 13½ ounces; for men 15 ounces. These figures are for the average man or woman, and may vary with body build, length of fingers, arm and wrist strength, etc. The "feel" of the racquet, plus all possible elimination of muscle strain due to excess weight of the racquet, too small or too large handle, etc., are the main factors in racquet selection. The make and style are matters of individual preference. The strings may be gut, silk, or nylon. Silk and nylon are excellent for damp climates, and are within the usual price range desired by a beginner. Gut is preferred by most expert players, although some college players express a definite liking for nylon.

Care and Repair. A tennis racquet should be kept in a press and a moisture-proof covering when not in use. It should be stored in a dry place when weather prevents play. This prevents rotting of strings and warping of the frame. Broken strings should be replaced immediately.

NETS

Selection. The nets are usually furnished by the school, and are made of tarred hemp, although cotton or string nets are used in gymnasiums, and where the cost of a regulation net is prohibitive. Steel nets for use the year around are becoming popular since they are not affected by weather changes, and require less upkeep.

Care and Repair. Tennis nets should be stored during inclement weather, and thoroughly dried before storing. Nets strung by rope should be loosened after each period of use. Tarred hemp nets strung on a wire cable need not be loosened. Steel nets may be left on the court the year around.

Breaks in the nets or wire backstops should be mended immediately, or replacements made if necessary.

BALLS

Selection. The balls selected should bear the official seal of approval of the United States Lawn Tennis Association.

Care and Repair. Tennis balls should be kept dry, and replaced if the cover becomes worn, or they begin to "float" when hit. The vacuum seal on a can of balls should not be broken until the balls are to be used.

COURTS

Selection. Because of the expense of upkeep on clay and lawn courts, school courts are usually of asphalt, cement, or some composition material; therefore the lines are of paint rather than cloth, steel tape, or wet or dry lime.

Care and Repair. Courts should be swept as often as necessary to keep them free from dirt, leaves, and any pools of water or piles of snow left on them, due to improper drainage. All cracks in the court should be mended immediately.

COSTUME

The tennis costume should be all white. Freedom of movement, comfort, and good taste are the only other requisites. Low white tennis shoes are preferable, worn with one heavy pair or two light pair or medium weight socks. Visors or light caps are also worn to protect the eyes from the sun.

THE EASTERN FOREHAND GRIP

The Eastern Forehand Grip is the position of the hand on the racquet handle that is used by the majority of players in executing the forehand drive.

GRIP SUMMARY

The Eastern Forehand Grip may be obtained by placing the racquet on edge, with the racquet handle toward the body. Grasp the racquet as if shaking hands, the heel of the hand against the leather butt at the end of the handle. The knuckles are diagonal to the racquet handle and the fingers are spread up the handle as far as it is comfortable to do so.

GRIP ANALYSIS AND ILLUSTRATION (Plate 4a, b, c, d)

Top View: Shaking hands with the racquet, knuckle of thumb nearer wrist placed just to the left of the top edge of the racquet handle. Knuckle of index finger closest to wrist, placed on top edge of back plate of the handle.

Right Side View: Fingers spread comfortably. Knuckles slant across handle.

Left Side View: Heel of hand against leather butt. Palm of hand on back of handle.

Bottom View: Heel of hand against leather butt. Firm grip.

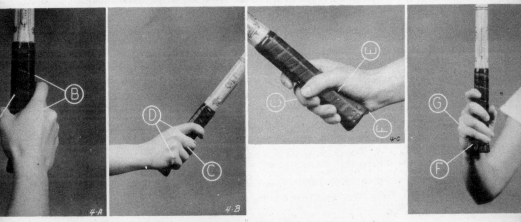

Top View. Right Side View. Left Side View. Bottom View.

Open Face of Racquet: Hitting surface slants upward.

Closed Face of Racquet: Hitting surface slants downward.

Flat Face: Short racquet strings perpendicular to court; long strings parallel to court.

GENERAL TEACHING AIDS

    I. How to Obtain the Eastern Forehand Grip. (Plate 5a, b)

    II. Keep the racquet head slightly higher than the wrist.

    III. Be sure this grip is the one best for each individual before advising its exclusive use.

IV. Do not hold students too rigidly to the supposedly orthodox grip. See VARIATIONS of racquet grip.

V. Teach checking points from VERBAL AIDS.

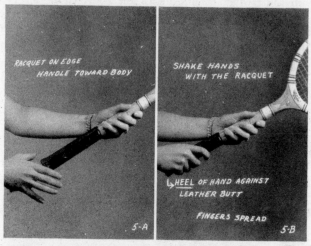

Racquet on Edge, Handle Toward Body. Shake Hands with Racket. Heel of Hand Against Leather Butt; Fingers Spread.

VERBAL TEACHING AIDS

A. Knuckles of thumb nearer wrist placed just to the left of the top edge of the racquet handle.

B. Knuckle of index finger closest to wrist, on top edge of back plate of the handle.

C. Spread fingers comfortably.

D. Knuckles of fingers slant across the handle.

E. Palm of hand on back of handle.

F. Heel of hand against leather butt.

G. Firm grip, not too tight.

VARIATIONS

1. Each individual using the Eastern Forehand Grip may vary slightly from the instructions given.

2. Each individual should be allowed such variations, provided these variations increase the effectiveness of the forehand strokes for that individual.

3. Body build, length of fingers, style of game, physical handicaps, wrist strength, and muscle leverage may influence variations in grip.

ADVANTAGES OF THE EASTERN FOREHAND GRIP

1. Maximum power behind stroke.

2. Excellent for returns at all levels.

3. No need for changes in grip for all forehand strokes.
4. Strength of hand is behind the racquet.
5. Good for use on any kind of playing surface.
6. This grip does not demand an exceptionally strong wrist; therefore *it is especially recommended for use by girls and women.*

EASTERN BACKHAND GRIP

The Eastern Backhand grip is the position to which the hand is moved from the Eastern Forehand grip, in order to execute a backhand stroke.

GRIP SUMMARY

Assume the Eastern Forehand Grip. Turn the hand to the left or backward on the racquet handle about a quarter of a turn. The palm of the hand is now more nearly on top of the handle and facing downward. The first knuckle of the index finger is on the top plate of the racquet handle. The leather butt is underneath the hand. The thumb is extended up the handle if further support is needed, or wrapped diagonally around the handle. The opposite face of the racquet meets the ball than that used in the forehand drive.

GRIP ANALYSIS AND ILLUSTRATION (Plate 6a, b, c, d)

Top View: Palm of hand on top of racquet, facing downward. First knuckle of index finger on top plate of handle.

Right Side View: Fingers spread comfortably. Heel of hand against leather butt.

Left Side View: Thumb extended up handle, or wrapped diagonally around the handle.

Bottom View: Leather butt underneath hand. Firm grip, but not too tight.

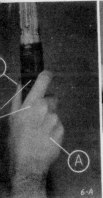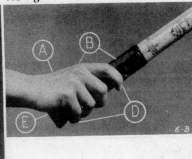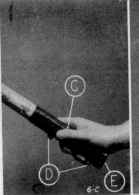

Top View. Right Side View. Left Side View. Bottom View.

GENERAL TEACHING AIDS

I. How to obtain the Eastern Backhand Grip. (Plate 7a, b)

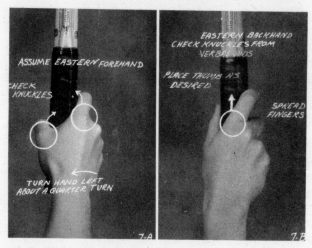

Eastern Forehand Grip. Eastern Backhand Grip.

II. Keep the racquet head slightly higher than the wrist.

III. Allow beginners to attempt all grips before selecting one for exclusive use.

IV. Do not hold students too rigidly to the supposedly orthodox grip. See VARIATIONS.

V. Teach checking points from VERBAL AIDS.

VERBAL TEACHING AIDS

A. Palm on top of racquet, facing downward.

B. First knuckle of index finger on top plate of racquet handle.

C. Extend thumb up the handle or wrap diagonally around the handle.

D. Spread fingers comfortably.

E. Leather butt underneath the hand.

F. Firm grip, not too tight.

VARIATIONS

1. Each individual using the Eastern Backhand Grip may vary slightly from the instructions given.

2. Each individual should be allowed such variations, provided these variations increase the effectiveness of the backhand strokes for that individual.

3. Body build, length of fingers, style of game, physical handicaps, wrist strength, and muscle leverage may influence variations in grip.

4. Unless a *woman* has a very large hand and exceptionally strong grip, the *thumb is probably more advantageously placed up the handle*, rather than diagonally around it, in all backhand strokes.

Advantages of the Eastern Backhand Grip

1. Maximum power behind stroke.
2. Excellent for returns at all levels.
3. No need for changes in grip for all backhand strokes.
4. Strength of the hand is behind the racquet.
5. Good for use on any kind of playing surface.
6. This grip does not demand an exceptionally strong wrist, and allows for aid from the extended thumb; therefore it is *especially recommended for use by girls and women.*

WESTERN FOREHAND GRIP

The Western Forehand Grip is the position of the hand on the racquet handle that is used by players who prefer to play on courts where the ball bounce is high.

Grip Summary

Assume the Eastern Forehand Grip, first knuckle of index finger at the top edge of the back plate of the racquet handle. Change to the Western Forehand grip by turning the hand to the right until the first knuckle of the index finger reaches the *lower edge* of the back plate of the racquet handle. Spread the fingers as far as it is comfortable to do so.

Grip Analysis and Illustration (Plate 8a, b, c, d)

Top View: First knuckle of index finger reaches lower edge of back plate of the handle. Main portion of thumb is on top of the handle.

Right Side View: Racquet may be laid flat and picked up in this position.

Left Side View: Thumb tip continues around handle. Fingers may close together, or spread comfortably. This depends upon the size of the hand.

Bottom View: Heel of hand against leather butt.

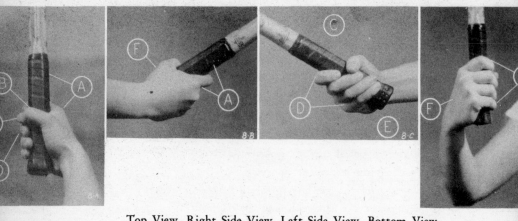

Top View. Right Side View. Left Side View. Bottom View.

GENERAL TEACHING AIDS

I. Teach the Eastern Forehand Grip before presenting the Western Forehand Grip.

II. Present the Western Forehand Grip in terms of the Eastern Forehand Grip.

III. How to obtain the Western Forehand Grip. (Plate 9a, b)

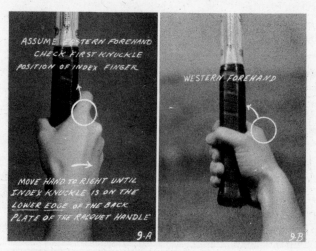

Eastern Forehand Grip. Western Forehand Grip.

NOTE: This reviews the Eastern Forehand Grip as well as demonstrates its relationship to the Western Grip on the racquet handle.

VERBAL TEACHING AIDS

A. First knuckle of index finger reaches lower edge of back plate of racquet handle.
B. Main part of thumb on top of handle.
C. Thumb tip winds around handle.
D. Fingers may be close together or spread comfortably.
E. Racquet may be laid flat and picked up to obtain this grip.
F. Firm grip, not too tight.

ADVANTAGES

1. Allows for great severity and power on the high forehand strokes.
2. Very little change in grip is needed for the backhand stroke.

DISADVANTAGES

1. Tends to develop the undercut or slice stroke on the backhand.
2. Awkward for use on low balls on forehand stroke.
3. Requires greater wrist strength than is found in the average player.
4. *Not recommended for women* due to the demand for an exceptionally strong wrist.

WESTERN BACKHAND GRIP

1. Grip remains about the same. The fingers may spread a little more, and the thumb may move up on the racquet handle.
2. The wrist turns, and the return is made with the same side of the racquet as is made on the forehand drive.

THE CONTINENTAL FOREHAND GRIP

The Continental Forehand Grip is the position of the hand on the racquet handle that originated in Europe and requires little change for the backhand stroke.

GRIP SUMMARY

Assume the Eastern Forehand Grip. Change to the Continental Forehand Grip by turning the hand to the left until the first knuckle of the index finger is on the right edge of the top plate of the racquet handle. Spread the fingers as far as it is comfortable to do so.

GRIP ANALYSIS AND ILLUSTRATION (Plate 10a, b, c, d)

Top View: First knuckle of index finger on right edge of top plate of handle. Hand placement is just to the left of the Eastern Forehand Grip.
Right Side View: Fingers spread comfortably. Knuckles slant across the handle.

Left Side View: The thumb is diagonally around the handle.

Bottom View: Heel of hand against leather butt. Forefinger spread to hook around handle.

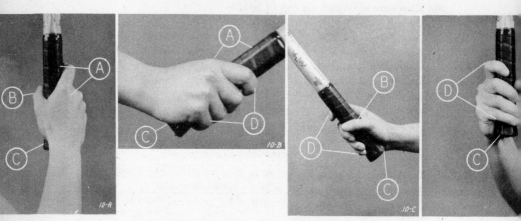

Top View. Right Side View. Left Side View. Bottom View.

GENERAL TEACHING AIDS

I. Teach the Eastern Forehand Grip before presenting the Continental Forehand Grip to the students.

II. Present the Continental Forehand Grip in terms of Eastern Forehand Grip.

III. How to obtain the Continental Forehand Grip. (Plate 11a, b)

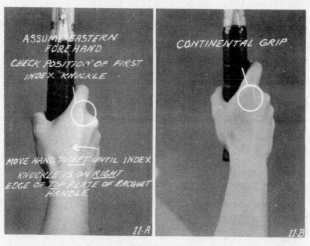

Eastern Grip. Continental.

NOTE: Teach all grips from the Eastern Grip. This reviews the Eastern Grip; gives the relationship of the Eastern Grips to the other grips; fixes the Eastern Grip in the minds of the students; and demonstrates to the students the variations in their grips to the Eastern, Western, and Continental Grips.

VERBAL TEACHING AIDS

A. Index knuckle on right edge of top plate of racquet handle.
B. Thumb may be straight up or diagonally across the handle.
C. Heel of hand near butt of racquet handle.
D. Spread fingers comfortably.

ADVANTAGES

1. The Continental Grip is good for low bouncing balls.
2. No change is made for the backhand grip.

DISADVANTAGES

1. The Continental Grip is not effective for high bouncing balls.
2. The balls cannot be hit as hard with the Continental Forehand Grip as with the Eastern Forehand Grip.

CONTINENTAL BACKHAND GRIP

1. The grip remains the same. The fingers may spread a little more, and the thumb moves a little more in back of the handle of the racquet.
2. The opposite face of the racquet is used in hitting the backhand returns than is used for the forehand returns.

NOTE: The Eastern Grip will be referred to in all further explanations since it has the least number of disadvantages of any of the three grips discussed, and is the grip preferred by the majority of American players. If another grip is preferred, substitute that grip wherever the Eastern Grip is advised.

HALF-SWING VOLLEY RETURN

The half-swing volley return is used to start the ball for a rally, to get the ball back to the opponent for service, and in setting up balls for student practice.

SKILL SUMMARY

Grasp the racquet with the Eastern Forehand Grip. Assume a position with the left side to the net, weight on the right foot. Hold the racquet horizontally opposite the right thigh. The ball is in the left hand and is tossed about two feet away from the body, about the height of the hip. As the ball is tossed, swing the racquet forward to contact the ball, and transfer the weight to the left foot by means of a step toward the net on the left foot.

The racquet finishes at shoulder height, and the follow through is made in the direction in which the ball was hit.

SKILL ANALYSIS AND ILLUSTRATION (Plate 12a, b, c, d)

Count 1. Eastern Forehand Grip. Left side to net, weight on right foot, racquet horizontal and opposite right thigh. Ball in left hand.

Count 2. Toss the ball two feet away from the body, hip high, and make a very slight backswing.

Count 3. Swing racquet forward to contact ball.

Count 4. Transfer weight to left foot. Follow through in direction ball is sent. Finish with racquet at shoulder height.

Count 1. Count 2. Count 3. Count 4.

GENERAL TEACHING AIDS

I. Review grip to be used, preferably the Eastern Grip, and check all grips for errors.

II. Explain and demonstrate the half-swing volley return.

III. Face the same direction as the class and lead them in practicing the racquet swing and follow through. Do not use balls, although the left arm should be used as if tossing a ball.

IV. Individual practice, instructor checking errors.

V. Divide class into buddies or partners. Partners opposite each other across the net, may now practice with balls. The instructor checks for errors. Practice this return first while quite close to the net. Later move back. After skill increases practice for ball placement.

VI. Buddies form into teams, A and B on opposite sides of the net. Team A hit, team B retrieve. Reverse when each member of team A has hit two balls. One point is scored for each successful hit into area requested by opponents. Five areas are designated in the following diagram. No one area should be called more than two times in succession, and never the same numbers for the same player. (Plate 13)

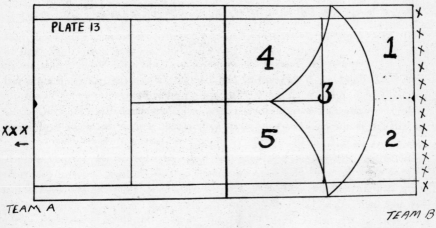

Team Drill. PLATE 13.

Verbal Teaching Aids

A. Swing racquet in a short backswing, no further back than right hip.
B. Toss ball directly out in front of body, two feet out hip high.
C. Line up center of racquet with ball.
D. Swing racquet in a horizontal plane, racquet face opened slightly.
E. Hit ball while it is in the air. (*Do not let ball bounce.*)
F. Ball flight is upward in direction.
G. Contact ball before it reaches knee height.
H. Racquet finishes at shoulder height.
I. Transfer weight from right to left foot as the forward swing is started. (*Should be a natural movement.*)

Advantages

1. Valuable in learning to co-ordinate transfer of body weight, meeting the ball squarely, using the correct grip, and the horizontal racquet swing.
2. Courteous stroke for returning balls to opponent; less chasing after balls.
3. Aids in learning accurate ball placement.
4. Useful stroke for beginners, intermediate, advanced, and professional players.
5. Easiest stroke for beginners to learn.

THE FOREHAND DRIVE

The forehand drive is a stroke used to catch the opponent out of position, to move the opponent to the back court, and for ball placement. It comprises 50% of all tennis strokes used in a game, and is useful in both offense and defense. The flat forehand is valuable for its speed, and the top spin drive for its difficult bounce.

SKILL SUMMARY

Assume the Eastern Forehand Grip. Stand with the left side to the net, feet about 18 inches apart, and parallel to the net. Draw the racquet straight back in line with the ball (see also Circular Backswing under TEACHING AIDS), weight on the right foot, as the ball approaches. The left arm acts as a balance as the backswing is completed. Hyper-extend the wrist, and rotate the trunk away from the net. Pause slightly at the end of the backswing. Start the racquet forward in line with the ball, the head of the racquet slightly higher than the wrist. Transfer the weight to the left foot, and keep the right arm straight and the wrist locked as the ball is hit. Keep the eyes on the ball at all times. Turn the shoulders into the shot, and continue to move onto the left foot as the follow through is made. Follow the flight of the ball as far as possible, and finish the follow through slightly higher than the point of contact with the ball, usually at shoulder or above shoulder height.

SKILL ANALYSIS AND ILLUSTRATION (Plate 14a, b, c, d, e)

Count 1. Assume the proper grip and stance, and begin backswing in line with the approaching ball.

Count 2. Complete backswing, pause slightly, transfer weight to left foot, and begin forward swing.

Count 3. Contact ball, right arm straight, wrist locked, racquet head above wrist level.

Count 4. Turn shoulders into shot and begin follow through.

Count 5. Complete follow through at or near shoulder height.

Count 1. Count 2. Count 3.

Count 4. Count 5.

GENERAL TEACHING AIDS

I. Be sure the half-swing volley return is learned before proceeding to the forehand drive. Insist upon the use of this return in all further lessons and practice periods.

II. Explain and demonstrate the performance technique of the forehand drive. Use a self-toss out beyond the left foot, step into the shot, and hit the ball before it bounces. Use a follow through in the direction of the ball flight. Do not confuse the students with the complete follow through and racquet turn-over.

III. Face the same direction as the class and take them through a short period of drill in the forehand drive, without the use of a ball. Allow them to continue and check for errors.

IV. Divide the group into partners. One person tossing the ball out beyond the left foot, and swinging through with an imaginary racquet. The other person holding a hand in the correct position toward which the ball should be tossed, and catching it. Partners reverse duties each time.

V. Partners assume opposite court positions attempting to coordinate the ball toss and the racquet swing as demonstrated by the instructor.

VI. After this has been perfected, attempt a self-bounce and a forehand drive.

VII. *Footwork Drill.* Students step or run forward or back, laterally left or right, or diagonally left or right for a forehand or backhand drive, as commanded by instructor. The object is to place the correct side to the net as quickly as possible. No balls are used, and the distance to be covered is controlled by the instructor. Use as many combinations of movement as possible.

VIII. Partners now may toss balls to each other. Students must move toward the ball to return it with a forehand drive.

IX. Partners or instructors use the half-swing volley return to right side of student, who attempts a drive from a hit ball.

X. Allow students to rally, using the forehand drive.

XI. Repeat practices using complete follow through. (This adds Count 5 from the SKILL ANALYSIS, where just 4 counts had been used previously.)

XII. THE BACKHAND DRIVE SHOULD BE TAUGHT AT THE SAME TIME AS THE FOREHAND DRIVE, AND PRACTICED AS MUCH OR MORE THAN THE FOREHAND DRIVE.

VERBAL TEACHING AIDS

A. Weight back on backswing.

B. Weight forward on forward swing.

C. Keep away from the ball. (*Crowding ball causes cramped elbow swing.*)

D. Arm straight and wrist locked as ball is hit.

E. Racquet head higher than wrist. (*Low racquet head causes a scoop shot and a high ball.*)

F. Stroke the ball. Carry it forward on the racquet. (*Do not jab.*)

G. Take racquet back in line with the ball.

H. Follow through at or near shoulder height. (*Complete follow through.*)

I. Start backswing immediately.

J. Pause at end of backswing. (*Keeps forward swing from being rushed.*)

K. Body at right angles to net. (*Left side toward net.*)

L. Move into stroke with body. (*Power and balance.*)

M. Fling racquet at ball on forward swing. (*Straightens arm.*)

N. Keep balls low. (*6 inch net clearance, ball landing near base line.*)

TEACHING AIDS COVER DAYS, AND SOMETIMES WEEKS OF INSTRUCTIONAL MATERIAL. DO NOT ATTEMPT TO MAKE THE STUDENT PROCEED TO FURTHER INSTRUCTION UNTIL THE PREVIOUS LESSONS HAVE BEEN MASTERED. AVOID SPEEDING INSTRUCTION IN ORDER TO COVER A CERTAIN AMOUNT OF MATERIAL EACH DAY. CLASSES DIFFER IN ABILITY TO LEARN QUICKLY.

VARIATIONS

1. THE RETURN OF A SHOULDER HIGH FOREHAND DRIVE.
(Plate 15a, b, c, d)

2. THE RETURN OF A KNEE HIGH FOREHAND DRIVE.
(Plate 16a, b, c, d)

NOTE: The technique of performance remains essentially the same. The higher the ball, the less knee flexion is required. In both instances the racquet is lined up behind the ball, and the follow through is higher than the position at which the ball is met. Note in the return of the knee high ball, the knee flexion, and the erect upper trunk. In both cases the racquet is parallel to the court in the correct horizontal swing.

Count 1. Count 2. Count 3. Count 4.

Count 1. Count 2. Count 3. Count 4.

3. The forehand drive may vary to the degree a player is "out-of-position," off balance, under physical handicaps, at variance in body build from the average player, at variance in age, sex, stamina, etc., from other individuals.

4. Every forehand drive should adhere as closely as possible to the approved performance technique. The instructor should use personal knowledge of the student and the game in order to judge as accurately as possible, the value of the variations adopted by each individual. This would apply more particularly to intermediate and advanced players. Beginners would vary in the majority of cases according to physical abilities, since the fundamentals of each stroke are quite uniform.

5. Other variations are as follows:

Backswings:

Straight: (Recommended for beginners.) (Plate 17)

The racquet is held slightly higher than the wrist, and is brought straight back in line with the ball. A slight pause detaches this swing from the forward swing, and the forward swing is made straight forward in line with the ball.

Circular: (Used by intermediate and advanced players.) (Plate 18)

Straight Backswing. Circular Backswing.

The racquet head is held slightly higher than the wrist level and is lifted up and back, hesitates, and swings straight forward in line with the ball. This keeps the elbow away from the body, and is more rhythmical. This is *not* recommended for the beginner, because it is harder to separate the backswing from the forward swing of the racquet, and more difficult to meet the ball squarely.

Spins. Various spins may be imparted to a stroked ball, and will be discussed more fully under chops and slices; however intermediate players may learn to impart top spin to a forehand drive. This is done by starting the forward swing slightly below the ball and finishing above it. This decreases the speed of the stroke, but gives a greater margin of safety in net clearance, and is more difficult to return due to the tricky bounce. This should not be used exclusively but in addition to, the flat forehand drive.

Impact. It is a well-known fact that players of different abilities contact the ball at different points in its bounce.

    A. *Beginners:* Contact ball as the bounce descends. Approximately waist high.

    B. *Intermediates:* Contact point at top of bounce.

    C. *Advanced:* Contact ball as it ascends the bounce.

An individual's game is therefore speeded up each time the ball is contacted nearer the advanced player's point of contact, or on the ascending portion of the bounce.

> NOTE: Beginners should wait for the ball until the fundamentals of the forehand and backhand drives are learned. Moving forward or back for balls when first learning, makes for hurried shots, elbow cramping, and jabbed or hit balls, rather than the stroking that is desired.
>
> Advise the students in large classes to take advantage of their free time to use the backboards, handball courts, and tennis courts for extra practice periods.
>
> Exceptionally difficult cases may require extra instruction if the instructor has the necessary time for additional individual attention outside the class period.
>
> The Tom Stow stroke developer is also good, but is not discussed here since few schools have such equipment. The same technique of performance and careful teaching apply for such professional, or school-made, teaching aids as in the student-teacher relationship.

ADVANTAGES

1. The Forehand and Backhand Drives are the basis of all tennis.
2. Forehand Drives comprise 50% of all tennis strokes used in a game.
3. Good ground strokes are the basis of good tennis.
4. High degree of accuracy is attainable. The average WOMAN player needs to *emphasize accuracy*, rather than speed in the forehand drive. Less arm and shoulder girdle strength make it impossible for most women to hit the ball as hard as a man.

THE BACKHAND DRIVE

The backhand drive is a stroke used in defense, although once mastered, it is also used for offense. It is a basic tennis ground stroke, that is used to move the opponent to the back court. As in the forehand drive, top spin may be imparted to give the ball a tricky bounce.

SKILL SUMMARY

Stand with the right side to the net; shoulder and hips at right angles, and feet parallel to the net. Carry the weight evenly on the balls of the feet, and grasp the racquet in the Eastern Backhand Grip. Swing the racquet back in line with the ball, the racquet head well above the wrist, elbow flexed, and transfer the weight to the left foot. As the backswing is taken, rotate the body away from the net so that the ball can be seen over the right shoulder. Pause slightly at the end of the backswing, transfer the weight to the right foot. and swing the racquet forward to meet the ball. Contact the ball with the racquet face flat, and rotate the body toward the net as the ball is hit. Keep the wrist firm and the arm straight at impact. The weight is well forward at impact, and the ball is met well to the right of the front foot. Follow the ball flight with the racquet and arm, and finish out away from the body, and well above the net to insure net clearance.

SKILL ANALYSIS AND ILLUSTRATION (Plate 19a, b, c, d, e)

Count 1. Assume the correct grip and body position. Begin backswing in line with the approaching ball.

Count 2. Complete backswing, pause, transfer weight to forward foot, and begin forward swing.

Count 3. Contact ball, wrist firm and arm straight.

Count 4. Turn shoulders into shot, and begin follow through.

Count 5. Complete the follow through toward the line of ball flight and well up above the net.

Count 1. Count 2. Count 3.

Count 4. Count 5.

General Teaching Aids

I. Teach the Backhand and Forehand Drives Together.

II. Explain and demonstrate the backhand drive.

III. Follow the Same General Teaching Aids for the Backhand Drive as Are Listed for the Forehand Drive.

IV. Rally using both forehand and backhand drives.

V. *Singles Rally Game.* Score as in tennis. No service. Outside boundary lines of the singles court only are used. One student begins the rally with a half-swing volley return, and continues putting the ball into play after each point, for the full game.

NOTE: It is taken for granted that the instructor has already given a brief history of tennis, instruction in the general aspect of the game, and initial instruction in scoring.

Three Strokes Are Generally Recommended for Beginners in Tennis Where the School Situation Must of Necessity Shorten the Period in Which Any One Sport Can Be Played. These Are the Forehand Drive, the Backhand Drive, and a Service, (one or two types). For this Reason it is Necessary that the Instructor Use Every Possible Means of Changing the Class Procedure with Drills, Practice, Lead-Up Games, Competition, Etc., in Order to Maintain Interest in Instruction and Practice. It may also be necessary to add to the Teaching Aids presented for these skills; however quite a lengthy and interesting period of instruction could be organized from those presented.

Verbal Teaching Aids

A. Change to Eastern Backhand Grip. (*Failure to do so, opens racquet too far, causing a weak hit.*)

B. Watch the ball.

C. Right side to the net.

D. Swing back immediately.

E. Backswing in line with the ball. (*See circular backswing.*)

F. Watch footwork.

G. Look at the ball over the right shoulder.

H. Keep away from the ball. (*Crowding causes a shot that resembles a push.*)

I. Pause between back and forward swing.

J. Shift weight forward before racquet hits ball. (*Failure to do so checks the speed of the racquet.*)

K. Meet the ball to the right and in front of the forward foot. (*Insures a free, large swing, and a maximum of speed and power in the stroke.*)

L. Forward swing meets ball with a flat racquet.

M. Firm wrist, straight arm at impact.

N. Follow through higher than point of impact and above net to insure clearance.

VARIATIONS

1. THE RETURN OF A SHOULDER HIGH BACKHAND. (Plate 20)
2. THE RETURN OF A KNEE HIGH BACKHAND. (Plate 21)

Count 4. Count 4.

NOTE: The technique of performance remains essentially the same. The higher ball requires less knee flexion. In both instances the racquet is lined up behind the ball and the follow through is higher than the position at which the ball is met. Notice the knee flexion and the erect upper trunk in the return of the knee high ball.

3. Every backhand drive should adhere as closely as possible to the approved performance technique. The instructor should use personal judgment in relation to the value of each individual's variations from the regular form. This would apply more particularly to the intermediate and advanced players. The form for beginners is more or less uniform in the basic fundamentals, and would be more apt to vary according to physical abilities.

4. Spins and impact points are the same as those discussed under the forehand drive.

ADVANTAGES

1. Backhand and forehand drives are the basis of all tennis strokes.
2. Good ground strokes are the basis of good tennis.
3. If the backhand is learned as well as the forehand, no weak side is apparent to an opponent.
4. Average *women players should work toward accuracy of ball placement*, since less arm and shoulder girdle strength prohibits the speed and power developed by men in the forehand and backhand strokes.

SERVICE GRIPS

The position of the hand on the racquet to facilitate delivery of the service, is the service grip. (Plates 22, 23)

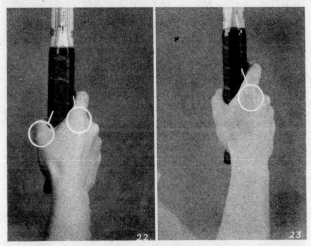

Eastern Forehand Service Grip. Continental Service Grip.

    A. The Eastern Forehand Grip is used for a service grip by many players. It is especially recommended for beginners and average players, since there is less tendency to cut across the ball due to failure to straighten the racquet as the ball is hit.

    B. The "service grip" or the Continental is often referred to as the professional grip, because it is used by ranking players. This grip imparts more top and side spin to the service than does the Eastern Service Grip.

SERVICE STANCE

The service stance is the position assumed by the player in order to begin the service. (Plate 24)

    A. Feet behind baseline.

    B. Left foot forward. (Approximately three inches behind baseline.)

    C. Right foot back.

    D. Feet comfortably spaced, and in line with or parallel to the service court for which the service is intended.

    E. Side toward the net.

    F. Racquet head held high.

    G. Balls in left hand.

READY POSITION

The ready position is the receiving stance the player assumes while waiting for the service or an opponent's return. (Plate 25)

Service Stance. Ready Position.

A. Feet comfortably spaced.
B. Weight evenly distributed on balls of both feet.
C. Racquet throat resting lightly in the left hand.
D. Knees only slightly flexed.
E. Body leans forward from the hips.
F. Eyes on server and the ball.

THE SLICE SERVICE OR ORDINARY TWIST

The slice service is a stroke used to put the ball into play in which very little speed or spin is imparted to the ball.

SKILL SUMMARY

Assume the service stance and Eastern Service Grip. Transfer weight to right foot, allow racquet head to drop toward court, and toss the ball to the right of the head and shoulder. The height of the ball toss depends upon the individual's racquet reach. Bend the right elbow and raise the hand to approximately the height of the right ear. This hyper-extends the wrist and the racquet head hangs slightly below the wrist, and behind the back. Bring the racquet head up and around the outside, and slightly over the ball, while the weight shifts naturally to the left foot. The body turns toward the net as the weight transfers. The face of the racquet is slanted when impact with the ball is made, and the right arm is not quite fully extended. Follow through toward the line of ball flight until the racquet comes down and across the body to the left, and the momentum carries the body still further around so that the right shoulder and foot point toward the net. The right foot may pass the baseline *after* the ball is hit, although the weight is supported entirely by the left foot until the follow through is made.

SKILL ANALYSIS AND ILLUSTRATION (Plate 26a, b, c, d)

Count 1. Drop racquet back and toss ball. Transfer weight to right foot.
Count 2. Slight loop of racquet head.
Count 3. Forward swing and impact with the ball.
Count 4. Follow through.

Count 1. Count 2. Count 3. Count 4.

Do Not Return a First Service if it is a Fault. Offer Opponent a Re-Play of Stroke if a Fault is Touched or Returned.

GENERAL TEACHING AIDS

I. Explain and demonstrate the Slice Service. If possible present a large illustration in addition to the demonstration. Demonstrate in both left and right service courts.

II. Discuss the foot fault rules and penalties. See official guides for rules.

III. Check service grips and proper stance.

IV. *Class Drill No. 1.* Raise racquet straight above head to check proper ball height. Practice dropping racquet back, and adducting wrist, and tossing ball to proper height.

V. *Class Drill No. 2.* Place racquet behind head, racquet head hanging slightly below wrist, wrist hyper-extended, and out from right ear. Toss ball and attempt forward swing, ball contact, and follow through. Practice against backboard or wire netting.

VI. Check individuals in class drills for stance, grip, starting position, height of ball, fling of racquet, and shoulder rotation and follow through.

VII. Drill 2 over nets, and into right and left service courts.

VIII. After the ball is being served quite regularly into the service court from the "racquet-behind-the-shoulder" position, teach the backswing as a separate unit. On command one, the students drop racquets to side, adduct the wrist as in Drill 1. On command two, the students bend the elbow, hyperextend the wrist, and allow the racquet to drop slightly below the wrist and behind the back. Toss the ball up on the command one.

IX. Attempt the full service. Use commands one to four as outlined in the SKILL ANALYSIS. Practice first without balls. Practice with balls against wire netting or backboards. Practice across the net and into both right and left service courts.

X. Practice complete service, partners calling for service to either forehand or backhand, catching the ball, and trying to serve as directed by previous server. One point for each correct response to command for position of the service.

XI. Repeat above with partners attempting to return the service.

XII. Review game, scoring, foot fault rules, and allow game to be played. Students try to win their service game. Check and correct errors made during the game.

Verbal Teaching Aids

A. Watch the ball.
B. Left foot forward, right foot back.
C. Toss the ball higher than the racquet can reach.
D. Toss the ball to the right of the head and shoulder.
E. Hand head high, racquet head slightly below wrist on backswing.
F. Transfer weight to forward foot. (*Should be an automatic movement.*)
G. Hit the ball at the greatest possible height.
H. Throw racquet across and over the ball, let the racquet head lead.
I. Arm slightly flexed in forward swing.
J. Swing racquet down and across body to the left.
K. Rotate shoulders toward net on follow through.
L. Follow through completely, opposite left knee.
M. Step forward with the right foot at the completion of the follow through.

Variations

1. FLAT SERVICE: (See page 257.)
2. AMERICAN TWIST SERVICE: (See page 260.)
3. REVERSE TWIST SERVICE: Imparts top and left to right spin on the ball. It is difficult to execute and is seldom used.
4. CHOP SERVICE: Imparts back spin, and low bounce to the ball. This service is a short service. The chop service is an inferior, slow service, and is used by players unable to co-ordinate other types of service.
5. CUT SERVICE: Imparts a left curve to the ball, which draws the receiver off the court when a serve is made in the right court. It is easy to execute and takes an opponent by surprise if used infrequently amid other types of service. The spin imparted gives a low, crooked bounce to the ball.

ADVANTAGES OF THE SLICE OR ORDINARY TWIST SERVICE

1. Does not tire the server.
2. Accurate, makes for good placement service.
3. Once mastered, service games have less double faults.
4. Universally used by top flight women players, because it is not tiring.
5. It is easy to learn.
6. An excellent second service if the Cannonball, or Flat service is attempted and missed on the first serve.
7. Excellent for both balls, when flat service is not "working" normally.

DISADVANTAGES OF SLICE SERVICE

1. Easily returned unless placed in the far corners of the service court.
2. Inexperienced receiver soon learns to return the service if it is used exclusively.

THE FLAT SERVICE

The flat service is a stroke used to put the ball into play in which great speed and little spin is imparted to the ball. This service is commonly called the Cannonball Service, and is usually used for a first service in an attempt to serve an ace.

SKILL SUMMARY

Assume the service stance and the Continental Service Grip. Transfer the weight to the right foot, and allow the racquet head to drop toward the court as the left hand starts the ball toss. Toss the ball straight up and slightly to the right of the head. This toss is more to the left of the toss for the slice service. Raise the hand and racquet until the right elbow is opposite the right ear, and the racquet head hangs down toward the court, and behind the back from a hyper-extended wrist. Transfer the weight to the left foot, straighten the left leg, and arch the back to add power to the stroke. Bring the racquet up to meet the ball, and contact the ball with the racquet face flat, and arm fully extended. Turn the body into the shot, and continue forward in the follow through. Follow through toward the line of flight and down and across the body to the left side.

SKILL ANALYSIS AND ILLUSTRATION (Plate 27a, b, c, d)

Count 1. Drop racquet head toward court, toss ball as weight transfers to right foot.

Count 2. Raise racquet and complete circular loop of racquet as back is arched to add power to the stroke.

Count 3. Transfer weight to forward foot and meet the ball. Begin follow through.

Count 4. Follow through to the left side.

Count 1. Count 2. Count 3. Count 4.

USUALLY AN INTERMEDIATE OR ADVANCED SKILL.

BE SURE AN OPPONENT IS READY BEFORE SERVING.

Ace: Service or return so placed that it is impossible for the opponent to touch the ball.

GENERAL TEACHING AIDS

    I. Explain and demonstrate the Flat Service.

    II. Follow same general procedure and drills as described for the slice service.

        1. Major points of difference in the flat service as compared to the slice service.

            (a) Racquet drops farther back on Count 2. (Compare illustrations.)

            (b) Side to net position more pronounced.

            (c) Contact made with racquet face flat.

            (d) More pronounced arch in back.

            (e) Racquet arm straight at impact.

    III. Those students who have difficulty with the "fling" of the racquet at the ball, let them throw the ball over the net into the correct service court with an overhand throw. This will give them the feel of the wrist snap, shoulder and trunk rotation, and forward step of the foot in the finish of the follow through.

VERBAL TEACHING AIDS

    A. Weight on back foot, side to the net.

    B. Drop racquet head toward court. (*Arm straight and relaxed.*)

C. Ball toss straight up and slightly to the right of the head.

D. Rotate arm outward and raise hand up and back until the elbow is opposite the right ear.

E. Racquet head hangs behind back, racquet head toward court, and wrist hyper-extended.

F. Arch back.

G. Transfer weight to forward foot. (*Should be a natural movement.*)

H. Straighten left leg.

I. Raise racquet head to meet ball. (*Hang of racquet head and swing automatically complete racquet loop behind the back.*)

J. Racquet face flat at impact.

K. Right arm straight and fully extended.

L. Turn body into shot.

M. Eyes on ball at all times.

N. Follow through down and across the body to the left.

O. Right foot steps forward at the end of the follow through.

VARIATIONS

1. A variation of the Cannonball service may be used for beginners and is merely a straight service, with no attempt at speed, ball slice, or spin. (Plate 28a, b, c, d)

Count 1. Count 2. Count 3. Count 4.

A. Major points of difference.

    (a) Less back arch.

    (b) Less speed imparted to the ball.

    (c) Racquet speed less.

    (d) Less turn away from net.

ADVANTAGES

CANNONBALL SERVICE

1. Excellent first service.
2. Used in an attempt to score an ace.
3. Speed of service makes it difficult to return.
4. Excellent surprise attack after slice or twist services.

BEGINNERS FLAT SERVICE (Variation)

1. Form of Cannonball service is learned without the inaccuracy caused by attempting excessive speed.
2. The full racquet movement becomes a natural motion.

DISADVANTAGES

CANNONBALL SERVICE

1. Speed causes inaccuracy.
2. Tiring service due to amount of energy expended. Few women can use this service continuously even for a first service, because of the fatigue factor. It is recommended that women learn this service, but use it only as a surprise attack, unless continuous use can be made of it without undue fatigue. This fatigue is usually caused in women, by weak back muscles.
3. Fatigue from this service causes a loss of control and accuracy in the net and long court game.

THE AMERICAN TWIST SERVICE

The American Twist service is a very popular service because of its high arc, and its high and tricky bounce.

SKILL SUMMARY

Assume the service stance and Continental Grip, weight on the back foot. The backswing and racquet loop are approximately the same as in the flat service; however the ball is tossed above and to the left of the head. The feet remain in the same position as in the flat service, but the greater trunk rotation causes the back to turn a little more to the net. The direction of the ball toss causes a greater back arch in order to contact the ball. The racquet is raised up in order to come across the top of the ball. As the ball is hit, the racquet moves from left to right, and the follow through is on the right of the body. The right foot steps forward as the body turns toward the line of flight in the follow through, just as in the other services.

SKILL ANALYSIS AND ILLUSTRATION (Plate 29a, b, c. d)

Count 1. Drop racquet head toward court, toss ball, weight on back foot.

Count 2. Raise racquet, rotate trunk, arch back, and complete racquet loop.

Count 3. Ball impact.

Count 4. Follow through to the right side.

Count 1. Count 2. Count 3. Count 4.

An Intermediate and Advanced Skill.

Check the Net Height Before Starting Play, Never During the Service, Unless Net Comes Down During Play.

General Teaching Aids

I. Explain and demonstrate the American Twist Service.

II. Follow the same general procedure and drills as described for the slice service.

    1. Major differences in American Twist and Slice services.
      (a) Greater back arch.
      (b) Body turns more, placing back to net.
      (c) Ball toss above and to left of head.
      (d) Racquet comes across top of ball from left to right.
      (e) Follow through on right side.
      (f) High arc in service.
      (g) Ball bounces to left as it comes from court.
      (h) Tremendous spin on ball, and a high bounce.

III. Watch students for correct follow through. Hitting the right leg is caused by failure to move the racquet far enough to the right on the ball contact from left to right.

Verbal Teaching Aids

Use the Same Verbal Aid for Identical Points in this Service and the Cannonball Service.

    A. Ball toss above and to the left of the head.
    B. Body turns away from net. Back toward net.

C. Contact ball across top and hit from left to right.
D. Follow through on right side.
E. Turn body into shot.
F. Arch back, therefore more knee flexion.

VARIATIONS

(See other types of services discussed.)

ADVANTAGES OF AMERICAN TWIST SERVICE

1. Tricky ball bounce, difficult to return.
2. High arc, gives time for server to go to the net.
3. High ball bounce.
4. Quite accurate.
5. A good second service.
6. Not as tiring as the Cannonball service.

DISADVANTAGES

1. Great back arch tiring for some women due to weak back muscles.

CALL "FAULT" OR "OUT" FOR INCORRECT SERVICE IF NO UMPIRE
IS AVAILABLE. PLAY THE GOOD SERVICES, DO NOT CALL THEM.

THE LOB

The lob is a high, lofted ball which lands near the baseline or just
out of reach of the player at the net. The former is a deep lob; the
latter a short lob.

SKILL SUMMARY

Since there are a number of ways of executing a lob, it is difficult to
present a single skill summary. For this reason, the SKILL ILLUSTRATION below
will show a lob made with a swing similar in many respects to the forehand
drive. The others not discussed in this summary will be illustrated under
VARIATIONS of the lob.

The lob may be made with either a forehand or a backhand stroke,
and the grips for both are the same as those used for the drives. The normal
side to the net position is maintained. The backswing is slow and short. The
forward swing may be horizontal to the court, as illustrated below, or the
racquet head may point toward the court. The lob may also be executed with
a chop stroke. In all cases the backswing is lower than the ball, and the impact
is made underneath the ball. The forward swing may be made with an arm
movement as in the drives, or by a wrist snap or flexion. The wrist snap gives
a feeling of tapping the ball; the arm swing of lifting it easily or gently. There
is little transfer of body weight and the follow through is very short. In fact
after impact, the racquet seems to stop; however it continues in an upward
direction for a very short distance.

Forehand: (Plate 30a, b, c)

Count 1. Count 2. Count 3.

Backhand: (Plate 31a, b, c)

Count 1. Count 2. Count 3.

DEEP LOBS LAND A MAXIMUM OF THREE FEET FROM THE BASE LINE. SHORT LOBS LAND JUST OVER THE NET AND OUT OF OPPONENT'S RACQUET REACH.

GENERAL TEACHING AIDS

I. Explain and demonstrate the forehand and backhand lobs, using a horizontal swing. This is recommended for initial instruction, because it more nearly resembles the strokes learned previously.

II. Student drill imitating slow demonstration by the instructor. Perform both forehand and backhand lobs without the ball.

III. Divide the students into fours. No. 1's stand at the baseline; 2's at the opposite baseline; 3's and 4's on opposite sides of the net. Using a self-bounce, the No. 1's lob (short). No. 4's hold racquets up in air, and stop balls that do not go high enough. No. 3's retrieve the balls that do not go over the net. No. 2's retrieve correctly placed lobs. Drill repeated with No. 2's lobbing, 3's holding up racquets, etc. Change court positions frequently. Instructor checks for errors.

IV. Repeat above drill for deep lob, moving net players back to center of service court. Baseline receiver checks ball landing for approximate distance from baseline.

V. Use same or different drills with self-toss, thrown ball, half-swing volley return, and finally rally using lobs.

Verbal Teaching Aids

A. Side to net.
B. Short, slow backswing. (*Too much force places ball out of bounds.*)
C. Horizontal forward swing.
D. Locked wrist and straight arm.
E. Meet ball underneath. (*Square or top contact, sends ball too low.*)
F. Raise racquet short distance upward after impact. (*Not raised far enough, ball falls short; raised too far, ball out of bounds.*)

Variations

Lob With Racquet Head Low and Use of Wrist Snap.

Forehand: (Plate 32a, b)

Count 1.   Count 2.

Backhand: (Plate 33a, b)

Count 1. Count 2.

NOTE: The lob is often used to gain time in order to get back into position. Many times this means the lob must be hit when the normal side to the net position is impossible. Practice may be quite correct according to available standards; however the game situation presents conditions far removed from class drills in supposedly "good" form. This makes it difficult to present any one type of lob as the best, or even a number of types of lobs that will be "workable" under all conditions. "Scrambling" of player, and accommodation of a stroke to reach a ball are certainly justified in the game situation and allow little time for the use of correct form. Add to this the variations necessary for each individual, and the lob appears to have more possible variations of execution than any other tennis stroke. The one general rule that can be applied is accuracy in ball placement, and disguise of execution whenever possible. In other words, place the ball out of an opponent's reach, and keep the opponent from anticipating the stroke.

ADVANTAGES

1. Excellent defensive stroke.
2. Useful in attack due to the surprise element in a well executed lob.
3. Gains time for returning to position, or resting momentarily after an exchange of running shots.
4. Drives opponent from net, and allows time for player who lobbed to reach the net.
5. Confuses opponents in a doubles game.
6. Breaks up rhythmic driving by opponent.

1. Offensive short lob in hands of a novice is dangerous. Should be used sparingly, and as a surprise attack.
2. Unless disguised, opponent may anticipate the lob.
3. Inaccurate placement usually results in a loss of a point.

Let Service: Ball touches net and continues into proper court. On first service, 2 more balls may be played. On second service, one ball may be re-served.

Let Ball: Ball touches net and continues in bounds on opposite side of court. Ball is good and still in play.

Net Ball: Ball played into net. Fault and loss of point on a return, and on a second service.

VOLLEY

A volley is any stroke played before the ball touches the court. It is usually made from a position near the net or at some point within the service court area.

SKILL SUMMARY

(As in the lob, other types of volleys will be presented under variations.)

Assume the Eastern Grip, and maintain if possible, a side to the net position. Swing the racquet back, racquet head higher than the wrist, weight evenly distributed. Step forward to the forward foot and meet the ball well out in front of the body. Follow through toward the net and finish with the racquet head above the net. This is a volley used for attack, and the ball is hit into the back court, and near the feet of the opponent.

SKILL ANALYSIS

Count 1. Short backswing, side to net, weight evenly distributed.
Count 2. Forward swing, weight on front foot, impact well out in front of the body.
Count 3. Follow through toward and above net.

SKILL ILLUSTRATION

Forehand: (Plate 34a, b, c)

Backhand: (Plate 35a, b, c)

INTERMEDIATE AND ADVANCED SKILL.

GENERAL TEACHING AIDS

I. Review forehand and backhand drives.
II. Explain and demonstrate the punch volley.
III. *Class Drill No. 1.* Partners: No. 1's toss ball to No. 2's forehand

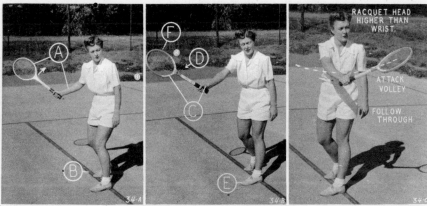

Count 1. Count 2. Count 3.

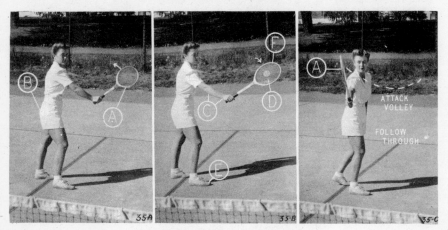

Count 1. Count 2. Count 3.

and backhand. No. 2's attempt to volley. Partners 3 and 4 retrieve balls. After 5 volleys each, both forehand and backhand, partners 3 and 4 come to the net, while 1 and 2 retrieve balls.

 IV. *Class Drill No. 2.* Half-swing volley return to player at net. Net player volleys. Change after 5 to 10 volleys. Change with players retrieving balls.

 V. *Class Drill No. 3.* Same as above; however the half-swing volley return is replaced by a forehand drive from the back court. Change after 5 volleys.

VERBAL TEACHING AIDS

 A. Racquet head higher than wrist throughout stroke.

 B. Weight evenly distributed. Side to net if time permits.

 C. Arm straight, wrist locked. (*Loose wrist causes inaccurate shots, due to change of racquet face at ball impact.*)

D. Ball met well out in front of body.

E. Weight on forward foot.

F. Racquet head open if necessary for net clearance. (*More necessary in low shots just over net.*)

VARIATIONS

STOP VOLLEY

> *Forehand:* (Plate 36)
>
> *Backhand:* (Plate 37)

Forehand Stop Volley. Backhand Stop Volley.

A. Major points of difference from punch volley.
  1. No swing, racquet held to meet ball.
  2. Racquet may "give" slightly when ball is hit.
  3. "Lay away" shot, or a certain point due to ball placement, speed, and surprise element.
  4. Racquet face usually open, since stop volleys occur close to and below the net.
  5. More knee flexion.

SLICE VOLLEY

> *Forehand:* (Plate 38a, b)

Backswing Stop Volley. Ball Contact and Follow Through.

Backhand: (Plate 39a, b)

Backswing. Ball Contact and Follow Through.

A. Major points of difference from the punch volley.
   1. Racquet hits back of ball and moves across it, from outside to inside.
   2. Ball bounces low and to the right or left.
   3. More wrist movement.
   4. Backswing is upward and back, elbow flexed.
   5. Racquet face flat, and moves forward and downward.
   6. Finish of follow through is near forward foot.

BEND THE KNEES TO REACH A LOW VOLLEY. DO NOT LOWER RACQUET HEAD BELOW THE WRIST.

CHOP VOLLEY

Forehand: (Plate 40a, b)

Backswing. Ball Contact and Follow Through.

Backhand: (Plate 41a, b)

Backswing. Ball Contact and Follow Through.

A. Major points of difference from the punch volley.
   1. Little follow through.
   2. Contact back of ball and hit downward. (*As if using a hatchet.*)
   3. Greater speed attained in volley.
   4. Usually a defensive volley.
   5. Ball given back spin.

VOLLEY OF A HIGH BALL

Forehand: (Plate 42)

Backhand: (Plate 43)

Forehand Volley of a High Ball. Backhand Volley of a High Ball.

A. Major points of difference from the punch volley.
   1. Forward swing is downward.
   2. Ball hit sharply.
   3. Greater speed attained in this volley.
   4. Usually a certain point.

ADVANTAGES

1. Excellent offense tactic and usually a sure point.
2. Surprise element and speed of placement.
3. Variety in strokes.

DISADVANTAGES

1. May be caught by a lob or a hard line drive if the court is not covered quickly enough.
2. There is some conflict of opinion upon the fatigue factor in continuous net play. Many men and women find it more tiring due to the running necessary to move up and back from the net. Others find it less tiring, because a point may be made in less time. Since the modern game encourages net play, it is recommended for all players of both sexes; however each individual should decide for or against using it in actual play. In this way the fatigue factor can be controlled by each individual.

OVERHEAD SMASH

The Overhead Smash is a stroke resembling the service in which a lob or an exceptionally high bouncing ball is returned with as much speed as possible, directly down toward the opponent's court.

SKILL SUMMARY

The overhead smash is very similiar to the service, although the player must move into the correct court position, hit a ball returned by the opponent, and reach the ball at the highest possible point. Possibly a little more wrist action is apparent due to the fact that the ball must be angled more sharply downward due to the close position to the net. Many players prefer to take this shot with a jump into the air, taking both feet off the court as the ball is hit. Others prefer the feet on the court to insure control and accuracy in ball placement. Although both types have been used by champions, the leap probably adds greater force to the shot, because the ball is hit at a higher point and can be hit downward at a sharper angle.

SKILL ANALYSIS AND ILLUSTRATION (Plate 44a, b, c, d)
(After run to proper hitting position.)

Count 1. Weight on right foot, racquet head dropped toward court.
Count 2. Racquet raised to start circular loop. Racquet head hangs down back as in the flat service.
Count 3. (Jump if desired.) Body turns into shot as ball is hit. Wrist snaps (flexes) quickly.
Count 4. Follow through to the left side of the body, and finish facing the net, ready for the next shot..

Count 1. Count 2. Count 3. Count 4.

INTERMEDIATE AND ADVANCED SKILL.

WATCH THE BALL.

GENERAL TEACHING AIDS

I. Review Flat (Cannonball) Service.

II. Explain and demonstrate the Overhead Smash.

III. *Class Drill:* No. 1 lobs ball; No. 2 attempts an overhead smash; No. 3 and 4 retrieve ball. After five attempts No. 2 lobs; 1 smashes. Change with 3 and 4, etc.

IV. Above drill may be performed with tossed balls if lobs are inaccurate.

NOTE: More than 4 players on the court, make this drill situation dangerous.

V. Play a doubles match. One point given for each successful lob and smash performed.

VERBAL TEACHING AIDS

A. Weight on right foot, side to net.

B. Drop racquet head toward court.

C. Rotate arm outward and raise hand up until racquet hangs behind back.

D. Arch back.

E. Jump. (*If desired.*)

F. Contact ball as high as possible.

G. Racquet flat as ball is hit.

H. Fast wrist snap or flexion.

I. Right arm straight and fully extended at impact.
J. Turn body into shot.
K. Follow through down and across body.
L. Land facing the net, ready for the next shot.

ADVANTAGES

1. Usually a certain point.
2. Speed.

DISADVANTAGES

1. Continuous smashing tiring, especially for women.

CHOP

The chop is a stroke used to return excessively fast drives. It is primarily a defensive stroke; however if used as a drop shot, the stroke may be used advantageously as offense, provided the opponent is as far back as the baseline, or out of position.

SKILL ILLUSTRATION

Forehand: (Plate 45)

Backhand: (Plate 46)

Forehand. Backhand.

A. Major points of difference in the chops and drives.
1. Backswing flexes arm above shoulder.
2. Hit is made down back of ball.
3. Follow through is short. (*Even shorter than the slice.*)
4. Similar to a hatchet stroke.
5. Wrist locked. (*Differs from the slice, not the drives in this respect.*)

TEACHING AIDS

I. Follow the same procedure as for the GENERAL and VERBAL AIDS for the drives. One to five from the list above may be used as part of the VERBAL AIDS.

VARIATIONS

1. DROP SHOT: Same as the chop only hit more slowly and carefully so as to barely drop over the net. This should score a point when used correctly.

ADVANTAGES

1. Defense for fast balls.
2. Breaks rhythm of opponent's drives.
3. Good angled shot.

DISADVANTAGES

1. Less speed.
2. Little value as a deep shot.

SLICE

The slice is a stroke used to hit high bouncing balls, down toward the court, and to impart a decided spin to the ball.

SKILL ILLUSTRATION

Forehand: (Plate 47a, b, c)

Backhand: (Plate 48a, b, c)

A. Major points of difference in the slice and the drives.
1. Backswing higher and shorter.
2. Racquet face slanted back.
3. The stroke is made underneath and across the back of the ball.
4. Forward swing is down from high to low.
5. More wrist and elbow action.
6. Follow through is lower.

TEACHING AIDS

I. Follow the same procedure as for the GENERAL and VERBAL AIDS given for the forehand and backhand drives. The six statements listed above may be used for some of the VERBAL AIDS.

ADVANTAGES

1. Excellent offensive stroke.
2. Hits high bouncing ball downward toward court.
3. Surprise element of bounce due to ball spin.
4. Good deep shot, difficult to return.

Count 1. Count 2. Count 3.

Count 1. Count 2. Count 3.

DISADVANTAGES

1. Less speed.
2. Easy to volley.
3. Over-use affects performance of flat drives.

HALF-VOLLEY

The half-volley is a defensive stroke used when caught out of position for any other kind of a return. It is merely placing the racquet, with the face open, directly in behind the ball, so that immediately upon contact with the court, the ball bounds off the racquet strings, and over the net.

SKILL ILLUSTRATION

Forehand: (Plate 49a, b)

Ball Contact. Follow Through.

Ball Contact. Follow Through.

Backhand: (Plate 50a, b)

A. Very little time for a backswing.

B. Racquet placed behind ball, and near or on court.

C. Eyes on the ball.

D. Racquet face open.

E. Weight transfer is less pronounced the closer the player is to the net.

F. Backcourt half-volley must have weight transfer as in the drives.

G. Follow through is low and extremely short.

1. Defense against balls bouncing at feet.

STRATEGY FOR BEGINNERS

Introduction. The forehand drive, the backhand drive, and the flat service variation discussed previously, with the possible addition of the slice service, are the strokes generally taught a beginner during a school class in tennis. This makes court strategy quite a simple problem when compared to the complexity of the net or all court game.

Singles. One general rule that may always be applied is to watch for and play an opponent's weaknesses. If the backhand is weak, play to the backhand. If the opponent is slow in covering the court, aim for the corners of the court, so a running shot will have to be made, or hit a baseline drive and then a short shot over the net. If an opponent moves from the left to the right as a return is made, return the shot in the direction *from* which the opponent is moving. Win your service. Avoid serving double faults. Serve to get the opponent off court, and then place a return to the opposite side. Avoid showing weakness to an opponent. Know the correct court position, and move to that home spot after each return.

Doubles. Play to an opponent's weakness. Hit to the corners to draw an opponent out of the court. Hit down the center to confuse opponent's team work. Drive to any space not covered by opponents. Know your correct court positions, and return to them if possible when a return is made. Be responsible for own half of court. If partner is pulled out of position, protect the rest of the court. Center balls are taken by the player who has a forehand shot at the ball.

> NOTE: In any school class situation the number of students oftentimes makes doubles play a necessity; however singles may be played by using just half of the court, thus allowing more balls to be played by each individual during the class period.
>
> As soon as possible in the teaching situation, devise a competitive game or modification of tennis. Students want to play, and they will drill with more enthusiasm if given a chance to use what they have learned in a game situation.
>
> Court tactics, or strategy, for the intermediate and advanced players must necessarily become more complex, due to the greater number of strokes learned. Any number of books listed at the end of this chapter contain excellent discussions of court strategy in both the doubles and singles games. Space does not permit its further discussion in this chapter.

Specific items for use in the general activities listed below, may be found in the Teaching Aids for each skill, as well as in the further references listed.

SUGGESTED CLASS ORGANIZATION

SUGGESTED ACTIVITY

Initial lessons

1st three weeks.

APPROXIMATE
TIME

Arrive and Dress	10 minutes
Roll Call and Preliminaries	3 minutes
Game, History, Equipment, Rules Discussion	5 minutes
Review	15 minutes
Explanation and Demonstration of New Material	8 minutes
Class Drill	9 minutes
Individual Activity	5 minutes
Shower and Dress	5 minutes

4th through 8th week.

Arrive and Dress	5 minutes
Roll Call and Preliminaries	2 minutes
General Discussion	3 minutes
Individual Rally and Warm-Up	10 minutes
Explanation and Demonstration of New Material	5 minutes
Class Drill	10 minutes
Game Situation	15 minutes
Individual Activity	5 minutes
Shower and Dress	5 minutes

9th through 12th week.

Arrive and Dress	5 minutes
Roll Call and Preliminaries	2 minutes
General Discussion	3 minutes
Individual Rally and Warm-Up	10 minutes
Explanation and Demonstration of New Material	5 minutes
Class Drill	5 minutes
Game Situation	20 minutes
Individual Activity	5 minutes
Shower and Dress	5 minutes

CLASSIFICATION OF PROGRESSION OF STROKES FOR BE-GINNERS, INTERMEDIATES, AND ADVANCED INSTRUC-TION

BEGINNERS:	INTERMEDIATES:	ADVANCED:
(Three Stroke Game)	(Net Game)	(All-court Game)
Forehand Drive	Volley	Chop
Backhand Drive	Lob	Slice
Flat or Slice Service	Overhead Smash	Half-Volley
	American Twist and	Other services
	Cannonball Service	

FURTHER REFERENCES

1. Ainsworth, Dorothy S.; Broer, Marion R.; Goss, Alice G.; Goss, Gertrude; Jennings, Evelyn; Pitkin, Bertha A.; Ryder, Florence: *Individual Sports for Women.* W. B. Saunders and Company, Philadelphia and London, 1943, 392 pages.
2. Beasely, Mercer: *How to Play Tennis.* Doubleday, Doran and Co., Inc., New York, 1933.
3. Brown, Mary K: *Streamline Tennis.* American Sports Publishing Company, New York, 1940, 112 pages.
4. Budge, Donald: *Budge On Tennis.* Prentice-Hall, New York, 1939.
5. Driver, Helen I: *Tennis For Teachers.* W. B. Saunders and Co., Philadelphia, Pa., 2nd edition, 1941.
6. Jacobs, Helen Hull: *Tennis.* A. S. Barnes and Company, Publishers, New York, 1941.
7. National Section on Women's Athletics: *Individual Sports Guide.* Official Sports Library for Women, A. S. Barnes and Company, Publishers, New York, 1945-46.
8. Vines, Ellsworth: *A Quick Way To Better Tennis.* Sun Dial Press, Allen J. Hall Company, 1939.

VIII

INDIVIDUAL SPORTS
MOTIVATION

Introduction. The use of the phrase "Individual Sports Motivation" may be misleading since the activities presented in these few pages, are generally organized after instruction has been received, and some skill attained, in individual sport techniques. The nature of the activities, their popularity as leisure time activities, and their co-recreational values, make motivation of interest in learning almost unnecessary.

This material is presented very briefly, and is offered to aid students in forming a working basis for incorporating original ideas in a recreational program in individual sports. It is taken for granted that previous instruction has been received in intramural organization, administrative policy, and program planning. For this reason, no attempt has been made to present any detailed discussion of policies, objectives, and organization.

Clubs. All recreational clubs should be open to any students desiring to join; therefore membership rules should not be necessary. Officers should be student elected, and usually include a president, vice-president, and secretary. The president's duties include arranging for use of the gymnasium and equipment, calling meetings, and conducting general club administration. The vice-president is responsible for arranging contests, tournaments, teams, novelty events, and special social activities. The secretary posts all announcements, handles all correspondence, keeps club records and membership, and arranges for tournament officials. This organization is quite generally used and may be enlarged if desired.

The subject of club dues is a controversial one, and need not be discussed, since it is felt that each school should control club finances according to the school administrative policy. In general, the payment of dues would seem unnecessary, and in some cases, might prevent student membership. (Plate 1)

Insignia and awards are quite commonly used in club programs and tournaments. Their use is usually a matter of departmental policy;

BADMINTON CLUB.

however they are not necessary to the success of a program. Awards if given, should have little monetary value, and should be presented to teams and clubs rather than to individuals. A club insignia, worn by all club members, is not as great an issue in club administration as the award problem. Individual awards tend to place undue emphasis on winning and upon individual play, while club insignia sometimes increases the group feeling and team play. If a choice must be made, and a tangible object denoting club competition felt necessary by student members, insignia would seem more democratic, and less detrimental to the objectives of a recreational program.

Sports Nights. Many educators are becoming quite concerned about the increasing number of extra-curricular clubs open to student membership, and recommend a reduction in number. The objection is raised because of set meeting times that involve the time of many students nearly every night of the week, particularly if more than one club is joined. For this reason, and for many others, sports nights and sports days, are increasing in popularity.

Student leaders, with the aid of the physical education instructor, plan the program, and arrange for officials, dates, facilities, and equipment prior to the sport night. Competition is arranged in two ways. Students may be placed on teams as they register for play, or groups may enter as a team. No insignia or awards are used in this type of program.

Open House. Open house resembles the sports night in organization, scoring, and competition. The major difference is in the fact that the public is invited to attend, although no charge is levied for watching the games.

Competition. Competition in individual sports does not present as great a problem as the team sports program. This is due to the type of game rather than to the vigor with which the players compete. The type of competition, as well as the amount, is governed by the policies of each physical education department; however it is recommended that the standards and policies of the National Section on Women's Athletics be thoroughly studied and their regulations used for setting any policies in regard to competition, particularly if the competition is co-recreational or for women only.

Tournaments.

Ladder. (Plate 2)

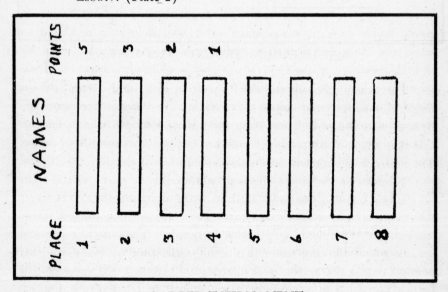

LADDER TOURNAMENT.

The player below may challenge the player directly above, and if the game is won, may exchange places with the loser. If the game is lost, the loser must challenge and win from, the player below before the player above may be re-challenged.

Points for the end of the tournament: award 5 points to the first place winner, 3 points for second place, 2 points for third place, and 1 point for fourth place.

Single Elimination. (Plate 3)

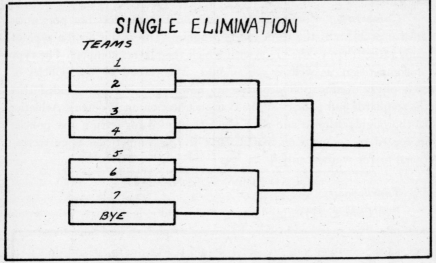

SINGLE ELIMINATION TOURNAMENT

The example chosen for the illustration in Plate 2 above, is for a single elimination tournament of 7 teams. This necessitates one bye. Byes are determined by computing the nearest multiple of two, (in this case it is 8), and subtracting from this number, the number of teams. The figure thus obtained designates the number of byes.

Winners in the single elimination tournament move to the right on the bracket, and the losers are out of the tournament.

Round-Robin. (Plate 4)

Round-Robin tournaments provide opportunity for each player or team to play every other player or team. For this reason it is excellent for a recreational program in sports competition. The example above is one of many different ways of forming a playing schedule. This particular schedule is for five teams. The letters designate the teams, and the numbers designate the order of play. In other words, the number 1 indicates the first two games to be played. From each No. 1, read up and across to find the teams competing, in this instance A versus B, and C versus E. The next games are figured from No. 2. These are A versus C and B versus E, etc.

ROUND-ROBIN 5 TEAMS					
TEAM	A	B	C	D	E
A	X	1	2	3	4
B	1	X	3	4	5
C	2	3	X	5	1
D	3	4	5	X	2
E	4	5	1	2	X

ROUND-ROBIN TOURNAMENT.

Publicity. General publicity for the individual sports program is desirable. This may be obtained by means of posters, and school and city newspapers. Publicity of any kind should reflect the spirit and policy of the recreational program. Teams and program should receive the publicity rather than individuals.

Motivation boards that present a daily, seasonal, and yearly record of team and club competition create interest in the recreational program. (Plate 5, 6)

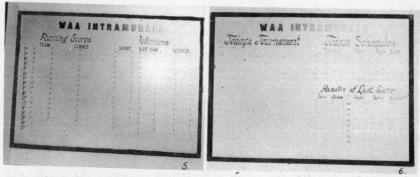

WOMEN'S ATHLETIC ASSOCIATION INTRAMURAL BOARD.
SCHEDULE BOARD.

These, plus the bulletin board, provide the daily schedule of games, and announce the winners of each day of competition, as well as the points scored by the teams. (Plate 7)

Further information concerning all of the subjects so briefly discussed, may be obtained from intramural text-books, and the Official Sports Guides published for the National Section on Women's Athletics by A. S. Barnes and Company.

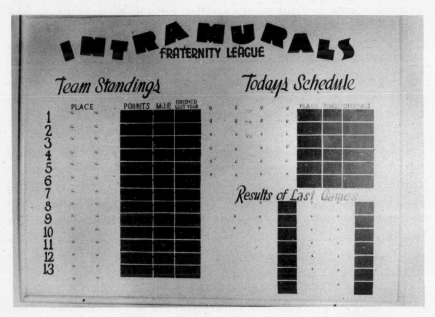

FRATERNITY LEAGUE INTRAMURAL BOARD.

Specific Problems in Class Organization. Generally speaking, the need for co-educational sports instruction becomes apparent through the leisure time activities of student personnel. Voluntary participation in co-recreation activity during periods of free play is a good indication of the enthusiasm with which such a program will be received. If this voluntary participation is not apparent, the specific problems in class organization become even more complex, and must be carefully studied and planned if the program is to be successful.

The initial organization of co-educational sports instruction in colleges and universities is a simple one, since students may register for specific courses. In the majority of secondary schools the system of class segregation leaves little choice to the student, and becomes a matter of departmental policy in that classes are arranged according to time rather than instructional units. This makes co-operative planning imperative, and the problems of program emphasis, class numbers, and sex distribution become paramount.

Program Emphasis. The amount and kind of activity chosen for a sports instruction program for both men and women should remain a departmental problem; however the tendency, once the program has gained momentum, is toward over-emphasis. This should be carefully guarded against or many of the social and recreational values are lost. The boys particularly, need the more strenuous activities of their own physical education programs, and over-emphasis of co-educational instruction decreases their interest in this type of activity.

Class Numbers and Sex Distribution. The number of students enrolled in any one class becomes more of a problem in individual sports instruction than in team sport instruction, since the nature of the activity permits fewer players to participate in an actual game situation. For this reason class numbers should be kept as low as possible for each school situation. Secondary schools find this a difficult problem in individual sports instruction, and thus recreational play and club programs have progressed faster than co-instructional programs. Until a system of registration and sports requirement program can be evolved for the secondary school physical education, the problem of co-educational instruction in any type of activity can be solved in only two ways. The first is by means of a club or recreational program; the second by dividing already existing classes into two divisions and sending half of the women students to the men's instructor, and half of the men students to the women's instructor. In attempting the latter solution, four factors are important: first to insure equal numerical distribution of the sexes; second to segregate the classes as equally as possible into similar age, grade, or growth and development groupings; third to divide the classes into beginners and advanced groups and place these groups in the same class; and fourth to require an official costume which will prevent self-consciousness in regard to personal appearance.

This self-consciousness is much more apparent on the secondary level, and a great deal of it can be overcome by encouraging voluntary participation in periods of free play.

Game Modification and Class Drill. Actually the instructional problems in co-educational sports classes are not much more difficult than in a class of only one sex, once the organization and segregation have been completed. The two major points of importance are game modification and class drill.

Game modification, while more particularly a problem of extra-curricular competition, becomes an instructional problem when mixed tournaments or games are played within a class period. Girls rules and length of games are recommended for this purpose. This insures equal opportunities of play for the girls, since boys rules and game length may create undue fatigue, which would in turn be detrimental to enthusiastic play.

Drill in sport skills is definitely a problem in any type of class situation. The amount and kind of drills presented should be decided by each individual instructor. The final decision should be based upon the kind of class, the student personnel, the size of the class, and student interest. In co-educational classes, the instructor will usually find that the men will drill more willingly and over longer periods than the women. This is due to the fact that the men feel it necessary to excel, and are therefore eager to drill provided results or progress can be measured. Women tire quickly of drill and appear more eager to play the game immediately and thus experience its social and recreational stimulation. For these reasons, student reaction should be carefully watched when drills are in progress in a co-educational sports class.

Other instructional problems may appear in individual school situations; however they should be quite easily solved through the co-operative efforts of the men's and women's physical education staffs.